Religion, Gender, and Kinship in Colonial New France

Religion, Gender, and Kinship in Colonial New France

Lisa J. M. Poirier

Syracuse University Press

Copyright © 2016 by Syracuse University Press
Syracuse, New York 13244-5290

All Rights Reserved

First Edition 2016

16 17 18 19 20 21   6 5 4 3 2 1

∞ The paper used in this publication meets the minimum requirements of the American National Standard for Information Sciences—Permanence of Paper for Printed Library Materials, ANSI Z39.48-1992.

For a listing of books published and distributed by Syracuse University Press, visit www.SyracuseUniversityPress.syr.edu.

ISBN: 978-0-8156-3488-1 (hardcover)
978-0-8156-3473-7 (paperback)
978-0-8156-5386-8 (e-book)

Library of Congress Cataloging-in-Publication Data
Names: Poirier, Lisa J. M., author.
Title: Religion, gender, and kinship in colonial New France / Lisa J. M. Poirier.
Description: 1st [edition]. | Syracuse : Syracuse University Press, 2016. |
    Includes bibliographical references and index.
Identifiers: LCCN 2016029451 (print) | LCCN 2016032695 (ebook) |
    ISBN 9780815634881 (hardcover : alk. paper) | ISBN 9780815634737
    (pbk. : alk. paper) | ISBN 9780815653868 (e-book)
Subjects: LCSH: New France—Religion. | Jesuits—New France—History.
Classification: LCC BL2520 .P65 2016 (print) | LCC BL2520 (ebook) |
    DDC 971.3/1701—dc23
LC record available at https://lccn.loc.gov/2016029451

Manufactured in the United States of America

For my beloved mother
Claire Germaine (Babineau) Giuliani
1941–2013

Contents

Acknowledgments - *ix*

1. Introduction: *Disjunctive Valuations and New Orientations* - *1*
2. Étienne Brûlé - *18*
3. Joseph Chihoatenhwa - *73*
4. Thérèse Oionhaton - *127*
5. Marie Rollet Hébert - *175*
6. Conclusion - *196*

Appendix 1: *Kin Replacement in the Jesuit Relations* - *205*
Appendix 2: *John Steckley's Translation of Joseph Chihoatenhwa's Prayer* - *209*
Appendix 3: *Poems to Marie Rollet Hébert* - *213*
References - *219*
Index - *227*

Acknowledgments

First and foremost I would like to thank my teacher, Charles H. Long, to whom I am vastly indebted. His groundbreaking scholarship in the history of religions is the basis for this work, and his longstanding encouragement is the fundamental reason for its completion.

I also thank Jennifer Reid, who is both a role model and a dear friend. Her abiding support and guidance are invaluable to me.

This manuscript has directly benefited from the scholarly expertise of Phil Arnold and Amanda Porterfield, and the editorial expertise of Deborah Manion and the staff of Syracuse University Press. I thank them all.

I am deeply grateful for the fine colleagues I had in the Department of Comparative Religion at Miami University in Oxford, Ohio, especially Peter Williams, Liz Wilson, Jim Hanges, Julie Gifford, Scott Kenworthy, Geoffrey McVey, and the late Harold Forshey. I fondly remember their kindness, generosity, and conviviality.

I am also grateful for all of the wonderful new colleagues I have in the Department of Religious Studies at DePaul University in Chicago. While I must single out for special thanks Kay Read, Frida Furman, Khaled Keshk, and David Wellman, I would like everyone in my department to know how much I value their collegial support and friendship.

Special thanks must be given for the tangible assistance I have been provided by Syracuse University, Sweet Briar College, Miami University, and DePaul University. Fellowships and grants are crucial to the process of research and publication, and I am delighted to say that these institutions have been unstintingly supportive of my work.

I would also like to express my gratitude to Mary Denney and Michael Van Dorpe for their extremely valuable administrative assistance.

I am most deeply thankful to Jes Fowler, upon whose loving patience and unwavering support I can always depend, and without whom I could never have seen this book through to completion.

Finally, I am thankful to and proud of my students, who always rise to the occasion. They are the reason for my work, and they give me great hope for the future.

Religion, Gender, and Kinship in Colonial New France

1

Introduction

Disjunctive Valuations and New Orientations

When one crosses a border, one declares what is of value. This is, of course, a contemporary phenomenon, having to do with national boundaries, duties, value-added taxes, and permissible personal exemptions. Even gifts must be declared. What is of value is determined by the customs office of the nation in question. While the operations of a customs office are not of interest in this work, the existence of borders and the phenomenon of value are of central concern. Declaring what is of value will serve as a central analytic metaphor, as well as a defining activity of the persons here examined.

The focus of this work is not the present, but the early decades of the seventeenth century. The location in question is not a customs office, but the geography of Wendat country in particular, and the geography of a colonial enterprise called New France. Wendat country was an area of land bounded by Matchedash Bay to the north, Nottawasauga Bay to the south, and Lake Simcoe to the east.[1] This area is in the southeastern corner of Lake Huron's Georgian Bay. "The Huron villages were concentrated in an area that measured no more than 35 miles east to west and 20 miles north to south" (Trigger

---

1. The residents of this geographical area referred to themselves with the term "Wendat," which has been variously translated as "Islanders" or "Dwellers on a Peninsula" (Trigger 1988, 26, 436n3). My preferred translation is "People of the Peninsula," and I shall use this designation interchangeably with "Wendat." Their term for their traditional land base was Wendake, which I will use, along with "Wendat country."

1988, 30). New France was much larger, of course, consisting at this time of a vast but undetermined and largely unmapped area beginning at the Atlantic coastline of what is now eastern Canada and continuing as settlements along both sides of the St. Lawrence River. At its zenith, New France comprised Le Canada (the present-day Canadian provinces of Quebec and Ontario), L'Acadie (the present-day Canadian provinces of New Brunswick, Nova Scotia, and Prince Edward Island), and La Louisiane (most of the American Midwest and portions of the Canadian West).

In the first half of the sixteenth century, the explorers Giovanni da Verrazano and Jacques Cartier first claimed North American lands in the name of France. In 1605 Pierre de Gua, Sieur de Monts, obtained a monopoly of trade and settlement from Henry IV and founded, with Samuel de Champlain, the first permanent settlement, at Port-Royal. Subsequent settlements, such as Quebec, were established as fur trading posts. Champlain's strategic alliance with the Native inhabitants of this geography, particularly the people of the Wendat confederacy, who had wide-ranging trade networks, greatly enhanced the fur trade. Although the fur trade was the economic center of the colonial program, the French colonial enterprise also mandated the implantation of an agricultural society modeled on the French seigneurial system, and most significantly for this study, the conversion of indigenous peoples to Roman Catholicism.

In the course of exploring the cultural borders crossed in this historical period and in this geographic area, I will illustrate the ways in which new religious identities, new orientations, emerged as products of the material exchanges of human beings performed during the first decades of the French and Native encounters in Wendat country and in New France. The various discourses operating within the context of colonialism created disjunctive valuations and geographical displacements of the persons involved in these exchanges. I suggest that the earliest French disruptions of and incorporations into Native kinship structures presaged the genocidal structure of settler colonialism. Native responses to these French interventions into Native religio-social structures were clear and legible. Native people recognized relational inequalities and remedied imbalances by attempting to strengthen their relationships with sacred power. In these unsettling and disruptive times, Native people rejected the commodification of human beings, and insisted upon the creation and maintenance of relationships that embodied what they valued: reciprocity. In the first substantive contacts and exchanges between French explorers and settlers and the various indigenous peoples of these lands, new human orientations emerged, as persons were exchanged between families and communities, and as relationships between French and Native people were ritually created and cemented. These new religious orientations contributed in a constitutive and essential fashion to the ideational construction of the Americas and of modern subjectivities, both Euro-American and Native American.

Charles H. Long has defined "the cultural contact situation itself as a religious locus" (Long 1986, 63). In the early contact situation between the Europeans and Natives to be studied here, each attempted to incorporate the other into their respective material and symbolic universes. Champlain, following the agenda of Henry IV, desired to draw the Wendat into the French social, economic, and religious systems; his aims were the identification and acquisition of lands to settle, the establishment of networks of trade, and the religious conversion of the people indigenous to those lands. The French Recollets, and later the French Jesuits, were not as overtly concerned with the establishment of trade relationships. In fact, they prohibited themselves from personally engaging in the fur trade, and most of them saw the effects of trade as directly undermining their mission. However, they were quite obviously concerned with the incorporation of the Wendat and other indigenous groups into French religious and social systems. The people of the Wendat confederacy were also desirous of drawing the French into their cultural systems. Because the Wendat kinship system was the basis for social, economic, and religious relationships, the adoption of certain French persons was a central and important strategy for the Wendat to establish alliances with the French. However, the interpretive languages employed and deployed by European colonial cultures, particularly those in which individualism and commodification were emergent values, did not and do not sufficiently encompass these Native strategies of exchange.

The French, for the most part, pretended an understanding of Wendat culture. They described and classified the indigenous inhabitants of all of New France with apparent ease. However, the true opacity to the French of the "specific and definitive empirical and imaginative language" of the Wendat system of exchange would prove to be the undoing of their colonial plans.[2] It would also greatly contribute to the eventual undoing of the Wendat confederacy.

French traders failed to comprehend the sacrality of exchange for the Wendat. Seventeenth-century European mercantilism demanded a secular imagination of material, insofar as "the market economy interpose[d] itself between persons, mediating direct awareness of social relations by the abstract laws of relationships between commodities" (Long 1986, 110). Instead, the Wendat system conferred religious meaning upon the materials exchanged between persons, and even upon the exchange of persons. Employing a Maussian hermeneutic, Wendat culture could be described as a "system of total services"; that is, as a cultural system in which reciprocal structures of exchange are established, and in which this system comprises and reflects the symbolic universe of the culture (Mauss 1967, 5–6). While the worldviews of the Recollets and the Jesuits clearly had the capacity to regard some material as sacred, certain matter (specifically, the commodity) was emphatically secular. The misunderstandings inherent in contact between cultures speaking different material and symbolic languages were catastrophic. Wendat culture as it existed prior to colonial contact was wrenchingly disrupted. French culture, too, was irreversibly impacted by the colonial project and its attendant material and symbolic profits and losses.

In pointing to these disruptions, it is essential to acknowledge the violence inherent in the colonial process, and the particular violences of

---

2. On the opacity of non-European empirical languages to European colonials, see Long 1986, 107.

these specific encounters. The works of Champlain and Gabriel Sagard, and the *Jesuit Relations*—the accounts composed by the colonialists themselves, which also contain the echoes and submerged voices of the people indigenous to what would become New France—vividly portray the bloody consequences of the arrival of the French in the Americas. The exploitation of Wendat trade networks in order to accommodate French desires for the land and its resources resulted in a marked increase in warfare between the Wendat confederacy and the Haudenosaunee confederacy to their south. In another sense, however, this particular contact situation occasioned creation as well as destruction.

The primary work of human beings may be the construction of meaning through the ideation of symbol. As J. Z. Smith has written, "society or culture is preeminently the construction of significance and order through symbolic activity." Smith continues, "Social change is symbol change . . . [and] social change may then be specified as the discovery or creation of new modes of significance and order" (Smith, 1993, 144). In colonial situations, social change is inevitable, both on the part of the colonizer and of the colonized. Insufficiently polysemic symbols lose their power and new symbols are, to paraphrase Smith, "discovered or created." I wish to illustrate how two men (a French man named Étienne Brûlé and a Wendat man baptized as Joseph Chihoatenhwa) and two women (Thérèse Oionhaton and Marie Rollet Hébert) became enmeshed in the machinations of these intercultural complexities and opacities. The people who lived through (and died because of) this colonial encounter were not merely tragic human footnotes to regrettable misunderstandings. These human beings responded creatively to the new situations in which they found themselves; they oriented themselves to their new material and symbolic landscapes in astonishing ways. Their new orientations, to self, to others, and to the sacred, were expressed in ways that can only be called "religious."[3] I intend to demonstrate that the recorded lives of these

---

3. The term "orientation" is here being used in the way that Long has outlined: "orientation in the ultimate sense, that is, how one comes to terms with the ultimate

human beings serve as particularly salient sites for the study of these processes of discovery and creation, these processes of transformation, reorientation, and revaluation.

I have stated that it is value with which I am most concerned. The determination of value, as articulated in my metaphoric reference to customs offices, can be done by nations, with specific reference to monetary systems and rates of exchange. The notions of value that will be explored here are not limited to the monetary, although French pistoles will appear. (Étienne Brûlé was recompensed by the French trading company at a rate of 100 pistoles annually.) Here, the most significant values are those values expressed by the actions of the persons whose lives provide structure to this book. When Étienne Brûlé chose to live among the Wendat, when he chose to refuse to assist the French religious Brother Sagard in composing a dictionary of the Wendat language, when he chose to remain in New France despite its occupation by the English, he articulated what he valued. When Joseph Chihoatenhwa, a singular Wendat man, claimed Christianity and affiliated with the Jesuits, when he recited his prayer, he articulated what he valued. When many Wendat women resisted baptism, when they dreamt alternative sacred realities, when they joined their families on French *réserves*, when they chose to run away from those réserves, they articulated what they valued. When Thérèse Oionhaton chose to affiliate herself with the Ursuline sisters and with French Catholicism, maintaining this connection even through her captivity among the Haudenosaunee (Iroquois), she articulated what she valued. When Marie Rollet Hébert joined her husband in settling the new colony at Quebec, when she brought into her household Native women and a "servant" from Madagascar, when she fed her fellow habitants during times of famine, she articulated what she valued.

Mindful of Long's concept of "signification," it is my foundational assumption that the methodological challenges presented to

---

significance of one's place in the world" (Long 1986, 7). This orientation is not only symbolic, but also profoundly material.

contemporary scholars examining moments in the history of colonial contact are great. Classifications, taxonomies, and descriptions of the religious modalities of non-Western "others" are characteristic of the post-Enlightenment disciplinary construction of knowledge, and it is an early manifestation of that sort of knowledge-gathering that is analyzed here. As early modern missionaries and explorers, including the Jesuits and Champlain, described and inscribed the lives of the non-Western people they encountered, they constructed objectified "others." It is both terribly ironic and brilliantly insightful that the People of the Peninsula, attempting to account for staggering numbers of dead, just-baptized kinspeople, accused the Jesuits of plotting and practicing murder by taking their names and writing them down in baptismal lists, and then tearing out these names (Thwaites 1896–1901, 19:129).

A similar problem of representation is also encountered by anyone attempting to study these colonial encounters. As Mary Keller has described this structural dynamic, "The scholar is constructed as an active agent and the agency of the people being studied is violently erased, their indigenous knowledge overridden by the imposition of interpretive frameworks" (Keller 2002, 12). Like the voices of the possessed women studied by Keller, the voices of the people inscribed and described by the Jesuits, especially those of the women, are "doubly lost" (Keller 2002, 13–14). It is not my intent to recover lost voices—that would be constructing yet another level of signification. Instead, I read closely the texts produced by French explorers and Jesuit missionaries, and seek within those texts evidence of moments in the lives of persons described and inscribed that articulate messages that run contrary to missionary and colonial programs. In other words, by reading against the texts, by remaining cognizant of the agendas of the French, and by seeking evidence of counter-narratives, I hope a clearer picture will emerge, a picture more attentive to the complexities and opacities of the colonial encounters and exchanges of Wendat country and New France.

Also, heeding the wise warning of Nicholas Thomas, I wish to stress that the analytical tools and descriptive categorizations employed and deployed here are not intended to ideologically polarize and historically staticize the cultures and people studied herein. "Now, in the late twentieth century, indigenous historians and metropolitan writers like myself can attempt to colonize the past through an interpretative scheme; but just as indigenous societies were never encompassed by colonizer's representations, or by the socioeconomic consequences of the world system, the past must remain refractory and partly intransigent before these projects (Thomas 1991, 82)."

However, it is in fact my intention to identify and describe the disjunctive languages, both material and symbolic, that shaped the initial decades of encounter between the French and the Wendat. Toward this end, I confine this analysis to a specific set of encounters between persons and cultures in a unique geography within a defined time period, and I endeavor to attend to those locative particularities.

On Exchange and the Emergence of New Orientations

Exchanges conducted between cultures in the context of colonialism may be understood as endeavors on the parts of both colonizers and colonized to incorporate the other into their respective material and symbolic systems. However, as materials passed from one culture to the other, they were necessarily abstracted from their original sites of meaning. When these materials were extracted, they were also revalued by the cultures that received them. For example, the beaver participated in an entirely different complex of meanings for the Wendat than it did for the French. Because of these revaluations, the materials could not totally recover their original located and contextualized meanings. In colonial situations, the exchanges between the colonizers and the colonized thus involved disjunctures in the understanding and valuation of the materials that were exchanged. It was because of these disjunctures of valuation that the possibility of the dislocation of these materials was introduced. The process of dislocation may be understood as having begun with the displacement of an object from its original network of meaning. When the object was thus removed, it was no longer necessary or practical to consider it as containing value only as it participated in its original milieu. It became possible to attribute to it a value independent of its former relational context. These new valuations typically recognized the object as carrying value not by virtue of its participation in its former constellation of relationships, but by virtue of its value as a potential means to an end. For example, by dislocating the beaver from its originary spatial and symbolic geography, it became possible to regard the beaver not as a material and symbolic participant in a network of Wendat relationships, but as a means by which profits could be made.

In the seventeenth-century colonial encounter between French colonizers and Wendat natives in the geography of what would become known as New France, human beings were among the materials exchanged. For the French, the exchanges of human beings took place within two discursive contexts: mercantilism and missionization. For the French, the exchanges of human beings were intended to extend each of these projects among the natives of New France. By sending French human beings to live among the Wendat, the French hoped to acquire, upon the return of these persons, interpreters with the ability to facilitate the projects of trade with and conversion of the Wendat. By receiving People of the Peninsula to live among the French, the French hoped to acquire converts to Christianity, who could also facilitate further missionization and trade. For the Wendat, exchanges of human beings were intended to create alliances, constituted and expressed through the extension of kinship relationships. By sending members of the Wendat confederacy to live among the French, and by receiving French human beings to live among them, the Wendat hoped materially and symbolically to establish and represent their kinship with the French, which would permit and even require mutuality in trade, assistance in warfare, and general extension of community. However, the transparency of these discourses should not be assumed. Rather, in recognition of the opacity of these discourses, this study purposely focuses on the sites and persons in which Native discourses came into conflict with French expectations and practices.

For these human objects of exchange, dislocation resulted in the creation of new religious orientations. These orientations are best understood as religious not only because they articulated value and expressed relationship to the sacred, but also because they served as sites of religious contestation. That is to say, the participants in the colonial exchanges within New France and Wendat country were clearly concerned with the ways in which these newly oriented persons could be made to conform with particular understandings of proper relationship to the sacred. The persons upon whom this study will focus are those who were to be fashioned by the French into interpreters and converts (significantly, often thought of as godchildren), and by the Wendat into kinspersons. These persons' bodies were contested sites. The pressing need for new orientations was created by the conflicting and overlapping discourses within French colonial and Native systems; these new orientations were created and expressed by those persons who were displaced from their original sites of meaning. Negotiating these orientations presented difficulties not only for those persons who were exchanged (the potential interpreters, converts, and kinspeople), but also for those persons, both colonizer and colonized, who were parties to these exchanges and witnesses to the fashioning of these new orientations.

The new orientations produced in the early decades of French and Wendat colonial encounters contain distinctively modern valences. These orientations, as products of dislocation and as self-consciously creative, are instantiations of modern subjectivities. This is not at all to imply a teleological view of history in which cultures are viewed as inexorably progressing toward one state or another. On the contrary, this analysis depends upon a Foucauldian understanding of the modern subject, which includes the dimensions of dislocation from social networks of meaning, as well as the internalization of power and control. A specifically Native construction of modernity will also be acknowledged and illustrated; this Native modernity resides in emergent senses of collective identity as opposed to emergent senses of individual identity. In short, my central contention is that the clashes of Wendat and French discourses, most notably in regard to strategies of exchange, in attempting to produce interpreters, converts, or kin, actually resulted in the articulation of distinctive and new religious orientations. The construction and negotiation of these orientations in the early decades of colonial New France stand as exempla of the central problems and possibilities of the Americas.

The Contexts of This Study

This study addresses a specific geography in the context of colonialism. Analyses of North American colonial encounters have been produced in profusion in the last four decades, and historians have been at the forefront of this trend. Scholars such as James Axtell and Francis Jennings provided some of the earlier works on Native responses to the European incursion and on the construction of colonial discourses of conquest, and although these scholars do attend to the complexities of intercultural encounters and colonialist assumptions, they often fall short in the analysis of the concept of conversion. Jennings examines and exposes colonialist ideology by attending primarily to European discourses of power (1976). Carole Blackburn's 2000 *Harvest of Souls: The Jesuit Missions and Colonialism in North America, 1632–1650*, which approaches the *Jesuit Relations* through the use of colonial discourse studies, has been essential to this book, and remains the best work of its kind. Although James Axtell (1990) has addressed the intercultural dimensions of Native-colonial encounters and exchanges, Kenneth Morrison has thoughtfully critiqued Axtell's inability to reframe the analysis by attending to a Native perspective. Kenneth Morrison's last monograph, *The Solidarity of Kin: Ethnohistory, Religious Studies, and the Algonkian-French Religious Encounter* (2002), attended closely to the ways in which the study of religion is critical in illuminating the crises and creations of the colonial period. This book takes inspiration from Morrison's final work, and is similarly invested in bringing a history of religions perspective to the analysis of the encounters and exchanges of colonial New France.

The second set of scholarly works with which this book is engaged are those exploring the history of New France itself. In the triumphalist shadow of the nineteenth-century work of Francis Parkman (1983), many contemporary scholars have labored to produce revisionist histories of New France. Scholarship in this field is quite plentiful and in the past was generally divided into two distinct categories: history (cultural, economic, or missionary) and ethnography. Traditionally, the histories addressed the persons and processes of European colonization, inclusive of encounters and exchanges with natives. The works of Marcel Trudel (see Trudel 1966 and 1973) and William J. Eccles (1998), both focused on French colonial activities, are perhaps the classics of this genre. Ethnographies, on the other hand, trace the histories of Native groups, employing archaeological research. Elisabeth Tooker's Huron ethnography (1991) is an early example of work of this type. In more recent decades, however, ethnohistories and histories focused upon intercultural encounter have appeared. Examples are the ethnohistories written by Conrad Heidenreich (1971), Howard Harrod (1984), and Bruce Trigger; the colonial histories composed by Denys Delâge (1993), Olive Dickason (1984), and Cornelius Jaenen (1976a and 1976b) use these to very fruitful effect, while Tracy Leavelle takes an instructively panoramic view in *The Catholic Calumet: Colonial Conversions in French and Indian North America* (2012).

Trigger's magisterial *The Children of Aataentsic: A History of the Huron People to 1660* (1988) is foundational to the present study, although it is critiqued for its uncritical acceptance and redeployment of European categories of thought. This book is also heavily indebted to the linguistic expertise of Michael Pomedli (1991) and John Steckley (1987; 1993; 2004); without their work in recovering and interpreting the Wendat language and the complexity of its religious referents, competent critique of any sort would be impossible.

In addition to its engagement with these secondary works, this book will engage most closely with the primary sources of the early colonial history of New France. These primary sources include the correspondences of the Jesuit missionaries from the years 1610 to 1649 included within the volumes published by Thwaites as the *Jesuit Relations* (1896–1901), and enhanced with additional documents in the several volumes published by Lucien Campeau as *Monumenta Nova Franciae* (1987–92); the two books produced by the Recollet missionary Gabriel Sagard (1866; 1968); the works of the explorer Samuel de

Champlain (1971); and the writings of the Ursuline sister Marie de L'Incarnation (1989).

The distinctive contribution of this book lies in bringing a hermeneutic grounded in history of religions to the particularities of the early decades of colonialism in New France. The history of religions perspectives advocated by Charles Long provides the foundation of this hermeneutical position. As demonstrated by Long, history of religions provides an exemplary set of analytical tools with which to interrogate the moments in which encounters and exchanges between cultures occur. Long points to the opacity of the other and to the sacred as critical parts of a successful hermeneutic. He also insists upon the necessity of a reflexive and self-critical positioning on the part of the historian of religions in the face of the opacity of the other. His insights are uniquely suited to an analysis of the new subjectivities produced by and within these discursive operations. Yet while Long points to the emergence of a modern subject in his analysis of the "double vision" of Pascal and the "veil" of DuBois, I locate modern subjectivities and complex religious orientations as emerging from the context of the colonial encounter itself.

A thoroughgoing history of religions perspective has yet to be brought to bear upon these particular persons and events in the study of colonial New France. Recently, Allan Greer's article on Iroquois conversion and identity (2003) and his substantial "dual biography" of Catherine Tekakwitha and her hagiographers, Fathers Chauchetière and Cholenec (2000; 2005); Emma Anderson's descriptive analysis of the "conversion" and estrangement of Pierre Pastedechouan (2007); and Erik Seeman's lucid 2011 study of the Wendat Feast of the Dead have made innovative and important contributions to the literature. While this work is inspired by and indebted to each one of them, it is Anderson's analytical grounding in a history of religions perspective that comes closest to the disciplinary positioning of this present work. I should note that just as Anderson has asserted, Richard White's notion of the "middle ground" (1991) is not applicable here. Anderson points to the French Recollet missionary agenda, which "sought nothing less than the total cultural and religious capitulation of native societies to their priestly authority" (Anderson 2007, 210). In addition, settler colonialism, understood as an historical and social structure that "strives for the dissolution of native societies" as it "erects a new colonial society on the expropriated land base" (Wolfe 2006, 388), is also not yet established during the historical period under study here. While the work of Frederick Hoxie (2008), Patrick Wolfe (2006; 2013), and Lorenzo Veracini (2010; 2013) will become quite relevant to the study of this geography after the 1650s, during the period under study here the French are laying the groundwork for the establishment of settler colonialist structures by attempting to alter Native social and religious structures of kinship and relationality by imposing other forms of relationship and other imaginations of matter in their stead.

When Champlain, the French explorer and soon-to-be settler, takes a Wendat man on board his ship, and in exchange allows one of his crew members to live among the Wendat, he is not simply participating in the Wendat kinship exchange that results in alliance. He has an alternative agenda that undermines and ultimately disrupts the intended equilibration of relationship. When Jesuit missionaries convince a Wendat man that if he wishes to participate in their relationships with sacred power, he should undergo the ritual of baptism and thereby become a part of their community, his existing Wendat kinship relationships are destabilized. When the Ursuline nuns provide a religious, ritualized model of relationality as a community of sisters, and when the women of the Hébert-Couillard family and other settler women serve as godmothers to Native women who seek to expand their kinship networks in order to seek safety and secure alliances, Native strategies of survival are co-opted.

Here, it is critical to note the gendered dimension of this socio-religious precursor to settler colonialism. Carol Devens's *Countering Colonization: Native American Women and Great Lakes Missions, 1630–1900* (1992) has served as a constant reminder that in colonial studies, it is imperative to take into account gender as an operative discourse. And as Bonita Lawrence contends, identity is always relational, and "[f]or Native people, individual identity is always being negotiated in relation to collective identity, and in the face of an external, colonizing society" (Lawrence 2003, 4). Lawrence's analysis points to Canada's Indian Act as one foundational example of the ways in which "Canadian regulation of Native identity created gendered notions of Indianness" (Lawrence 2003, 5). I wish to support her assertion with evidence of much earlier instances of gendered intervention into Native identities. In addition, I wish to echo Adam Barker's recognition that "colonization is motivated by an implicit individualism" (Barker 2010, 322) and, with Barker, to support Dale Turner's call for respect, as he defines it relationally, from a Haudenosaunee perspective: "[R]especting another person's intrinsic value means that you recognize that they have the right to . . . choose for themselves how to act in the world . . . [R]espect functioned in a communal context . . . [and] was reciprocated" (Turner 2006, 49).

In sum, I propose to bring an important interpretive strategy to this particular colonial encounter. I employ a methodology grounded in attentiveness to the religious valences of exchange, and in particular to the various sites of contact in which strategies of exchange are amplified. My aim is to locate and analyze the religiously significant orientations that emerge from the context of contact. This methodology has been seen in other recent works in the history of religions, such as Mary Keller's *The Hammer and the Flute: Women, Power, and Spirit Possession* (2002) and Jennifer Reid's *Myth, Symbol, and Colonial Encounter: British and Mi'kmaq in Acadia, 1700–1867* (1995), as well as in earlier works in colonial history, such as Fernando Cervantes' *The Devil in the New World: The Impact of Diabolism in New Spain* (1994).

It may also be worth mentioning that my mode of analysis is also indebted to studies of gift and exchange, including Marcel Mauss's *The Gift: The Form and Reason for Exchange in Archaic Societies* (1997) and Annette Weiner's *Inalienable Possessions: The Paradox of Keeping-While-Giving*. For shaping my understanding of "the modern," I also acknowledge Michel Foucault's *Discipline and Punish: The Birth of the Prison* (1995) and Philip Deloria's *Indians in Unexpected Places* (2004), especially for the latter's thoughtful presentation of varying types of evidence of the full participation of Native people in the construction of modernity.

Chapter 2 of this book is organized around the person of Étienne Brûlé, a French young man who crossed borders, engaged and exchanged with persons his compatriots disdained, and emerged with a new orientation and a new occupation. He was a translator of words, a translator of cultures, but also a translator of value. The understanding of value he embodied was as a commodity, and his translation of mercantilism was construed as treason to the Wendat. The chapter tracing Brûlé's journey through Wendat country and beyond is a chapter that attends to surface exchanges. It is a map of the movement of persons and things across a landscape, and on this map is marked a spot where a murder was done.

In many ways chapter 3 contains a deeper level of analysis. While it focuses on the person of Joseph Chihoatenhwa, a Wendat man who allied himself with the Jesuits, it is primarily concerned with linguistic exchanges and the production of a linguistic economy. It addresses the rhetoric and symbols of Jesuit success: a harvest reaped, a justification for monetary support of the enterprise, and the production of a new person/fiction by the Jesuits. However, the production of this person, Joseph Chihoatenhwa, is no mere literary achievement. This chapter traces the production of a new person/fact by Joseph himself. It examines his sacrifice of self in pursuit of the goal of preservation of relationships and community, and explores another murder mystery. This chapter also marks the emergence of indigenous hybridities—in the intended production of converts by Jesuits, in the production of rituals by the Wendat, and in the words of Joseph Chihoatenhwa.

Chapter 4 examines the experiences of Wendat women and further explores ideas about kinship in both French and Native societies. The chapter opens with mention of Thérèse Oionhaton, Joseph Chihoatenhwa's daughter, and focuses on the religiously inflected ways in which Wendat women created their own kinship networks in response to the displacement and bereavement they experienced during the colonial period. Here, the most difficult level of analysis is broached, because the voices and experiences of the women of Wendat country are often more deeply buried in colonial texts. In this chapter various modalities of resistance are explored, as women use traditional techniques (the dream) but also creatively deploy hybrid techniques to articulate their values and their losses. Landscapes and languages are shifted slightly in the examination of the public punishment of Innu women at the Sillery réserve. The seemingly contradictory strategy of maintaining kinship structures by altering them is identified, and is associated with women who appear to be converting to Christianity in order to remain in relation with other women. It will be demonstrated that through this activity, their female lines of communication and instruction are preserved. Most important, it is here that I explore and dismantle the concept of conversion and reread a Wendat myth of a lost sister.

The fifth chapter, which opens with the stories of the Hébert-Couillard women of the first settler families in New France, describes and interprets the orientation and kinship-creation strategies of immigrant French women. It identifies the gendered rituals and activities of godmothering as critical tools for negotiating the new relational landscapes in which these settler women found themselves, particularly in light of Marie Rollet Hébert's literal and metaphorical role as godmother of New France.

The conclusion of this work addresses the operations of gift and commodity, exchange and reciprocity, as constituents of authentic relationship; the persistence of the traditional and the emergence of opaque "visions of the vanquished"; and the differing valuations conferred upon the emergence of modern identities in both French and Native communities. In sum, here I articulate the implications that my analysis of one colonial moment might have in the broader context of studies of religions in the Americas.

2

Étienne Brûlé

Étienne Brûlé: Translator

Étienne Brûlé is an enigmatic figure in the colonial history of New France. At a time when many literate Europeans were carefully inscribing their experiences of a continent new to them, he left no journal, he wrote no history; indeed, it is possible that Brûlé was not literate.[1] Yet references to Brûlé appear in almost every primary source from the period 1608–33, and these references are never noncommittal; in every case they articulate particularly strong opinions. He was known by many, and many voices speak of him; Brûlé is invoked by explorer and by missionary, by European and by Native, by colonizer and by colonized. It is partially because of this passionate familiarity that Brûlé must be regarded as a crucial figure of his time and place. Yet there is more to this study than an historical reconstruction of the life and death of Brûlé.

Through Brûlé one may witness most clearly the terrible religious complexities of colonial New France. It is not only that Brûlé was chosen to serve as a mediator between cultures. It is not simply that Brûlé's actions in this role produced ethical pronouncements and moral judgments. The greatest significance of Brûlé is that he became

---

1. J. Herbert Cranston quotes Benjamin Sulté as venturing in his *Ottawa Journal* column, "Annals of the Ottawa," that Brûlé was indeed literate, asserting that Champlain intentionally recruited several educated young men to be trained as interpreters in New France. However appealing this conjecture may be, there is no proof of this to be found in primary sources (Cranston 1949, 5n).

both the material and the symbol through which colonial relationships were negotiated. Chosen by the French as *truchement*,[2] chosen by the Wendat people as kin, his presence enabled and, in the end, thwarted attempts to establish relationships. Early in his life in New France, in one momentous instance, he physically embodied intercultural exchange; after his death, his very bones provided the occasion of a religious conundrum for both the French Jesuits and the Wendat people. During his life in between those hopeful and fearful moments, Brûlé himself had to negotiate a new way of being in a new kind of world, a world fraught with hazardous limits and filled with perilous freedoms.

Voyages: Brûlé and Champlain

In 1608 the experienced navigator and cartographer Samuel de Champlain made his fourth voyage to the Americas; it was his third to the geographic area then known as New France.[3] Some scholars have ventured that Champlain may have been Protestant by birth, coming as he did from Brouage, "in the heart of the Huguenot country" (Bishop 1948, 5). Morris Bishop has also raised the interesting point that Samuel as a given name bespeaks Protestantism, especially since Roman Catholics of the time named their children after saints, "thus affording their offspring a personal advocate in heaven" (Bishop 1948, 5). In any event, Champlain was, by 1598, an experienced soldier in the

---

2. *Truchement* is the term employed in seventeenth-century French to signify "interpreter"; the literal meaning is "medium" or "means of expression." Valences of this term shall be explored later in this chapter.

3. In 1603 Champlain had established alliances with and wintered among the Wendat people, spending time at the settlements of Hochelaga (Montreal) and Stadacona (Quebec). Upon his return to France, he wrote a small book detailing his sojourn, and on the title page of that work referred to the geographic area he visited as "France nouvelle." Later that year, when Henry IV conferred upon Sieur de Monts the trading monopoly for that area, he formally christened "Nouvelle France" that region of the Americas between the fortieth and forty-sixth latitudes.

army of Henry IV. He had fought in Brittany against Spain and the Catholic League (Champlain 1971, 1:3), and he appears to have been at this time, like his monarch, at least nominally Catholic (Bishop 1948, 9–12). After the war, in 1599, Champlain secured employment through his uncle's connections and sailed with a Spanish convoy (on a chartered French transport, whose owners Champlain may have been representing) for New Spain (Champlain 1971, 1:3–5, Bishop 1948, 14–15). Upon his return, he engaged himself aboard the fleet of François Gravé, Sieur du Pont (also known as Pontgravé), an experienced trader and explorer of the St. Lawrence, and sailed to the Americas and back to France with him in 1603 (Champlain 1971, 1:91–469, Bishop 1948, 37–123).

In the year 1604, Pierre du Gua, Sieur de Monts, a Huguenot, had secured from Henry IV exclusive rights to the French fur trade in North America. He was also ordered by Henry to Christianize the inhabitants of the Americas and to establish French colonies there. De Monts hired Champlain as geographer and cartographer; de Monts engaged Pontgravé and his ship as well. A settlement was established on the St. Lawrence island they called St. Croix, but during that winter, thirty-nine of the seventy-five colonists died of scurvy. In the spring of 1605, all but three of the survivors of St. Croix returned to France. Champlain remained, and sailed with Pontgravé up and down the coast from what is now known as New Brunswick to what is now called Cape Cod. In need of establishing a winter settlement, they disembarked in November at Port-Royal, which was a long-established harbor and landing for Basque fishing fleets as well as the home of many Mi'kmaq people, including the famed chief Membertou. While Pontgravé sailed for France in the spring of 1606, Champlain again wintered in New France and did not sail for France until 1607. This, then, was a three-year voyage for Champlain (Champlain 1971, 1:225–469).

In the year 1608, de Monts had obtained from Henry IV a year's extension on his fur trading monopoly, and this time de Monts had given Champlain his first position of command. Champlain would serve as his chief lieutenant (representative) on this particular voyage.

Champlain quoted the entirety of the king's commission at the beginning of his account of that year, which he published in Paris in 1613. The commission points to what may be considered the four primary concerns of the king and of de Monts, and thus of his agents Pontgravé and Champlain: land, missions, settlement, and trade: "Upon the information which has been given to us by those who have come from New France regarding the good quality and fertility of the lands in that country, and that the inhabitants thereof are disposed to receive the knowledge of God, we have resolved to continue the settlement which had already been begun in those parts, in order that our subjects may go there and trade freely" (Champlain 1971, 2:5).[4]

Two of de Monts' ships sailed for New France in April 1608. The first ship, commanded by Pontgravé, sailed from the French port of Honfleur on April fifth. Pontgravé was to sail along the coast of New Brunswick, to negotiate and trade with Natives through the summer months and then to sail both ships back to France in the autumn. The second ship, carrying Champlain along with a group of trained artisans and young men, was to explore the St. Lawrence River and its tributaries, and return the ship to Pontgravé in the fall. Champlain's group was to stay the winter and further trading relationships with the various Native groups indigenous to the area. Étienne Brûlé, sixteen years of age at the time, was one of the young men accompanying Champlain (Champlain 1971, 2:3–9; Bishop 126–27).

Brûlé was born in the year 1592 at Champigny-sur-Marne, near Paris (Jurgens 1966, 130). He has been described as the son of peasant farmers (Cranston 1949, 7), but there is no clear evidence to confirm this as fact. It simply appears that Brûlé was one of the many young men of France who left their homes in this period to seek employment

---

4. I have chosen to retain, in most citations, the translations of the works of Champlain produced by Biggar et al. under the auspices of the Champlain Society (Champlain 1971). While these translations are smooth, they do sometimes tend to "improve" Champlain's language. When clarification or elucidation seemed necessary, I have rendered my own word choices in brackets. In some instances, I have chosen to employ my own translations, and these are designated as such.

on one of the ships headed to the Americas. Despite Sulté's aforementioned opinion on the matter (note 1), it is impossible to say whether his assignation to Champlain's ship was a matter of chance or of Champlain's particular design.

Champlain arrived in June at the harbor of Tadoussac, situated at the mouth of the Saguenay River. "By the end of the sixteenth century, Tadoussac . . . was the established rendezvous for the French traders and the . . . Montagnais and others of Algonquin stock" (Bishop 1948, 34).[5] However, demonstrating his commitment to another of the aims of Henry IV's commission, Champlain and several of his men moved on from that harbor. His efforts were directed toward finding suitable land upon which to establish settlement. He found this land at Quebec (Stadacona), and he and his men began to build their *habitation* there. However, Champlain's work was momentarily diverted by an assassination plot initiated by one of his artisans, the locksmith Jean Duval. Duval apparently intended to convince the men at Quebec to kill Champlain, take over the fort being built, and sell it to the Basques or Spaniards who were then at Tadoussac. Duval had already convinced three men to join his conspiracy, and these four together intimidated the rest into acquiescence. It is unclear whether Brûlé was among the men then at Quebec, but it is possible that he was. He was certainly not one of the primary conspirators. However, in Champlain's explanation of the plot, this tantalizing sentence appears: "In short, so successful were they in their intrigues with those who remained [at Quebec] that they would have attracted all to their side, *and even my lackey*, making many promises which they could not have fulfilled" (Champlain 1971, 2:26).[6] It is tempting to attribute Champlain's term (*laquay*) as a reference to the young Brûlé.

In any event, when Champlain discovered the plot, he captured the main conspirators by a ruse and had them bound and sent back

---

5. The "others" referred to here would include Naskapi and Attikamek. In this work, "Montagnais" will be referred to as "Innu," which is their preferred name for themselves and means "the people."

6. Emphasis mine.

to Tadoussac, where Pontgravé awaited and took them into captivity. Some days later, Pontgravé transported the captives back to Quebec, where they were tried. Four confessed, blaming Duval for instigating the conspiracy, while Duval confessed and asked for mercy. All were condemned to death for such treason, but only Duval was hanged on the spot. After execution, Duval's head was displayed on the highest pike of Champlain's fort. The other four were sent back to France on Pontgravé's ship, in order that de Monts might approve and carry out their sentences. This event was Champlain's first encounter with treason in New France, but it was not to be his last (Champlain 1971, 2:24–34).

Pontgravé sailed for France with his captives on September 18, while Champlain remained at Quebec with twenty-seven of his men. As they worked together to complete the habitation (which included lodgings, storehouses, a kitchen, and a garden, all surrounded by a moat), local Native groups gathered around the construction site and fished for eel. Champlain stored the inhabitants' catch for them and took the opportunity to "stud[y] their customs very particularly" (Champlain 1971, 2:45). He inquired as to their religious beliefs and concluded, "they would soon be brought to be good Christians, if one were to live in their country, as the majority of them desire" (Champlain 1971, 2:51). Champlain described in his journals the religious practices, marriage customs, and death rituals of the Innu people. He concluded that "they believe in the immortality of souls, and say that the dead enjoy happiness in other lands with their relatives and friends who have died" (Champlain 1971, 2:50). Champlain also portrays himself as ardently in pursuit of the stated aims of King Henry and of de Monts.

The winter Champlain and his men spent at Quebec was a difficult one. A few times, their fort was visited by Innu bands, who risked death by crossing the river to the French fort and arrived "so thin and emaciated that they looked like skeletons, most of them being unable to stand" (Champlain 1971, 2:54). The French fed them, as they had lain by a sufficient store for the winter. However, their food was not nutritionally adequate; twenty of the twenty-eight men died of scurvy and dysentery that season. The remaining eight consisted of Champlain, four unnamed men, the pilot Laroutte, and the two youngest: Nicolas Marsolet and Étienne Brûlé (Champlain 1971, 2:61–63).

Encounters: Champlain and the Arendarhonon Wendat

In June 1609 Pontgravé returned from France, and Champlain met him at Tadoussac. It was arranged that Pontgravé would remain to oversee the habitation at Quebec, and Champlain would take the opportunity to explore the Iroquois country, accompanied by some Innu men. Champlain states that his objective was exploration, but both he and the Innu (whom Champlain now calls *"nos alliez"* [our allies]), seem to have had other plans. The Innu men escorted Champlain to an island in the St. Lawrence then known to the French as St. Eloi, and on this island were waiting some two or three hundred Natives (according to Champlain's estimate). They were made up of a small nucleus of two distinct groups: the Wendat, specifically the Arendarhonon (the easternmost of the four groups comprising the Wendat confederacy[7]) led by Ochasteguin, and the Onontcharonon Algonkin led by Iroquet. The great part of Champlain's hundreds were local Natives hoping to have the opportunity to trade with the French (Trigger 1988, 248). The Onontcharonon had been in contact with Champlain ten months earlier, and since then had agreed to introduce to the French their trading partners and war allies, the Arendarhonon. The Arendarhonon Wendat were making their first overtures toward establishing an alliance with the French. Although Trigger has emphasized the interest of the Wendat in "winning renown by going to war with these strangers" (Trigger 1988, 248), it appears more likely that their primary motivation was to establish a trading relationship with the French unmediated by the Onontcharonon

---

7. The four confederated nations of the Wendat, were, in order from east to west, the Arendarhonon (Rock People), Attigneenongnahac (Cord People), Tahontaenrat (Deer People), and Attignawantan (Bear People).

and the Kichesipirini, who were at that time middlemen in all trade and contact with the French.

Upon Champlain's arrival, he was greeted with the presentation of gifts of furs. On the second day at St. Eloi, Champlain met with Ochasteguin and Iroquet in council. Champlain describes an oration by Iroquet, in which was recounted the meeting that had taken place ten months earlier between Champlain and Iroquet's son. At that meeting Champlain had apparently told this man that he and Pontgravé were willing to assist the Onontchataronon in warfare. The present council on St. Eloi was in anticipation of a war raid upon the Mohawk, and in expectation of French assistance in that expedition. Champlain replied by asserting that he was there precisely in order to conduct a war expedition against the Iroquois and invited all present to return with him to Quebec, "that they could see that I had no other intention than to make war; for we had with us only arms and not merchandise for barter" (Champlain 1971, 2:71).

In any event, all present returned with Champlain to Quebec, where five or six days were spent in ritual preparation ("dancing and feasting") for a war expedition (Champlain 1971, 2:72). At the close of preparations, Champlain outfitted twelve French men, and set out with Iroquet and Ochasteguin and their men down the Saint Lawrence River and down the Richelieu River toward Iroquois country. Upon reaching the St. Louis Rapids at Chambly, Champlain found that his small boat (*challoupe*) could not pass through. He sent all of his men except two back to Quebec and continued on in a canoe with those two. The war party, now pared down to about sixty men, continued portaging and canoeing until they came upon a large lake, which Champlain named for himself. They paddled and portaged from Lake Champlain to Lake George, eventually trekking to Ticonderoga. Upon meeting a group of Mohawks, Champlain immediately shot his arquebus and killed two men (whom he describes as *chefs*, or chiefs), while the Algonkin and Wendat killed a few men and took a dozen or so as prisoners. After the battle, the Wendat commenced the early stages of the ceremonial torture of one of their captives. Champlain, although asked to participate, refused and finally persuaded the

Wendat people to allow him to shoot and kill the prisoner. When he was dead, the Wendat men attempted to feed portions of the dead man's heart to their Mohawk prisoners. The victorious group then paddled and portaged back to the mouth of the Richelieu, where the Wendat people departed for Wendat country, the Algonkin people for their homes (presumably the Ottawa valley and its environs), and the Innu and the French to Quebec. Champlain wrote that "all separated with great protestations of mutual friendship, and they asked me if I would not go to their country, and aid them continually like a brother" (Champlain 1971, 2:104–5). A celebratory feast was held at Tadoussac, and some weeks later, on September 10, Champlain sailed for France. It is certain that Brûlé remained and wintered in New France, most likely at Quebec and Tadoussac (Champlain 1971, 2:72–107).

Champlain's encounter and war alliance with the Wendat confederacy is quite significant for this study, even though Étienne Brûlé was most likely not present during these events. The events of the summer of 1609 highlight a crucial disjunction between French and Wendat symbolic systems and cultural practices. For Champlain, an obvious way to establish amity and alliance with the Wendat was to assist them in warfare. "The French who visited the Huron country were accustomed to wars that were fought for territorial gain or commercial advantage, or because of religious differences. To their surprise, none of these motives played an important role in traditional Iroquoian warfare" (Trigger 1988, 68). The primary aim of warfare among Iroquoians was the taking of captives,[8] not the murder of enemies. War was conducted in order to achieve blood-revenge and to assuage the grief of those who had recently suffered the death of family members. The capture of prisoners was often the aim, because they could be taken as replacements for the deceased kinsperson and adopted into the bereaved families (Thwaites 1896–1901, 6:259, 17:65, etc.; Trigger

---

8. The term "Iroquoian" designates a Native linguistic group; members of the Haudenosaunee and Wendat confederacies were and are speakers of Iroquoian languages.

1988, 68–75). This understanding of warfare as a locus of reciprocity through which lost kinspeople may be replaced can be taken as evidence of a Maussian system of total services. In any event, Champlain seems completely to have missed the meaning of Iroquoian warfare, as his conduct in later war raids would demonstrate.

Champlain was also unable to discern the meaning of the Iroquoian practice of the torture of captives. As he recorded, he demonstrated his objection to the torture of the Haudenosaunee man, refused to participate, "went away from them as if angry at seeing them perform so much cruelty on his body" (Champlain 1971, 2:103), and was finally allowed to shoot the prisoner.

> The Europeans, judging from their own frames of reference and relying on their own moral assumptions, could not understand . . . the torture of captives and could not accept that soldiers . . . should suffer a death reserved in Europe only for the basest criminals . . . The native motivations, ritualistic satisfaction and value system were ignored. Frenchmen did not understand that in most Amerindian cultures retribution was "an act of inspired virtue," the highest expression of their moral system. (Jaenen 1976b, 139)

Iroquoian peoples did not understand torture as an expression of outright cruelty. Given the warrior complex that comprised the Iroquoian understanding of proper male behavior, prisoners, as warriors, were expected to conduct themselves with stoicism and to demonstrate their strength while bearing torture. Further, torture also functioned as an expression of kinship-based total exchange. Torture was the ritualized alternative to the adoption of prisoners taken in raids, and was conducted while ritually addressing the captive as a respected kinsman[9] (Trigger 1988, 73–75, Thwaites 1896–1901, 1:271–73, 4:199–201, 5:29–31, etc.).

A brief mention of the unusual attempt to feed the heart of the dead prisoner to the other captives may be warranted here. In Wendat

---

9. See appendix 1 for particular examples illustrative of the kin-replacement significance of the torture of captives.

practice, portions of the bodies of captured warriors were sometimes eaten by the Wendat people (Thwaites 1896–1901, 10:227, 17:75). "If the prisoner had been particularly brave before he died, the Huron would eat his heart, blood, and roasted flesh in order to be courageous also" (Tooker 1991, 38–39). In this uncommon instance, however, it appears that because of the fact that Champlain had deprived the Mohawk captive of his opportunity to demonstrate the strength and courage of a warrior, his heart was deemed unworthy of consumption by the victorious Wendat, and the dishonored organ was mockingly fed to the defeated Mohawk.

The greatest significance of this encounter, however, is that it begins to hint at the importance of trade to the Wendat. It will be recalled that the impetus behind the presence of Ochasteguin and his men at St. Eloi was the desire for unmediated trade with the French. Long before the arrival of Europeans, the Wendat had established a wide-ranging trade network. They traded with other Iroquoians also inhabiting southern Ontario: the Tionnontaté, the Neutral Nation, and further south the Susquehannock. They also traded with Algonkians to their north and east; in addition to the Onontchataronon, trade relationships were established with the Nipissing and Petite Nation Algonkin. For the Wendat, trade was also embedded in a network of social relations, understood as replications of kinship ties, and the exchange of goods was carried out largely in the form of reciprocal gift-giving. Such reciprocity was considered "an integral part of any friendly interaction, and ties between trading partners were modelled on those between relatives . . . Foreign tribes with whom the Huron did not have bonds of trade and reciprocity were automatically not to be trusted" (Trigger 1988, 64, 68). Champlain did at least note that he was asked to become "like a brother" to the Wendat. This request may be taken as an initial overture toward the foundation of a kinship relationship. It would not be until the following year, however, that kinship would be formally established between Champlain (and thus the French) and Tregouaroti, an Arendarhonon leader (and thus the Wendat confederacy).

Exchanges: Savignon and Brûlé

Champlain sailed again for New France in 1610, arriving in Tadoussac in April and proceeding directly to his habitation at Quebec. That winter had been a pleasant one on the St. Lawrence, for few remaining there had fallen ill, and no one had died. An Innu delegation soon arrived at the settlement and reminded Champlain of his promise to accompany them in war again. They began another war expedition in June, and this time it is certain that among Champlain's men was Étienne Brûlé. The French and Innu had planned to meet the Onontchataronon (Algonkin) and the Arendarhonon Wendat at the mouth of the Richelieu River, but upon arriving, they were met by an Algonkin man in a canoe, who told them that some Algonkin warriors had already fallen into battle with the Haudenosaunee and required assistance. Champlain and a group of Innu men hastened to their aid, and a prolonged battle ensued in which Champlain, employing his arquebuses, managed to put down the group of members of the Haudenosaunee confederacy. Champlain sustained an arrow wound in the battle. The Algonkin and Innu emerged victorious, taking fifteen prisoners whom they immediately tortured and killed. The next day the Arendarhonon Wendat and the Onontchataronon Algonkin arrived, led by Ochasteguin and Iroquet, respectively. They expressed regret that they had missed the battle, but these leaders immediately seized the opportunity to negotiate a formal trading alliance with the French (Champlain 1971, 2:115–38).

The most significant "trade" that took place at that point was the exchange of Étienne Brûlé for Savignon, the brother of Tregouaroti, an Arendarhonon headman. Champlain's motivation for desiring that Brûlé live among the Natives is quite clear. He had previously planned to allow members of his crew to reside with various indigenous groups in order that they become knowledgeable about various Native languages and customs, which would facilitate French ability to engage in trade. By his account, Champlain appears to have initiated with Iroquet the prospect of Brûlé's residence among the Onontchataronon.

Champlain also reports that the other Algonkin people were loath to accept Brûlé, on the grounds that Brûlé's death while in their care would initiate a mourning war between the Algonkin people and the French. Champlain states that he convinced the Algonkin headmen that this would not be the case, and that they offered Savignon in exchange for Brûlé. Champlain accepted Savignon, and the deal was done. Both parties promised to rendezvous the next June at the Lachine Rapids (Champlain 1971, 2:138–42).

Champlain, however, was unable to appreciate the intricacies or the complete ramifications of this exchange. The Onontchataronon Algonkin people had acted as mediators in introducing the Arendarhonon Wendat people to the French and were continuing in this role. It is true that they, represented by Iroquet, arranged the terms of the exchange, but it was an Arendarhonon Wendat man (Savignon) who was given to Champlain. "[S]ince Iroquet had introduced these two groups, the Onontchataronon were still officially viewed by the Huron as intermediaries between themselves and the French" (Trigger 1988, 262). This fact indicates that although Champlain did not realize it, Brûlé was to live among the Arendarhonon, not the Onontchataronon, and an alliance was being forged with the Wendat confederacy, not the Algonkin people, who seem to have perceived themselves as already in sufficient alliance with the French. Champlain's bond with the Onontchataronon was sealed when his men participated not once, but twice, in warfare against the Mohawk. Those raids had been carried out and coordinated by the Onontchataronon in retaliation for Mohawk trucebreaking (Champlain 1971, 2:69; Trigger 1988, 247). The exchange of Savignon and Brûlé was of tremendous import, as it formally began the unmediated alliance between the Wendat and the French, as symbolized by the establishment of a kinship relationship between the two. (It will be recalled that a year earlier, Arendarhonon leaders had asked Champlain to become "like a brother" to them.) In this exchange, Savignon, the brother of a Wendat leader, was given as a brother to Champlain, who then became the brother of Tregouaroti. Étienne Brûlé, most likely perceived as brother of Champlain, then became the brother of Tregouaroti, who thus became the kin of Champlain.

This interpretation of the event is upheld by the fact that the Wendat people are said to have understood the French as being members of one clan or nation, and therefore, "relatives of one another" (Trigger 1988, 262).

This exchange also had tremendous import for Brûlé himself. Granted, he had lived in New France for two years, but that was among men of his own country. Now he was to set off on a journey that would bring him far from his countrymen and to an uncertain fate. Champlain quite plainly states, however, that Brûlé was unafraid; witness his description of the exchange:

> I had a young boy who had already wintered two years at Quebec who desired to go with the Algonkins to learn the language. Pontgravé and I decided that it would be better to send him there than elsewhere, to learn what their country was like, see the great lake, observe the rivers and what people lived there, at the same time explore the mines and the rare things of those people and places, so that on his return we might be informed of the truth. We asked him if this would be agreeable; because it was not my wish to force him, but as soon as the request was made, he accepted the journey very willingly. (Champlain 1971, 2:138–39)[10]

It is impossible to surmise with certainty the reasons for Brûlé's desire to leave the habitation and to live with Natives. It is known that during his two years at Quebec, he had come into considerable contact with Natives, most notably Innu, and may have become favorably disposed toward Native people in general. Because Brûlé was around eighteen years old at the time, boyish enthusiasm may have played a part. He may have been motivated by a desire to be of assistance to Champlain; the explorer, with his royal commission, his entitlement to all trade profits, and his desire to settle the lands of New France, may have impressed the young man. He may have desired to establish himself as a trader, or he may have simply tired of living and working in the

10. My translation.

habitation at Quebec. Whatever his motivations might have been, this decision shaped the rest of his life and greatly affected the history of colonial New France.

Brûlé set out for Wendat country in a canoe on the twenty-fourth of June in the year 1610. The journey he took with some Wendat men began at the mouth of the Richelieu River, required negotiation of the treacherous Lachine Rapids to the long and dangerous Ottawa River (along which one encountered the Rideau and the Chaudiere falls), a portage to Lake Nipissing, on through to the French River, and finally into Lake Huron's Georgian Bay. Because Brûlé was formally the kin of Tregouaroti, he must have traveled through many central and western Wendat villages, eventually to arrive among the Arendarhonon, the easternmost of the confederated Wendat nations. He was the first European to traverse these rivers and this landscape. We have, of course, no record of his sojourn there.

Champlain, for his part, embarked for France in August, taking with him his new "brother" Savignon; they landed in Honfleur on September 27. While in France, Champlain, then forty-three, married a twelve-year-old girl named Hélène Boullé. Champlain left no journal of this period, but Lescarbot, who saw Savignon in Paris, noted Savignon's scorn for the way in which French men would argue with one another; "he would mock at them, saying that they were naught but women, and had no courage" (Lescarbot 1907–14, 3:22). As Trigger notes, "Wendat men did not engage in verbal disputes and were not supposed to interrupt one another" (Trigger 1988, 263). In later years, Sagard, a lay Recollet brother who lived among the Wendat people in 1632, noted that Savignon, then back among his people, discouraged others from sending children to France, averring that the French beat their children. Although Savignon reported that he was treated well while in France, he reported with disgust that the French injured and sometimes murdered people without regard for their guilt or innocence (Sagard 1866, 320–22). Trigger asserts that the words of Savignon as recorded by Sagard "represent the authentic reactions of an Indian, reared in a tradition of personal liberty and blood feud, to European concepts of legal and parental authority" (Trigger 1988, 264).

Significances: The Alliance Secured

In May 1611 Champlain sailed again for New France, along with Savignon. After arriving at Tadoussac, Champlain set out to meet the Arendarhonon and the Onontchataronon at the Lachine Rapids. Champlain arrived at the rapids on May 28, but found no one waiting for him there. He sent Savignon and another Native man ahead to look for the Wendat and Algonkin groups he expected to meet, but Savignon returned four days later without having seen them. While Savignon had been away, five boatloads of French traders arrived. They had heard that Champlain was meeting with Wendat and Algonkin representatives, and wished to participate in trade as well. As for Champlain, he had decided that the land near the rapids would make an ideal point of settlement, so he gave orders to his men to clear the land and begin building a second habitation, which he named Place Royale because it was less than a league distant from Montreal. Eventually, on the thirteenth of June, two hundred Wendat and Algonkin men arrived. They were led by Iroquet, Ochasteguin, and Tregouaroti, who brought with him Étienne Brûlé. Champlain wrote, "I also saw my boy, who came dressed like a [savage]. He was pleased with the treatment received from the [savages], according to the customs of their country, and explained to me all that he had seen during the winter, and what he had learned from the [savages]" (Champlain 1971, 2:188). It is unfortunate that Champlain did not see fit to write down the details related by Brûlé of his sojourn in Wendat country.

The next day the Wendat and Algonkin delegations called Champlain and Brûlé up to their encampment, specifically requesting that they come alone. Upon Champlain's arrival, they "expressed satisfaction at the kind treatment [Champlain] had shown to [Savignon], as if he had been [Champlain's] brother, which placed them under such obligations to be kind to me that in anything I desired of them, they would try to satisfy me; but they feared lest the other patches [trader's small boats] would do them harm" (Champlain 1971, 2:189). Champlain assured them that the traders would not hurt them, explaining that all the Frenchmen present served one king, whom Savignon had seen in

Paris. "After several harangues" (formal ritual addresses), the Wendat and Algonkin people together presented him with one hundred beaver skins. They then related to Champlain a rumor that they had heard: that Champlain had been negotiating with the Haudenosaunee confederacy and had planned to help the Haudenosaunee in warfare against the Wendat and Algonkin people. Champlain attempted to convince them that this was not so, and testified to the constancy of his friendship with them. After a long and friendly discussion about the features of the geography around the St. Lawrence and about the various peoples inhabiting that area, Champlain and Brûlé returned to their boat to spend the night (Champlain 1971, 2:186–92).

The next day the Wendat and Algonkin delegations built a large barricade around their encampment, explaining that it was for protection against enemy attacks. That night the Arendarhonon Wendat leaders alone sat in council, and sent for Savignon and Brûlé to join them. Hours later, around midnight, they sent for Champlain. They again expressed to Champlain their dismay at the group of traders who had come with Champlain. "They . . . said . . . that they were as kindly disposed to me as to their own children, and had such confidence in me that they would do whatever I told them, but that they much distrusted the others" (Champlain 1971, 2:194). They then reiterated their wish for Champlain to visit their country and to bring as many people as he liked, "provided they were under the leadership of one chief" (Champlain 1971, 2:195). With this, the Wendat leaders presented Champlain with fifty beaver skins and four wampum belts, which apparently represented fifty Wendat villages and the four confederated Wendat nations. The Wendat leaders requested that Champlain share these with Pontgravé. Champlain then assured them of his friendship, and proposed that he and fifty Frenchmen be escorted to Wendat country, where they would give gifts to the leaders who had sent the beaver skins. In addition, if they were to find that the land was arable, they would establish settlements. The Wendat leaders were pleased with Champlain's proposal and promised to do their part to bring it about. Champlain left at daybreak (Champlain 1971, 2:192–96).

The next day the Wendat and the Algonkin delegations indicated that they were going hunting and asked Champlain not to dismantle their encampment. Rather than leaving for a hunt, however, they left Savignon with Champlain and held council by themselves above the Lachine Rapids, where they knew Champlain's boat could not go. The morning after that, Iroquet and Tregouaroti came to fetch Champlain and Brûlé, brought them to the new encampment above the rapids, and proceeded to hold a feast. They explained that they believed the French fur traders amassed upriver had intended to kill them and thus would be leaving the next day. After the feast the Natives again left to hold council by themselves, but some hours later sent for Champlain and Brûlé. The Wendat and Algonkin leaders explained that the barricade they had built around their first encampment was not to defend against the Haudenosaunee, but to defend against the French traders who had followed Champlain. Again they requested that Champlain disallow traders from following him, and Champlain agreed. They then renewed their promise to guide Champlain to their country. This time, however, the promise was accompanied by the request that Champlain send another kinsman of his to live among them (Champlain 1971, 2:196–201).

The Algonkin group indicated that a trader named Bouvier had offered a young man (most likely Thomas Godefroy de Normanville) who was in his service to be this person, and had promised to pay the Natives well for taking this young man, "but that they had been unwilling to do so, until they heard from [Champlain] whether he should agree; for they were uncertain whether [Champlain and Bouvier] were friends" (Champlain 1971, 2:201). Champlain said that it was a matter of indifference to him whether they accepted this young man, but if Bouvier "made them good presents, I should be glad, provided the lad stayed with Iroquet, as they promised me he would" (Champlain 1971, 2:203). Upon the conclusion of this matter, and promising to return the next year, Champlain asked to be taken back to his boat. Bouvier's young man did indeed leave with the Algonkin group and Savignon was returned to his father, but Brûlé apparently stayed with the Arendarhonon Wendat group as well. Champlain soon left for Quebec (after meeting with the Kichesipirini Algonquians, led by Tessouat, and sending Nicolas de Vignau to live among them). After two months in Quebec, Champlain sailed for France (Champlain 1971, 2:203–14).

The repeated meetings with the Wendat delegation attended by Champlain and Brûlé testify to the complexity of the ritual sealing of a kinship relationship. It is notable that at first, the Onontchataronon were present, signifying acknowledgment of their role in introducing the Arendarhonon Wendat to the French, but that as proceedings continued, the Wendat wished to meet alone with Champlain and Brûlé. The Wendat's deep suspicion of the other traders indicates two things. First, the Wendat appear to have been told that the traders planned to attack them. It seems logical to posit that the Innu or Kichesipirini people may have spread a rumor to that effect, out of jealousy over the new relationship that had begun between Champlain and the Wendat confederacy; such a relationship would have negatively affected their profitable positions as middlemen in trade along the St. Lawrence. This new direct alliance had already eliminated the Onontchataronon Algonkin as intermediaries in the trading relationship. Second, the Wendat people seem to have had difficulty understanding that so many people could have been united under one person (then King Louis XIII). Indeed, that Brûlé and Champlain were called alone to councils, and that symbolic skins and wampum belts were presented to Champlain (who is only requested to share with "his brother" Pontgravé) together indicate that the Wendat finally decided to hold Champlain to be the leader of all the French present. These repeated meetings with Champlain and Brûlé also make clear that it was only these two persons that the Wendat trusted; for it was with them that they had become bonded in kinship. Finally, as Trigger rightly points out, the presentation of the fifty beaver skins and four belts indicated that the Arendarhonon Wendat were now representing all of the confederated Wendat nations. "The impression that is gained from [these meetings] is that the question of an alliance with the French had rapidly become an important issue within the Huron confederacy" (Trigger 1988, 268).

The specifically requested presence of Brûlé and Savignon at these councils highlights several important issues. Obviously they had both acquired a certain level of linguistic competence during their time with their hosts. Their presence was desired because their abilities as interpreters could be exploited, and finer points of negotiation could be more clearly expressed. Further, they had each experienced firsthand the cultural practices of their host groups, and could convey to their Native cultures their insights regarding things important in negotiations, such as geography, material wealth, social structures, and sites of power, as well as cultural expectations regarding conduct during the negotiations themselves.

Champlain's new awareness and appreciation of the effectiveness of Brûlé (and the practice of kin exchange generally) in securing an alliance with the Wendat confederacy become quite visible by virtue of his actions both during and after the councils. It will be recalled that immediately upon Brûlé's return on the thirteenth of June, Champlain had the young man "[explain] . . . all that he had seen during the winter, and what he had learned from the [savages]" (Champlain 1971, 2:188). Champlain had obviously learned of a valuable tool in establishing trade relationships. The fact that Champlain dissuaded the Wendat group from initiating kin exchange with Bouvier but allowed such an exchange between Bouvier and Iroquet demonstrated his intention to preserve his status as the sole "brother" of the Wendat for purposes of trade.

But perhaps most important, at least for the purposes of this study, Brûlé and Savignon's essential presence at these councils revealed that they were not only linguistic and cultural interpreters, but that they themselves represented and embodied the alliance being made. Their mutual adoption through the vehicle of kin exchange established the groundwork for an alliance by creating kinship ties between the French and the Wendat confederacy. The fact that they were taken to the home countries of each group both materially and symbolically located them within the cultures of the other. Their journeys to and inclusions within each other's societies across geographical space and over significant time inextricably linked each culture to the other.

Their presence in the binding place and moment definitively signified the alliance, because they were the material and symbolic loci of that alliance.

However, Champlain's cognizance of the religious significance of this moment was, if at all present, certainly dimmed by his differing valuation of the process of exchange. He had certainly begun to apprehend the efficacy of sending young men to live among Native societies. For at that time, Champlain's valued goal was securing a monopolistic trade relationship with the people of the Wendat confederacy. For him, the obvious surplus of such an exchange was the acquisition of an interpreter (truchement). Given that Champlain's religiosity overtly admitted the sacrality of only those things properly consecrated by priestly authority or by sacred tradition, and because seventeenth-century mercantilism secularized operations surrounding the acquisition of commodities, it is unlikely that Champlain had any perception of the religious import that, for the Wendat people, resided in the means of alliance. However, it must be carefully noted that as time passed, the overriding object of Champlain's exploration became colonization, with its accompanying aim of conversion of indigenous people. Champlain's words and actions in later years would demonstrate this goal. Yet for Champlain, commerce was a practice that stood apart from religion; one must commit one's efforts to one or to the other.

Journeys: Brûlé and Champlain

Champlain did not return to visit the Wendat people in 1612 as he had promised; economic and political circumstances forced him to remain in France. There are no written records of Brûlé's activities in New France from the years 1611 to 1615. Of the Wendat confederacy, however, this much is known: the years 1612–15 were filled with warfare waged in alliance with Algonkin groups against the Haudenosaunee confederacy. There were French traders other than Champlain with whom to deal, and during their journeys through the Ottawa Valley and down the Ottawa River to the St. Lawrence, the Wendat people were incessantly attacked by Haudenosaunee raiders. With mourning war being compounded by economic interest in and disputes over trading routes, the Wendat had good reason to revenge themselves upon the Iroquois. Despite the escalation in warfare, Wendat attention centered on matters of trade. Trade had developed to such an astonishing degree that the Arendarhonon Wendat people could not handle the huge French demand for furs, and willingly shared their trading routes and partnerships with the other three confederated Wendat nations, as was demonstrated by the four wampum belts presented to Champlain. "Of their previous right, they retained only the distinction of being the oldest and closest allies of the French" (Trigger 1988, 287–88). It is likely, then, that Brûlé did not remain solely with the Arendarhonon nation, but eventually went to stay with the Attignawantan nation, the westernmost, the most populous, the best-represented in council, and hence the most powerful nation in the confederacy. It is certain that by 1620 Brûlé had established as his primary residence the village of Toanché, "which was the Attignawantan's chief point of departure for the St. Lawrence" (Trigger 1988, 292; Jurgens 1966, 132).

When Champlain arrived in New France in 1615, he had with him four members of the Recollet order: Fathers Jamet, Delbeau, and LeCaron and Brother DuPlessis. He was fulfilling the missionary aims of his king and country. In the dedication of his published works describing the voyages of 1615–18, Champlain addresses King Louis XIII, averring that within this new volume, the king would see the well-founded reasons for Champlain's hopes for bringing the knowledge of God to the Natives of New France. Champlain describes his missionary effort as paramount, even as others hold monetary goals above religious ones. That Champlain's sense of religious mission had factored into his plan is clarified at the beginning of the volume, as he described his decision in 1615: "I thereupon concluded that I should be committing a great sin if I did not make it my business to devise some means of bringing [Natives] to the knowledge of God. And to this end I exerted myself to find some good friars, with zeal and affection for the glory of God, whom I might persuade to send or come themselves with me to this country to try to plant there the faith" (Champlain 1971, 3:16).

Champlain himself solicited funds and eventually was given a sufficient amount to equip the Recollet fathers for the voyage. On arriving in New France, Champlain deposited three of the Recollets at Quebec and brought Father LeCaron with him to meet the Wendat delegation at the Lachine Rapids. LeCaron was taken directly to Wendat country by the majority of the Wendat people present, and Champlain followed shortly thereafter with two Frenchmen and ten Wendat men who had remained at the rapids with him for a few days. One of these Frenchmen seems to have been Brûlé, who must have journeyed with the Wendat delegation that year to attend their expected annual meeting with Champlain. Thus Champlain made his journey up the Ottawa River to Lake Nipissing and on to the French River and Georgian Bay in the company of his "young boy," who by then would have been the most experienced and well-traveled truchement in all of New France.

After arriving in August in Toanché, a prominent Attignawantan village, Champlain was ceremonially conducted to other villages and to meetings with numerous Wendat leaders. Included among these villages was Caragouha, where Father LeCaron established himself. Champlain had no desire to find a residence, however, as he was impatient to accompany the Wendat men in warfare against the Haudenosaunee. Champlain stayed in Cahiagué, the largest Attignawantan settlement, for a few days, and was finally accommodated in his wish as contingents of Wendat men from all four nations as well as groups of their Algonkin allies began to arrive in force. After several more days of the ritual feasting necessary for warfare preparation, Champlain, Brûlé, the Wendat warriors, and the Algonkin men proceeded toward Iroquois country. As they journeyed, twelve of the "most stalwart" Wendat men decided to go ahead of the rest to the country of their other allies, the Susquehannock, to secure the assistance of five hundred of their warriors in the planned attack (Champlain 1971, 3:53–58). Étienne Brûlé asked Champlain's permission to accompany them. "[Champlain] readily agreed, since he was drawn thereto by his own inclination, and by this means would see their country and could observe the [people] that inhabit it" (Champlain 1971, 3:58).

As Champlain, the Wendat group, and their Algonkin allies proceeded toward Haudenosaunee country, they captured and tortured eleven Haudenosaunee men from a fishing party they had surprised. They then journeyed on to an Iroquois fortified village, which almost certainly was an Onondaga settlement in the vicinity of Syracuse, New York. Champlain attempted to coordinate the battle. However, the Wendat men and their Algonkin allies, not accustomed to European war plans or to taking orders, did not have the same aims in mind as did Champlain. While Champlain was intent upon seizing and destroying what he perceived as a fort, the Wendat and Algonkin groups desired "to harass the village, and, by threatening to set fire to its defences, to force the Iroquois warriors to come out and engage in hand to hand combat" (Trigger 1988, 312–13). For the Wendat people, warfare was an action in which bravery and skill could be displayed, but was ultimately about the reconstitution of family. For Champlain, warfare was about the acquisition of property, and thus he was unable to recognize the disjuncture between the French and Wendat understandings of the aims of warfare.

Witnessing what appeared to be an undisciplined and uncoordinated attack, Champlain shouted orders, but to no avail. His exasperation is clear in his description of his own role in the battle: "In vain I shouted in their ears and showed them as best I could the danger they ran through their lack of intelligence, but they heard nothing on account of the great noise they were making . . . it was troubling myself to no purpose to shout . . . my remonstrances were useless" (Champlain 1971, 3:72–73). After the battle Champlain again "addressed several complaints to them for the confusion that had occurred, but all [his] discourses availed as little as if [he] had been silent" (Champlain 1971, 3:75). Champlain's annoyance again revealed a critical disjuncture; not only were the French and Wendat understandings of the aims of warfare irreconcilable, but the manner in which this warfare was conducted illustrated another fundamental difference: the understanding of authority. Champlain had expected the Native men to acknowledge him as leader and to follow his directives; the Natives, however, were proceeding in their traditional manner, as a coordinated group, linked by their shared goals. Champlain's completely different goals effectively alienated him from this coordinated group. At the end of the attack, the Wendat and Algonkin men considered the raid to be over, but Champlain managed to convince them to wait four days for Brûlé to arrive with Susquehannock reinforcements in order to try again. However, these expected allies never arrived, and all began the journey back to Wendat country.

Champlain's perceived failure to successfully manage this battle irked him. His trek back to Cahiagué, made doubly difficult by painful arrow wounds in his leg and knee, allowed his anger to fester. He was angry with the Wendat and Algonkin warriors, and angry with Brûlé for not appearing with reinforcements. Upon reaching Wendat country, Champlain made known his wishes to be transported directly back to Quebec, which would involve a journey through Haudenosaunee-controlled territory. The Wendat leadership waffled, knowing well that such travel at this time would be ill advised, and to his initial regret, Champlain was forced to spend the winter in Wendat country. Champlain spent the winter traveling among the Wendat people and their allies (Champlain 1971, 3:76–170). In his examination of this period of Champlain's sojourn among the Wendat, Trigger rightly asserts that "Champlain's actions in the Huron country in the winter of 1615–1616 do not reveal him as a man who understood the Indians and knew how to deal with them, as many historians have claimed. Instead, they show him to be a man who not only understood very little about Indian ways but was too inflexible in his opinions to learn about them" (Trigger 1988, 329).

While Trigger draws from this solid observation the opinion that the alliance made between Champlain and the Wendat confederacy was "largely the result of Champlain accommodating himself, haphazardly and unwittingly, to the Huron conventions that had to be observed if a treaty were to be made" (Trigger 1988, 329), this conclusion seems to overstate the case. Even granting that Champlain was unusually fortunate in that his desire to gain an interpreter dovetailed with the Wendat cultural practice of kin exchange, it may have been Champlain's religious mission that prevented him from further "accommodating himself" to Wendat society. Champlain continually described and condemned the Wendat people as "without faith, without law, living without God and without religion like brute beasts" (Champlain 1971, 3:15–16).[11] While Fischer portrays Champlain as a humanist in pursuit of peaceful relationships between French and Native people (Fischer 2008), Champlain's Christianity was foundational to his understanding of the world. Even though experience of the wars of religion made him critical of religious intolerance, and even though in that sense his religion was rather inclusive, compared to other Europeans of his time, it is not the case that Champlain saw the beauty, complexity, and value of Wendat religion.

The next April Champlain received a bit of information regarding Brûlé, who had never returned from that errand to the Susquehannock. Champlain came across some of the Wendat men who had accompanied Brûlé on that mission, who told him that "they had left our interpreter on the trail, and that [Brûlé] had returned to the [Susquehannock] village [of Carantouan] for certain reasons which prompted him to do so" (Champlain 1971, 3:168). Here Champlain seems to be either unable to explain Brûlé's continued absence or loath to describe in print the reasons for it. It is notable that here Champlain did not refer to Brûlé in his usual terms, as "my young boy," but impersonally describes him as "our interpreter." Champlain still may have been angry with him for contributing to the failed (in Champlain's estimation) battle with the Haudenosaunee, but it is also possible that he was distressed at Brûlé's abandonment of his position among the Wendat people, in which he had been so useful to Champlain.

Two years later, in 1618, at the annual meeting of Champlain and the Wendat trade delegation at the Lachine Rapids, Brûlé arrived with the Wendat. Champlain interrogated him as to the reasons for his absence from the battle with the Haudenosaunee, and Brûlé told him

---

11. This is likely the first articulation of what became the famed refrain of many French speakers in their descriptions of Native cultures. Champlain has it as "*Ny foi, ny loi, sans Dieu et sans religion*"; the phrase would later become "*Sans foi, sans loi, sans roi.*"

quite a story. Champlain's record of this conversation is the only source of information regarding Brûlé's whereabouts for those two years. It is again evident in Champlain's account that Champlain's anger had not dissipated, but Brûlé's story was an astonishing one, so much so that even in his resentment, Champlain was moved to comment that Brûlé was "more to be pitied than blamed, on account of the mishaps that befell him on this mission" (Champlain 1971, 3:214). According to Champlain, Brûlé told the tale as follows.

On the route to the village of Carantouan, the primary village of the Susquehannock, Brûlé and his twelve Wendat companions came across some Iroquois men, killed four of them, and took two as captives. These two were taken to the Susquehannock people, who received them joyfully, marking the arrival of their Wendat allies with feasts and dancing. Brûlé had no trouble convincing the Susquehannocks to join the Wendat confederacy in battle against the Iroquois, but he did run into the difficulty of the length of their deliberative councils and subsequent ritual preparations for warfare. When he and the five hundred warriors arrived at the planned site of the raid, Champlain and the Wendat warriors had already completed their fight and had left the area. Upon finding no Wendat men in the environs of the Haudenosaunee settlement, Brûlé and the war party returned to Carantouan where "the said Brûlé was forced to remain and to pass the remainder of the autumn and all the winter, waiting for company and escort to return" (Champlain 1971, 3:217). If Brûlé had left for Wendat country alone, he would have had to pass unguided through "woods, forests, and dense and difficult thickets, and by marshy swamps, frightful and unfrequented places and wastes, all to avoid the danger of an encounter with [the Iroquois]" (Champlain 1971, 3:215). Brûlé related that he passed the time exploring areas to the south of Carantouan, "visiting the [people] and territories near that place, and making his way along a river which discharges on the coast of Florida" (Champlain 1971, 3:217–18). Here it appears to be quite possible that Brûlé's route took him along the Susquehanna River all the way to Chesapeake Bay, and that he visited several coastal islands. This journey was undoubtedly made in the company of the Susquehannock men on their annual trading expedition, and Brûlé returned with them to Carantouan in the spring.

That spring, Brûlé began his return to Wendat country, probably accompanied by Susquehannock men on their way to visit and trade. However, his party was attacked by the Haudenosaunee. Brûlé became lost in the forest for days and, exhausted and starving, he decided to follow a path "no matter where it might lead, were it towards the enemy or not, preferring to place himself in their hands through the trust he had in God, than to die alone so miserably; moreover, he knew how to speak their language, and this might bring some advantage to him" (Champlain 1971, 3:220). Brûlé finally encountered a Haudenosaunee fishing party (most likely of the Seneca nation), spoke with them, and

> they smoked together, which is their custom when they and their acquaintances visit one another. They seemed to have pity and compassion on him, offering him every assistance; they even brought him to their village where they entertained him and gave him something to eat. But as soon as the people of this place heard of it, to wit, that an Adoresetouy had arrived, for so they call the French, which name is equivalent to saying "iron men," they came crowding in great numbers to see the said Brûlé, whom they took and brought to the lodge of one of the principal chiefs, where he was questioned. They asked him who he was, whence he came, what cause had driven and led him to this place and how he had got lost, and further whether he were not one of the French nation which was making war on them. Thereupon he made reply that he belonged to another better nation that was desirous only of their acquaintance and friendship, which they refused to believe, and rushed upon him, and tore out his nails with their teeth, burned him with red-hot firebrands, plucked out his beard hair by hair, contrary nevertheless to the will of their chief. And in this emergency one of the savages spied an *Agnus Dei* which he had hung about his neck, and on seeing it, asked what he had thus hanging at his neck, and tried to seize it and tear it off, but the said Brûlé said to him (in a resolute voice): "If you take it and put me to death, you shall see that immediately afterwards you and all your house will die suddenly"; to which the savage paid no attention,

but pursuing his evil purpose tried to seize the Agnus Dei and tear it from him, and all together were prepared to put him to death, after first making him suffer many pains and tortures which are usually practiced by them upon their enemies. But God who had mercy on him would not permit it, but in His providence caused the sky which had been clear and fine suddenly to become overcast and to be filled with thick heavy clouds, which ended in thunder and lightning so violent and continuous as to be something strange and awful. This storm so frightened the savages, because it was unusual to them, and also because they had never known the like, that it distracted them and made them forget their wicked intentions with regard to Brûlé, their prisoner, and they left and forsook him, yet without unbinding him, not daring to approach him. This gave the sufferer an opportunity to use gentle words to them, calling to them and representing the harm they were doing to him without any reason, making them understand how angry our God was with them for having thus ill-treated him. Then the chief approached the said Brûlé, unbound him and brought him into his lodge, where he cleaned and doctored his wounds. After this, there were no dances and feasts or rejoicings to which Brûlé was not summoned, and after having spent some time with these savages, he determined to withdraw to our quarters and settlement. And taking leave of them he promised them to make them friends with the French and their enemies, and to make them swear friendship with one another, and said that with this object he would return to them as soon as he could. On his departure they conducted him four days journey from their village, whence he came to the country and village of the [Attignawantan] which I [Champlain] had already visited, and there the said Brûlé remained some time. Then resuming his journey to us he passed along [Lake Huron] and went by boat along its shores some ten days . . . and the said Brûlé would have proceeded farther to explore the lie of these regions as I had given him instructions, had it not been for a rumour of war preparations among them which caused him to hold this plan in reserve to another time. After he had told me his story I gave him hopes that his services would be recognized, and encouraged him to keep to this good intention until our return, where we should more and more have the means of doing something wherewith he would be pleased. This is indeed the whole account and narrative of his journey after he left me. (Champlain 1971, 3:213–26)

Shortly after the telling of this tale, Brûlé departed for Wendat country, and Champlain sailed for France.

As engaging as this story is, historians, most notably Trudel (Trudel 1973, 227–29), have seen fit to doubt its veracity. It does appear ridiculous that the Seneca people would have been terrified by a thunderstorm. There is, then, the distinct possibility that Brûlé shaped his story expressly to impress Champlain, and to excuse his absence from the raid and from Wendat country for so long a time. It is especially interesting that Brûlé, if he did indeed invent or embellish, chose to express his deliverance from death by torture as miraculous in nature. It is particularly interesting that Brûlé chose, in his narration to Champlain, to invoke the spiritual power represented within and symbolized by his Agnus Dei. It is not at all impossible that Brûlé calculatingly chose to appeal to Champlain's own religiosity.

However, certain details of Brûlé's story ring true. "[I]t is clear that the Iroquois council chiefs, who generally exerted a moderating influence in intertribal relations, managed to rescue Brûlé from his tormentors" (Trigger 1988, 307). His subsequent treatment as an honored guest may reveal the actual motivation behind the decision of the Seneca headmen to preserve Brûlé's life. Brûlé's knowledge of the Wendat language and familiarity with Iroquoian cultural practices would have clearly demonstrated to the Seneca people that he had been in relationship with the Wendat. At that time, just as the Wendat confederacy was dominating the northern trade networks and materially benefiting from alliance with the French, the Mohawk nation was establishing a similar relationship with the Dutch along southern routes and raiding Wendat trade routes with regularity. Unlike their Mohawk allies to the east, the Seneca nation was not "as well situated for trade with the Dutch, or for raiding the Ottawa Valley . . . Hence, the council chiefs were interested in exploring the possibility of establishing a trading relationship with the French" (Trigger 1988, 307). Cultivation of Brûlé would have appeared to the Seneca people as an excellent move toward that goal. Brûlé's admitted accompaniment of a Seneca group on trading ventures to the south only buttresses this interpretation.

Brûlé's disclosure to Champlain of his promises to "make [the Seneca nation] friends with the French and their enemies [the Wendat confederacy]" was daring in that this arrangement would have been unacceptable to Champlain at that time, because it would have jeopardized French-Wendat relations and exacerbated Wendat-Haudenosaunee hostilities. However, Brûlé may have presented this to Champlain as idle promises made in order to leave Seneca country with Seneca assistance and goodwill. In any event, whether sincere or idle, his promises coupled with his actions (most important, his trading expeditions with the Seneca group) reveal Brûlé's emerging independence from Champlain's agendas, both mercantile and missionary.

Trade: The Wendat and Brûlé

Champlain never again visited Wendat country, nor are there any records of Champlain personally dealing with the Wendat delegations at the annual trade encampments. After the year 1616, these trade meetings no longer took place at the Lachine Rapids, but at the mouth of the Richelieu River or at Trois-Rivières, and sometimes as far upriver as Quebec. Champlain stayed at Quebec during each of his subsequent voyages to New France and concentrated his efforts upon the building of that settlement. Trade with the Wendat people was conducted by representatives of whichever French trading company was granted the monopoly that year.

Trigger rightly observes that the most important feature of Wendat life during the period 1616–29 was the staggering ascendance of their engagement in trade (Trigger 1988, 335). The Wendat made yearly trips down the Ottawa River to encampments along the St. Lawrence in order to supply the French with animal furs, principally beaver. Trigger estimates at ten thousand the number of beaver skins supplied annually by the Wendat confederacy, which would amount to approximately "two-thirds of all the furs that were traded along the St. Lawrence at that time" (Trigger 1988, 337). The relocation of the primary trading sites meant longer voyages for Wendat traders. The huge proportion of trade performed by the Wendat people became resented by the Innu and Algonkins, who sometimes raided and sometimes taxed Wendat canoes passing through their territories along the Ottawa and St. Lawrence Rivers (Trigger 1988, 341–42). The Wendat traders were made to placate these nations with gifts, thereby giving them a piece of the new source of trade through the redistribution of goods and maintaining their previous kinship-based trade relationships.

The Wendat confederacy had been in control of wide-ranging trade networks well before the arrival of the French. The traditional trade that they conducted with northern nations such as the Ottawa and the Nipissing expanded along with trade with the French. These nations, which were more nomadic than the Wendat (who lived in semipermanent villages), had historically hunted more game than the Wendat and had come to trade their game for Wendat-grown corn and Wendat-manufactured wares. With the explosion in Wendat-French fur trade, the demand for furs from the Nipissing and Ottawa grew. As a result, these northern nations hunted and trapped more game, cultivated less corn themselves, and became increasingly dependent upon the Wendat trading network (Trigger 1988, 354). The Wendat too at first had expanded their hunting and trapping, so much so that by 1630 the beaver population within Wendat country had been extinguished (Trigger 1988, 350). The Wendat nations then used their corn and the objects they received in trade from the French in order to further exploit these trade networks, and were so effective in their expansion that the Wendat language became the language of trade "not only . . . around the shores of Lake Huron, but in trade as far east as the Ottawa Valley and possibly as far west as . . . the shores of Green Bay, Wisconsin" (Trigger 1988, 65).

The dramatic escalation of Wendat-French trade brought a number of French traders and trappers to Wendat country. These Frenchmen, like Champlain and Brûlé, assisted the Wendat confederacy in warfare against the Haudenosaunee and in protecting Wendat villages against attacks, which "permitted the Huron men who normally remained [at home during the summer trading season] to guard their villages to engage in trading activities" (Trigger 1988, 339). This arrangement was also in harmony with the Wendat cultural practice of association of trade with kinship. "[I]ndividual Huron traders were anxious to establish special personal relations with them. In particular, they hoped to adopt or conclude matrimonial alliances with these visitors, either of which meant that the French entered into kinship with a particular Huron family" (Trigger 1988, 365). The traders, truchements, and *coureurs de bois* (woodsmen) who integrated themselves into Wendat society by marrying Wendat women may have enhanced the Wendat family's social prestige, improved the Frenchman's own chances of linguistic mastery of the language of trade, and formed a trading connection from which both sides could benefit.

Given the burgeoning significance of trade for both the Wendat and the French, these men were of great value to all; and among these Frenchmen, those of greatest importance were the truchements. This was, of course, Brûlé's position. Further, Brûlé seems to have been the sole truchement among the Wendat for several years (Trigger 1988, 367). "[H]e was hired by the trading company to work and live among the Huron as their agent" (Trigger 1988, 369), he was expected to accompany the Wendat delegation on the annual trading expeditions to the St. Lawrence, and he was expected by both the trading company and Champlain himself to explore the geography in and around Wendat country and report back his findings.[12] "So important was Brûlé's work judged to be that he was paid more than 100 pistoles a year,[13] which was many times the wage of an ordinary

---

12. Trigger has ventured the possibility that the prototype of a pre-1638 manuscript map of the Great Lakes "may have been based on information supplied by Brûlé." See Trigger 1988, plate 29, 371.

13. This salary was documented by the Jesuit Father Lalemant in the year 1626 (Thwaites 1896–1901, 4:209), which demonstrates that this salary was paid to Brûlé by de Mont's company. It was not until 1627 that his trade monopoly was revoked and transferred by Louis XIII to the expressly Catholic La Compagnie de Cent-Associes.

employee of the company and almost equal to Champlain's salary" (Trigger 1988, 369).

Brûlé had to have been aware of his material value. He was obviously regarded as an essential employee by the trading company, and he was certainly valued by the Wendat confederacy as its visible symbolic kinship link to the French. The consequences of his position among the Wendat people would have provided him an additional material benefit: the company of Wendat women. Trigger writes of the early traders and coureurs de bois who lived among the Wendat in the years 1616–29:

> These early *coureurs de bois* . . . were delighted by the frankness of native sexual relations and enjoyed seducing Huron women and being seduced by them. In spite of their reservations about the physical appearance of the French, [Wendat] girls appear to have made themselves available to these visitors, whom they no doubt found interesting because of their novelty, as well as because they were able to give them European goods as presents . . . The popularity of the French did not elicit expressions of jealousy from Huron men, because promiscuity was characteristic of youth and the Huron frowned on the public expression of jealousy and on men trying to restrict the sexual freedom of unmarried women. Promiscuous behavior was therefore not incompatible with good relations between the French traders and the younger men with whom they lived and worked in the Huron country. (Trigger 1988, 367–68)

One may go even further than simply stating that sexual liaisons were "not incompatible" with good relations. First one must take into account that in Wendat culture, trade routes were owned and controlled by the families of the men who discovered the routes, and all of the main routes during this time of an explosion in trade were held by prominent heads of individual clan segments. As Trigger himself points out, "No other [Wendat] was supposed to trade along [a proprietary] route without first receiving permission from the head of the family that had legal title to it . . . Such control . . . provided the headmen with an important means of acquiring wealth, which in turn could be used to validate their high status within their tribes" (Trigger 1988, 65). Taking this a step further, it is quite possible that the leaders of clan segments who were owners of trade routes would indeed have encouraged the young women of their families to enter into sexual and even marital relationships with French traders. Certainly a trader who was made a kinsman in this way could have been prevailed upon to favor his family's route. And, as Trigger observes, "if marriages were contracted with women from influential families, they would have enhanced the prestige of individual French traders" (Trigger 1988, 368).

The Wendat traditional systems of trade, at least in the first years of colonialism, expanded to encompass an increasing number of participants. Exploitation of traditional trading relationships and extension of these trading relationships to the French brought about an astonishing increase in material wealth for the Wendat and their trading partners, but most perceptibly for the French. In the specific case of the Wendat confederacy, however, the vast increase in trade also brought about quite negative consequences. For instance, Wallis Smith asserts that the traditional matrilineages of the Wendat were severely compromised by the growing dependence of the Wendat and their neighbors on trade, a traditionally male-centered activity. The heightened valuation of male labor resulted in a disruption of balance in power between the genders among the Wendat, and resulted in devastating societal consequences. These societal shifts will be explored further in chapter 3. However, it is quite clear from the contemporary records that in those years the truchement Brûlé benefited both in salary and in female companionship. He was not just a symbol of the French-Wendat alliance, but a paradigmatic locus of the material surpluses generated by that alliance.

Mission: Sagard and the Wendat

The traders were not the only Frenchmen who settled among the Wendat. Father LeCaron, who had spent the winter of 1616–17 at the Attignawantan village of Caragouha, returned to Wendat country in

1623, accompanied by two other members of the Recollet order, Father Nicolas Viel and the lay brother Gabriel Sagard. While spending the intervening time at Quebec, LeCaron and the Recollets had begun to shape their policies and intentions regarding the conversion of the Wendat. One of the major principles of conversion, according to the Recollets, was that sedentary Native people, like members of the Wendat confederacy, were more amenable to conversion than were non-sedentary Natives (Sagard 1866, 793). As early as 1616 Champlain had spoken with LeCaron, and they had agreed that conversion would also be best achieved if French families were settled alongside the Natives, "and by good example . . . incite them to correct living" (Champlain 1971, 3:145). In his work published in Paris in 1632, Sagard declared that "unless colonies of good virtuous Catholics are established in all these savage countries, Christianity will never be quite strongly rooted in them, though men of the religious life should give themselves all the trouble in the world . . . [S]avage tribes . . . need an example of a virtuous life in order to see themselves therein" (Sagard 1939, 176).

Sagard, aware of this program when he arrived in Wendat country in 1623, began to compose a dictionary of the Wendat language intended to aid other missionaries to the area, but also to prepare those families whom he eventually hoped would "make a home there and live like Christians" (Sagard 1939, 9). It has been posited that it is unlikely that Sagard acquired sufficient command of the Wendat language to compose such a dictionary, given that he spent only the winter of 1623–24 in Wendat country. Percy J. Robinson, in his "Note on Sagard's Dictionary," has written that "Étienne Brûlé, who had been for many years among the Hurons, probably assisted [Sagard and LeCaron] in obtaining their first knowledge of the language; if this is so the dictionary remains as an interesting memorial of an obscure person" (Sagard 1939, xlvi). However, as later events will reveal, Brûlé was actually unlikely to have assisted Sagard, at least not very much. Like other interpreters, he did not care to share his knowledge of indigenous languages. Truchements came to guard their positions jealously; after all, their livelihoods depended on their monopolies on these skills.

If Brûlé indeed was helpful to Sagard in the composition of his dictionary, Sagard did not express his gratitude. Sagard did, however, provide a brief account of Brûlé's explorations: "The interpreter Brûlé assured us that beyond the Freshwater Sea [Lake Huron] there was another very large lake which empties into it by a waterfall, which has been called 'Saut de Gaston' [Gaston Falls, at Sault Ste. Marie], of a width of almost two leagues, which lake and the Freshwater Sea have almost thirty days journey by canoe in length, according to the account of the savages, but according to the interpreter Brûlé's account, they are four hundred [French] leagues in length" (Sagard 1866, 328).

Brûlé guided and assisted Sagard in his difficult canoe journey back to Quebec, and even then Sagard showed no great affection for Brûlé, although he did acknowledge Brûlé's instrumentality in obtaining a dog for the party to eat (Sagard 1968, 263). Indeed, to Sagard, it was the example of Brûlé that most clearly illustrated the necessity for establishing Catholic families in Wendat country.

In his later work, Sagard related a tale illustrative of the irreligiosity of Brûlé. He reported that "Brûlé was not devout. . . ." In fact, he had trouble recalling his prayers, and on one of his adventures, "finding himself in . . . great peril of death, for prayer he said his *Benedicite*" (Sagard 1866, 338).[14] Sagard took the trouble to relate his opinion of Brûlé to Champlain, speaking of "the bad life which most of the Frenchmen had led in the country of the Hurons; and among others the interpreter Brûlé, who was given a hundred *pistoles* a year to incite the savages to come to trade. It was a very bad example to send such evil-living persons, who should be severely chastised; for this man was recognized as being very vicious and given to women. But what will not be done in the hope of gain, which undermines all other considerations?" (Champlain 1971, 5:132).[15]

---

14. The *Benedicite* is, of course, "grace"; it is the prayer of thanksgiving said before meals. Yet as Cranston has observed, "One wonders whether Brûlé was not pulling the credulous Brother's leg" (Cranston 1949, 87).

15. Translation mine.

Champlain certainly came to agree with Sagard. According to Champlain, Brûlé, no longer in his sole employ but now a well-paid facilitator of trade, had been corrupted by the evils of the fur trade and its profits, and was now a poor Christian and a womanizer.

Sagard and Champlain were not the only inhabitants of New France becoming angry with Brûlé. In 1625 Henri de Lévis, Duc de Ventadour, an extremely zealous Catholic, "arranged, at his own expense, to send three Jesuits to Quebec" (Trigger 1988, 404). These Jesuits, Fathers Charles Lalemant, Enemond Massé, and Jean de Brébeuf, were not only engaged as missionaries, but also "were armed with special powers to curb the interpreters, whom the Recollets had long complained were interfering with their mission work" (Trigger 1988, 404). Marsolet, the truchement of the Innu people, was first to be targeted. He was ordered by General Emery de Caën (the present trading monopoly holder) to return to France. Lalemant relates the tale of Marsolet's reprieve:

> The General was ordered by his associates to send him back to France, or else to reduce his wages; and he [Marsolet] begged him so earnestly . . . that the General was compelled to use imperative authority, and to tell him that his wages would not be reduced, to make him stay this year, and in fact he remained, to our great satisfaction. This interpreter had never wanted to communicate his knowledge of the language to any one, not even to the Recollet Fathers, who had constantly importuned him for ten years . . . And yet he promised me [to teach Lalemant the language] . . . and he kept his promise faithfully during that winter. (Thwaites 1896–1901, 4:211)

Trigger correctly interprets this passage as signifying that while the Jesuits were determined to punish the truchements for refusing to assist in their missionary efforts, the traders, de Caën in particular, fought their deportation (Trigger 1988, 405). Lalemant, in the passage above, demonstrates that although de Caën succeeded in keeping Marsolet in New France, the Jesuits still managed to secure his linguistic assistance.

Another interpreter, however, was not so easily persuaded to teach the missionaries the language they desired to learn, and despite the opposition of de Caën, the Jesuits managed to arrange his deportation back to France. According to Lalemant, "we deemed it necessary for the good of his soul" (Thwaites 1896–1901, 4:215). But the night before his deportation, "he was taken with a severe attack of pleurisy and was put to bed . . . [so] that the ships were obliged to go back without him" (Thwaites 1896–1901, 4:215). Trigger believes that this truchement was Brûlé (Trigger 1988, 405). It also appears, through a close reading of Lalemant's letter, that the Jesuits may have engineered a ruse in order to achieve their goal of learning from the interpreter. Lalemant's description of this incident follows:

> The great God showed his Providential designs very propitiously then; while [the interpreter] was with us, he was taken with a severe attack of pleurisy and was put to bed, so nicely and comfortably, that the ships were obliged to go back without him, and by this means he remained with us, out of all danger of ruining himself; for it was the fear of this which had caused us to urge his return. You will readily understand that during his sickness we performed every act of charity for him. It suffices to say that, before he recovered from this sickness, in which he expected to die, he assured us that he was entirely devoted to us; and that if it pleased God to restore his health, the winter would never pass by without his giving us assistance, a promise which he kept in every respect, thank God. (Thwaites 1896–1901, 4:215)

The truchement's deportation was thus averted. Whether or not this was Brûlé, it is certain that Brûlé eventually was made to go back to France, most likely through the influence of the Jesuits. In 1626 he accompanied an Attigneenongnahac Wendat young man named Amantacha as his personal interpreter. Amantacha remained in France until 1628, but Brûlé does not appear to have stayed with him through this period; he seems to have returned to New France that same year (Trigger 1988, 405).

In 1608 Champlain had referred to Brûlé as "my young boy." He was then pleased with the youth who went willingly with the Wendat people to learn their language, who facilitated communication between Champlain and the Wendat leaders, who accompanied him on his war expeditions, who served as the very means of alliance between Champlain and the Wendat confederacy. By the 1620s, however, Brûlé's conduct was impeding Champlain's redrawn agenda. He was refusing to cooperate with missionary aims by tutoring the Jesuits in the Wendat language. To the missionaries and to Champlain, he was not of religious value. This young man, who was still regarded by the Wendat as the material evidence of kinship alliance with the French, and who would have been a valued relation in any Wendat trading family, was completely desacralized, even demonized, by Brother Sagard, by the Jesuits, and by Champlain. The evidence of Brûlé's continued participation in and profit from the fur trade constituted a betrayal of Champlain and of God, and moreover had reduced him, in the eyes of the Recollet brother, the Jesuits, and the mission-conscious Champlain, to the level of an unholy commodity.

Treason: Champlain and Brûlé

As has been mentioned, after 1618 Champlain was quite involved with continuing the establishment of his habitation at Quebec. He had moved his wife to Quebec in 1620, and had since been lobbying the king and court for assistance with colonization, with few results. "In 1627 the population of Canada still consisted of less than one hundred [French] persons—clerks, interpreters, and missionaries . . . not one of them could be called a genuine settler" (Zoltvany 1969, 3). By this time Champlain was a veteran of many battles with de Monts' monopoly-holding merchant companies, including Les Marchands de Rouen et St. Malo, which held the monopoly from 1614 to 1620, and with La Compagnie de Caën, which operated from 1620 to 1627. These companies were generally administered by Huguenots with purely mercantile goals and with no interest in agricultural settlement or in conversion of the Natives.[16] However, in 1628 the monopoly held by de Caën was revoked by the monarchy, and Cardinal Richelieu, a staunch opponent of Protestantism, caused Louis XIII's official charter to be given to La Compagnie de Cent-Associes (Company of One Hundred Associates). This company was composed in great part of French Catholic aristocrats with interests in a semifeudal rather than a purely mercantile New France. The Cent-Associes had been given a charter that, to Champlain's delight, mandated that in exchange for a perpetual monopoly on the fur trade and a fifteen-year monopoly on all other commerce, they were required to finance and arrange the settlement of four thousand agricultural settlers in New France by 1643. Unfortunately for Champlain's plans, however, in the Cent-Associes first year of operation, the war between England and France reached the shores of the Americas.

An English merchant, Gervase Kirke, had secured a commission from Charles I of England to seize New France, which they called Canada, from the French. He sent his three sons, David, Thomas, and Louis, across the Atlantic to carry out this plan. David Kirke intercepted four ships full of settlers that the Cent-Associes had sent, including a ship on which Amantacha was sailing back to New France. Amantacha was held by the English, who "were told that he was the son of a native 'king,' [and] thought he might be useful to them" (Trigger 1988, 456). Kirke then blockaded Champlain's habitation at Quebec. The traders and other inhabitants at Quebec managed to survive the winter of 1628–29 by fishing and digging for roots, but in July 1629 Louis and Thomas Kirke forced their surrender. The French inhabitants of Canada were rounded up, and all prepared to leave for Europe. But there were a few of the defeated French who refused to leave Canada, and thus, at least in the eyes of loyal French returnees, decided to go over to the side of the English. Champlain

---

16. By far the best and most lucid survey of the succession of merchant companies in New France is Marcel Trudel's *The Beginnings of New France, 1524–1663* (1973).

saw two of these Frenchmen standing with the English conquerors at Tadoussac. Both of these men were interpreters, and one of them was Étienne Brûlé (Champlain 1971, 6:1–98). The other was Nicolas de Marsolet, the truchement living among the Innu. Champlain was enraged, and recorded the declamation he delivered to the two men, as well as their responses.

> I saw Étienne Brûlé, *truchement* of the Huron, who had put himself in the service of the English, and Marsolet, with whom I remonstrated regarding their infidelity toward their King and their country. They replied that they had been taken by force (which is not believable, since in that situation one would expect disservice rather than fidelity). I said to them, "You say that they gave each of you one hundred *pistoles* and some trade rights, and having promised them complete fidelity, you remain without religion, eating meat on Friday and Saturday, engaging in debauchery and licentious libertinage? Remember that God will punish you if you do not make amends. You have no relative or friend who would say the same thing to you; they rather, would hurry to bring you to justice. If you only understood that what you are doing is displeasing to God and to all the world, you would have a horror of yourselves! You who have been raised from little boys in these parts, now selling those who have put bread in your hands! Do you think you will be esteemed by this nation? No, I assure you, for they only use you out of necessity, and will always be watching your actions, because they know that when you are offered more money than they pay you, you will sell them even more quickly that you did your own nation. When they learn enough about this land they will chase you off, because one only uses traitors for a short time. You are losing your honor; you will have fingers pointing at you in all places, wherever you may be. They will say, 'Those are the ones who betrayed their King and sold their country.' It would be better for you to die than to live in the world in this way, for whatever may come, you will always have a worm gnawing at your conscience." Then I said even more on the subject. They said to me, "We know very well that if they had us in France we would be hung. We are very sorry for that, but the thing is done. We have mixed the cup and it must be drunk. And we have

resolved never to return to France; we will not give up our lives." O poor excuses [exiles?],[17] you will now be forced to keep traveling, and if you are caught, you run a great risk of being taken and punished. (Champlain 1971, 98–101)[18]

Shortly after this incident, Brûlé secured the return of Amantacha to his father, Soranhes, and returned with the two of them to Wendat country. Champlain, on the other hand, was taken by the Kirkes and shipped to England. Ironically, given that the war on the continent between the French and the English had ended in April, and Quebec had fallen to the Kirkes in July, Champlain was returned to France in December 1629, and Quebec was formally returned to the French in 1632 (Champlain 1971, 6:143–85).

Champlain's recorded "remonstrances" to Brûlé and Marsolet are remarkable for several reasons. His new sense of mission and the clear opposition he drew between religion and mercantilism are overtly in evidence here. According to Champlain, the treason of the truchements consisted not only in their betrayal of their king and country by going over to the side of the English, but also in their being "without religion," ignoring meat fasts and engaging in (presumably sexual) "debauchery and licentious libertinage." They had, Champlain averred, betrayed their religion. Although he did not specifically mention their reluctance to assist the Jesuits in learning indigenous languages, for this would be a reference to past behavior, he did in

---

17. The Champlain Society scholars note that "Pour donner le vrai sens de ce passage ambigu il faudrait peut-être rattacher les mots: 'l'on ne laissera pas de vivre,' à ce qui precede, et lire ensuite: — 'Ô pauvres excuses! que si,' etc. (voy le debut de cet entretien). A la rigueur, on pourrait voir dans ce mot *excusez* une 'formule polie de contradiction'; mais cette civilité ironique est rare chez notre auteur. Ou bien, c'est peut-être une faute d'impression, qui aura mis *excusez* pour *exilez*." I have chosen to place into the mouths of Brûlé and Marsolet the phrase "l'on laissera pas de vivre," and have indicated the possibility that Champlain intended the use of "exiles" rather than "excuses."

18. Translation mine.

this way address their irreligiosity. Although Champlain did not quite use this specific terminology, he may also have been accusing Brûlé and Marsolet of having done the unthinkable: of becoming Natives themselves. The two men indeed had chosen to remain among their adoptive kin rather than return to Europe. It may be ventured that in the eyes of Champlain, Brûlé and Marsolet, in negotiating with the English, had actively chosen a Native identity over a European one. They had certainly elected to abide in Native land.

Again and again Champlain accused the truchements of selling: selling themselves "for one hundred *pistoles* and trade rights," selling those who "put bread in their hands" (Champlain himself?), selling their honor, and selling their country. He predicted that since they have made this mercantile choice, they would also be expected by the English again to sell out to the highest bidder. He described the consequences of such a sale: the truchements will become symbols of treason for all who see them; fingers will point at them wherever they may be. They will be described as the men who sold their country. For Champlain, these young men began their careers as truchements by serving as means of alliance. But the specific material concerns of the trading companies in the colonial process have disillusioned Champlain. Brûlé, through his participation in trade and through his rejection of what Sagard and Champlain considered to be true religiosity, can be and has been bought and sold.

Yet Brûlé's position is also made clear in Champlain's record of this incident. He was clearly choosing not to leave New France; not to leave Wendat country; not to lose his means of livelihood and his way of life. He had been sent to France with Amantacha just two years before, and appears to have returned with haste. "We will not give up our lives," said the truchements. This statement may be interpreted in at least two ways. They may have been indicating that they would avoid France, and thus avoid being hung. The other possible interpretation is that the truchements were refusing to leave what had become their homes and refusing to give up what had become their lives.

Kinship: The Feast of the Dead

In 1632 France returned the Jesuits to Quebec, and in 1634 Father Jean de Brébeuf returned to Wendat country, where he had lived for three years prior to the fall of Quebec. In Brébeuf's 1635 Relation (annual letter to his superiors in France), he described seeing "the spot where poor Étienne Brûlé was barbarously and treacherously murdered" (Thwaites 1896–1901, 8:93). The next mention of Brûlé by Brébeuf was in his 1636 Relation, and the circumstances of this reference are extremely interesting. The 1636 missive was sent to the superior of the Jesuit mission, Father Paul LeJeune. In the second half of this letter, Brébeuf submitted his most detailed observations of Wendat life. This portion of the letter contained chapters on Wendat myths of origin; ideas regarding the soul; their gods, superstitions, and faith in dreams; the order of their councils; their burial and mourning rituals; and their Feast of the Dead (Thwaites 1896–1901, 10:125–37). These chapters, as the aforementioned topics indicate, were categorized, named, and described in a thoroughly European and Catholic manner, but they remain the richest source of description of Wendat culture as it existed at that particular time.

In his chapter on polity and government, Brébeuf mentioned a change that he observed in Wendat governance: "formerly, only worthy men were Captains, and so they were called Enondecha, the same name by which they called the Country, Nation, District—as if a good chief and the Country were the same thing. But today they do not pay so much attention to the selection of their Captains; and so they no longer give them that name" (Thwaites 1896–1901, 10:232). Following this statement, Brébeuf corroborates observations regarding the Wendat practice of matrilineal inheritance made by Champlain in 1615, but only to a certain extent and also implying change. He stated that Wendat headmen "reach this degree of honor partly through election; their children do not *usually* succeed them, but *properly* their nephews and grandsons" (Thwaites 1896–1901, 10:233).[19] Here Brébeuf mentioned

---

19. Emphasis mine.

an additional requisite for accession to position: these nephews and grandsons are appointed "only in so far as they have suitable qualifications, and accept the position, and are accepted by the whole Country" (Thwaites 1896–1901, 10:233). According to Brébeuf, "there are even Captains to whom . . . matters of government are referred on account of their intellectual superiority, popularity, wealth, or other qualities which render them influential in the Country" (Thwaites 1896–1901, 10:233). These statements may be read in support of Wallis Smith's opinion that by the 1630s Wendat social structures had been visibly affected by contact with the French, and most specifically by the explosion in trade. Regarding Brébeuf's observations, Smith concludes,

> These statements certainly do not prove the absence of an operative kinship principle in the succession to political office, but they do indicate the intervention of non-kinship factors beyond what the Huron considered—or Champlain indicated—to be common or traditional in the functioning of their system . . . I would suggest that under the impact of the fur trade . . . the matrilineal system of succession had to a degree broken down and exogenous political contingencies were beginning to override the dictates of kinship . . . That is, there are indications that the strength of the matrilineal principles was waning. (Smith 1970, 195)

Further, in his 1636 Relation, Brébeuf also notes that rights to trading routes were held by the person who discovered them and were inherited by his children; indeed, it was "in this that most of their riches consist" (Thwaites 1896–1901, 10:225). This may be read as an indication of the possibility of individual male-headed family accumulation of wealth, and of the social power and prestige associated with wealth. Because of the increasing importance of and dependence upon trade for the Wendat, this factor may imply an ascendance in the cultural significance of agnatic inheritance in general.

This is not to say that individual profits derived from trade were not subject to redistribution. Brébeuf's description of the 1636 celebration of the Feast of the Dead revealed that this feast remained a traditional site of the redistribution of wealth. The Feast of the Dead was a rite dating from the middle Iroquoian period, which initially seems to have been a method of uniting clan segments in their own ossuaries (Trigger 1988, 147). As time passed, the Feast of the Dead was elaborated. It became a reinterment ritual that served as an important site of the redistribution of goods through feasting (*tabagie*), and as the recognition of trade alliances through the affirmation of kin relationships. These relationships were materially and symbolically expressed through the burial of the dead of several groups (clan segments, Wendat nations, and even non-Wendat nations) in a common site and in a shared ceremony. The Wendat name for this ritual was "Yandatsa," which translates as "the kettle" and refers to the ritual feasting. "From the kettle expression the Wendats generated a series of metaphors relating to cookery in order to describe the ritual: to 'stir the ashes beneath the kettle' meant to hasten the arrival of the Feast, and to 'overturn the kettle' meant to decide against having a Feast. The situation in 1636 was a divided kettle, an image that connoted selfishness rather than the highly respected trait of generosity" (Seeman 2011, 62–63).

Archaeological findings demonstrate that in the colonial period, as trade with the French increased, the proportion of trade goods interred along with the bones of the dead increased dramatically (Trigger 1988, 426–27). Brébeuf's 1636 record reported that some twelve hundred gifts were brought to this feast, and of these gifts, "forty-eight robes were used in adorning the [burial] pit. Each whole body had its robe, and some had two or three" (Thwaites 1896–1901, 10:303). Trigger states that archaeological examination of the ossuary seen by Brébeuf proved that it contained, in addition to the robes and in addition to indigenous objects such as shell beads and pipes, a large percentage of European-made goods, such as glass beads, knives, rings, kettles, iron axes, metal arrowheads, and iron cups (Trigger 1988, 427). It is safe to conclude that much of the elaboration of the Feast of the Dead was owing to European influence. Although Trigger maintains that this elaboration was "the florescence of a traditional feature of [Wendat] culture rather than a radical departure from it" (Trigger 1988, 427), Brébeuf made one observation in the context of this feast that stands as testimony to the extent to which Wendat culture and social structure were profoundly affected by the influx of European goods. This effect was expressed in terms of wealth differential.

> The Old Men and the notables of this Country, who had the administration and the management of the feast, took possession secretly of a considerable quantity [of the beaver skin robes]; and the rest was cut in pieces . . . and ostentatiously thrown into the midst of the crowd . . . It is only the rich who lose nothing, or very little in this feast. The middle classes and the poor bring and leave there whatever they have most valuable, and suffer much, in order not to appear less liberal than the others in this celebration. (Thwaites 1896–1901, 10:304–5)

It appears that "the Old Men and the notables" were the men who profited most from trade, and even in their participation in the ritual that comprised the ceremonial locus of redistribution, had begun to secretly preserve their wealth. This phenomenon only supports the conclusion that by 1636 Wendat culture had been affected profoundly by contact with the French. The trade routes owned by certain men had become the routes to maintainable wealth and prestige, and the ritual site of redistribution of goods had been compromised.

Further, the ability of certain Wendat men to accumulate and preserve wealth affected the processes of governing councils. Brébeuf reported that by 1636 the principal headmen, increasingly selected on the basis of their wealth and prominence in trade, held sway in councils. Brébeuf stated that the economic position of a headman was such that "in short, if they are successful in trading, they are richer than the others" and that "when someone, be he Citizen or Stranger, wishes to obtain something from the Country, the custom is to grease the palms of the principal Captains . . . The regret that some private individuals have for such irregularities, and the envy of other Captains who have not been called upon to share the booty, discourage the practice more than they like; they decry one another, and the mere suspicion of these secret presents stirs up sometimes great debates and divisions"

(Thwaites 1896–1901, 10:253). It appears, then, that the trade with the French enabled individual accumulation, but that the accumulation of individual wealth was resisted by some of the Wendat, as seen by their protestations of such "irregularities" as acquisition without redistribution. It also appears that the cultural imbalances caused by the expansion of trade were becoming expressed within the primary symbolic site of redistribution, the Feast of the Dead. Yet there was a further complication of the feast held in 1636.

At this particular feast, the primary headman of the Attignawantan, Aenons, asked Brébeuf if he wanted Brûlé's bones and the bones of another deceased Frenchman, Guillaume Chaudron, to be exhumed and reburied in the ossuary along with the Wendat dead. Brébeuf declined, on the grounds that Brûlé and Chaudron were baptized Christians, and thus it was forbidden for them to be buried among unbaptized people. However, Brébeuf added, it would be acceptable for them to be buried in a separate pit alongside the general ossuary, and that it would be fitting if baptized Wendat would also be buried there. Aenons, the headman of the northern Attignawantan, agreed to Brébeuf's proposal.

However, another difficulty arose. There was at that time a schism between the northern and the southern Attignawantan, and thus a controversy over where the feast of the dead should be held. The southern Attignawantan favored Ossosané, the traditional burial location in the south, and the northern Attignawantan preferred Ihonatiria, a major village of the north. A council was called to solve the dispute, and during deliberations Brébeuf was asked at which site he desired to have Brûlé and Chaudron reinterred. Brébeuf left the matter to the judgment of the council. After ritual exchanges of gifts, with Aenons and the southern headman each insisting that the other take the two Frenchmen's bones, Aenons finally articulated that he had no claim on the bones of Chaudron, which were then buried near Ossossané, but that

> as for the body of Étienne Brûlé, it belonged to him, since he had embarked him and brought him into the Country; and thus the bodies were divided . . . Thereupon someone said, in an undertone, that

it was very reasonable that they should render honor to his bones, since they had killed him. This was not said so discreetly as not to be heard by [Aenons] . . . After the Council, when we [the Jesuits] had left, he took notice of the reproach and had very high words with the [southern headman]; and finally ceased to lay any claim to the body of Brûlé, in order not to irritate and reopen this wound. (Thwaites 1896–1901, 10:309)

In the end, neither Chaudron nor Brûlé was exhumed, and Brébeuf frankly was pleased with this turn of events: "Truly there is reason here to admire the secret judgments of God; for that infamous wretch did not deserve to have this honor shown him; and, to tell the truth, we would have had much difficulty in resolving to make on this occasion a private Grave, and in transporting to consecrated Ground a dead man that had lived so scandalous a life in the Country, and had given to the Savages so bad an impression of the morals of the French" (Thwaites 1896–1901, 10:310–11). The detail Brébeuf provided of this incident also supplies some information about the feelings of both the French and the Wendat toward Brûlé, and supplements the few other existing records of the circumstances of the death of Brûlé.

One other record of Brûlé's death is contained within the writings of Sagard. He confirmed that Brûlé was killed by the Attignawantan, and that "this killing was done for the hatred they bore him, but I do not know what offence he committed against them. There were many years that he was living amongst them, following the customs of the country and serving as an interpreter, and all that he received as a reward was a painful death—a nefarious and unhappy end" (Sagard 1866, 431). Finally and perhaps most revealing, there is a reference to the death of Brûlé in Father LeJeune's Relation of 1641. Apparently, when Brébeuf made a missionary visit to the Neutral Nation, while he was away the Wendat had begun to wonder and to spread rumors about his motivation for that journey: "They said that he had gone to visit them [the Neutral Nation] in order to make them a present of porcelain collars [wampum] and arrowheads and to instigate their coming to complete the ruin of this country. Some warned us [Jesuits] privately to beware of this undertaking, as there had been no other cause for the murder of one of our Frenchmen, that occurred here some years ago, than just such journeys which made the country uneasy and fearful of a transference of trade" (Thwaites 1896–1901, 21:211). LeJeune was certainly referring to the murder of Brûlé, because he was the only French person the Wendat had ever killed. From this account, Trigger concludes that Brûlé's death was what he calls "a political assassination. Brûlé was killed because certain Huron knew or believed him to be dealing with the Seneca, or some other tribe whose rivalry the Huron feared" (Trigger 1988, 474).

In many respects, Trigger's analysis is good. The fact that murder among the Wendat is known to have taken place only in cases of retaliation in mourning war and in cases of just punishment for endangerment and betrayal of one's kin serves only to support Trigger's argument. However, as has been noted, the Wendat understood and practiced killing in terms of kinship. The creation of kinship relationships (in warfare, in torture, in adoption, and in alliance) was performed and understood by the Wendat as sacralized, as ritualized exchange. Kinship was not simply political, but was rather a religious modality of exchange. Given this, Trigger's interpretation of the death of Brûlé as a political assassination is incomplete. The murder of Brûlé was essentially a religious act. Brûlé, by initiating a relationship with the Seneca nation, had acted outside of the proper boundaries of kinship. He had acted as an independent agent, negotiating an irreligious exchange. He had acted as if exchange could be conceived as simply a matter of commodities and thus had betrayed the sacrality of his relationship with his Wendat kin.

It is necessary to examine the events of the year before Brûlé's death in order to attempt to ascertain his motives for such a betrayal of his Wendat kin. In 1632 England had ceded to the French all rights to the colonization of Canada. One might propose that upon learning of the return of the French, Brûlé hoped to make up for his treason of 1629 by securing new and profitable alliances, possibly through diverting Haudenosaunee trade with the Dutch into the hands of the French. On the other hand, it is possible that Brûlé feared for his life (or at least doubted his welcome in French-controlled trade) upon the return of the French to Canada. After all, his past actions had earned the curses of Champlain, as well as the censure of the Recollets and Jesuits. In this case, he may have considered attempting to ally with the Iroquois and seeking the employ of the Dutch. Trigger proposes both of these possibilities (Trigger 1988, 474). However, even upon admitting the possibility of each of these hypotheses, a definitive answer to the question of Brûlé's motivations remains elusive.

Symbol: Étienne Brûlé

This chapter has attempted to present the phenomenon of exchange as the mediative language between participants in the colonial encounters of early New France. The languages of exchange are perhaps most clearly articulated when they are contested, and in the years 1608–32 these contestations, brought about by the various colonial encounters, both materially and symbolically dominated the geography. Étienne Brûlé traversed boundaries; these boundaries were geographic, cultural, and symbolic. Brûlé was chosen to mediate exchanges, to translate between cultures, but his mediatory role placed him at the nexus of conflict. Because of his location on the interstices of culture, of language, of religion, of all modes of exchange, he became the site upon which colonial contestations were enacted.

The kinship-exchange language of the Wendat was opaque to Champlain when Brûlé was exchanged for Savignon. Champlain's impetus for such an exchange was the expectation of the production of a truchement. It is important to emphasize that the word *truchement* is not simply a term that may be precisely translated as "interpreter." The word *truchement* carries other, deeper meanings: it signifies a means, a medium, a means to an end, a vessel through which things might flow. Further, Champlain did not deliver a truchement to the Wendat; on the contrary, he desired that a truchement be produced. Champlain wanted the Wendat to transform Brûlé into a French route of entry into the Wendat spoken language. He hoped to employ this truchement as a means through which exchanges of material goods might be accomplished, and as a means through which alliances might be made in order to facilitate this flow of goods. He wanted an extension of himself that he could deploy farther into the Wendat landscape; he wanted this extension to return to him with knowledge of land, of resources, of peoples. He intended this truchement, this means, to be a channel through which these materialities would flow.

The Recollets and Jesuits also saw in Brûlé a means to an end. He was the vehicle through which they could acquire an indigenous language, and language acquisition was the essential first step in their program of missionization. Only after languages were possessed could a missionary instruct Natives in another language: that of Catholicism. The Jesuits in particular exercised whatever powers they had in order to accomplish that first acquisition. To them, if they could extract what they desired from Brûlé, they could then present what they understood as the gift of knowledge of God to the Wendat. Brûlé, however, was reluctant to embody that role for them; he did not desire to participate in that exchange. Therefore, evaluating him as expressly in violation of religiosity, the French missionaries (Sagard and Brébeuf in particular) configured Brûlé as symbolizing that which does not have value. He was not a religious Frenchman, nor was he supposed to be a "savage" Wendat man. He inhabited the boundaries of these cultures (and of the colonial experience), and thus signified both an absence—a lost soul—and a problematic presence.

The Wendat desired to bring the French into relationship with them. This relationship was symbolized and enacted by them through the construction of kinship relationships, and in order to establish such a relationship, they exchanged Savignon, one of themselves, for another young man whom they perceived to be a member of the kin grouping of Champlain. In this they were deceived. Champlain did not present Brûlé to them as a kinsman or as a gift, as something full of and rich in meaning, but rather as an empty vessel, needing to be filled. And when the exchange had been completed, Savignon was returned to them, but Brûlé, the empty gift, remained among them. In response, the Wendat reconfigured their ideation of what they received in exchange. They revalued their cultural system in order to exploit the exchange by shifting their cultural emphases in order to accommodate the material possibilities presented to them.

Given these shifting operative systems, Brûlé's was not the first treason. Perhaps the first was Champlain's empty gift. Perhaps Champlain's revaluation of the aims of colonization can be interpreted as a betrayal of what he had performed in previous years. Surely Brûlé was betrayed when, because he acted in ways in which he had been tutored (both by the Wendat and by the trading companies), he was vilified and even, for a time, exiled. His attainment of Champlain's initial colonial desires carried little meaning to Champlain when another set of colonial and missionary desires took precedence. Yet what Champlain interpreted as Brûlé's treason may also be understood as Brûlé's new religious orientation. He chose to remain where he was valued as an accomplished facilitator of trade. In addition to learning the spoken language of the Wendat, Brûlé had mastered the symbolic language of mercantilism. Brûlé, when choosing to stay in New France, was electing to remain within the site in which his value was still acknowledged. He understood that as a truchement, he could be a conveyor of material of value to merchants. Brûlé was accused of faithlessness, but in truth he had placed his faith in his ability to translate the commodity. But Brûlé had placed his faith in something else as well. In making the choice to remain within a Native geography, Brûlé demonstrated that he too had been transformed by the colonial process. In this sense, Brûlé also illustrated his new orientation, which was grounded in the kinship relationships that he had symbolized, but perhaps more concretely, in the familial status and resulting protections that had been given to him by the Wendat confederacy. He had no qualms about returning to Wendat country; he chose to accompany Soranhes and Amantacha on their journey rather than to accompany Champlain on his.

Yet it is also clear that Brûlé did not orient himself sufficiently to Wendat understandings of kinship; he betrayed the sacred responsibilities that had been given him as a kinsperson of the Wendat. The Wendat understood Brûlé's treason against them as a betrayal of the integrity of that kin relationship. Because he made kinship overtures to people who were already in a relationship of exchange with the Wendat confederacy—that of warfare—his offer of exchange would not have been simply a reduplication, but rather would have been a revaluation of that relationship. Further, his offer of a relationship of exchange could not have been carried out within the proscribed boundaries of ritual; it had not been approved culturally and could not be enacted symbolically. Brûlé, by acting outside of the approved system, was proffering an empty gift. Thus the murder of Brûlé was, in one sense, the elimination of the material and symbolic expression of the empty gift. In the end, Brûlé was not allowed to partake in the Feast of the Dead, nor was he buried in consecrated ground. He had chosen not to conduct himself as a member of the Wendat. Thus the body of the murdered Brûlé was, for both the Wendat and the French Jesuits, the material and the symbol that could not be incorporated; his body was the exchange that was refused.

Yet that which is refused does not disappear. This study has proposed that Brûlé incarnated what may be described as the most crucial material exchanges and symbolic changes in the earliest decades of colonial New France. In the figure of Brûlé, the contradictions and complexities of intercultural encounter were expressed; through him, negotiations of boundaries and exchanges of materials were enacted. Brûlé, who embodied the third term, that which stands between the colonizers and the indigenous people, was necessary for the creation of what the Americas would become. Himself a new and terrible creation, a person expressing and enacting an orientation different from those around him, Brûlé, although materially and symbolically rejected by the Wendat, by the Jesuits, and by Champlain, would be resurrected in the persons and in the symbols of the coureur de bois: those men who traversed the landscape, creating new kinds of relationships based on new understandings of materiality and of value. As the embodiment of skewed relationships, the ever-present reminder of incomplete and unequal exchanges past, the unclaimed and blood-soaked bones of Brûlé still color the land.

3

Joseph Chihoatenhwa

Joseph Chihoatenhwa: Convert

References to Joseph Chihoatenhwa appear in many documents of the early colonial period in New France. Just as the Jesuit missionaries to New France recorded the details of the controversy surrounding Étienne Brûlé's death, these missionaries also inscribed their versions of the specifics of Joseph Chihoatenhwa's life. However, just as fiercely as Brûlé was chastised, vilified, and damned in the writings of the Jesuits, Chihoatenhwa was praised, commended, and eulogized. Chihoatenhwa was portrayed so sympathetically by the Jesuits because he represented their greatest success: he was a Wendat man who became a steadfast convert. But perhaps most important, like Brûlé, Joseph Chihoatenhwa constituted, as a human being who was transformed through intercultural encounters and exchanges, both the material and the symbol through which colonial relationships were negotiated.

For the Jesuit missionaries, Joseph Chihoatenhwa was the physical embodiment of their success, the critical ingredient of their mission to evangelize the Wendat people. Father Lalemant, younger brother of Father Charles Lalemant, referred to him as "the leaven of the gospel that has made the whole lump of this new Church of the Hurons rise" (Thwaites 1896–1901, 17:47) and recognized him as the "Apostle" (Thwaites 1896–1901, 17:41, 19:51, 20:83) to his own people. After his own baptism, he brought many family members to the Jesuits to receive the sacrament. He accompanied Jesuit missionaries on evangelical journeys, assisting them by translating their message into Native languages. Moreover, Chihoatenhwa risked his own livelihood by using his trading relationship with the Tobacco Nation (Tionnontaté) in convincing that wary nation to allow the Jesuits into their villages. Finally, Chihoatenhwa, although castigated by other Wendat people and taunted with the name "The Believer," became the guardian and caretaker of the Jesuit chapel established at the village of Ossossané. He and his family stood as the leading Wendat Christians of that village, which, owing to the efforts of Chihoatenhwa and his family, became a predominantly Christian village and the center of the Jesuit mission to Wendat country.

Predictably, the Jesuit rhetoric deployed in praise of Joseph Chihoatenhwa was florid.

> Our Christian . . . is incomparably superior to all the others in knowledge of and pious affection to our mysteries and to the spirit of Christianity . . . this brave Christian, I say, did not fail on this occasion often to address the people, and to perform the duty of an elder brother by instructing and teaching his juniors with most special benefit and success, because he had at once intelligence, eloquence, integrity, reputation, the knowledge of our mysteries and the affection for them, in an eminent degree; so we are beginning to regard him as an Apostle rather than a Barbarian of these countries. (Thwaites 1896–1901, 17:41)

> He has done, this year, everything that one can expect from an excellent Christian; he has thrown himself into the apostolic occupation at the height of all these squalls, which he has always faced with the eye of faith. There is no region in the country where he has not assisted our Fathers in the publication of the Gospel; he has everywhere openly borne witness to the truth which he knows; and all these infidel peoples have been constrained to avow that the Faith and the law of God was not beyond their possibilities,—seeing a Huron like them, who from his birth has been nourished and brought up in the same customs as they, seeing him not only profess this Faith, and practice on all occasions the commandments of that great master of our lives whom we come to announce to them, but protesting openly that he is ready to die rather than offend in that matter his conscience. A spectacle truly worthy of God, and

one which no doubt has delighted all the angels, although this infidel land has not derived from it the advantage which so holy a zeal deserved. God grant him the grace to persevere even till death. (Thwaites 1896–1901, 19:259–61)

These encomia were not misplaced; according to the Jesuits, Chihoatenhwa served them well indeed. Not only did he serve their mission as a Native "Apostle" and translator, but he also served Jesuit rhetorical purposes by standing as a shining example of the success of the missions to the various Native peoples of New France. The letters in which Joseph Chihoatenhwa was so portrayed were published in France. Both the letters and their subject, Chihoatenhwa himself, became valuable propaganda for raising much-needed additional funding for the mission.

Thus the reports made by LeJeune and the other Jesuit missionaries must be read as the missionary propaganda they are. It is also essential that these documents be read with strict attention to their historical context. As Carole Blackburn has demonstrated, Jesuit claims of missionary success were often exaggerated in order to establish their own authority over the indigenous inhabitants of the area, and indeed, in order to justify the inegalitarian relationships they were establishing with the Native people they so desired to convert. Even further, Jesuit rhetoric was deployed in order to establish and nurture ties with European donors to the mission.

Yet, as Blackburn rightly argues, clear evidence of indigenous opposition and resistance to the Jesuit program is embedded in the *Relations*. The forms this resistance took were varied. Active antipathy to the Jesuit presence was expressed; in other circumstances, cultural relativism was invoked. While some antipathetic and relativistic responses will be enumerated here, the next chapter are primarily concerned with exploring the resistance implicit even in evident embrace of the Christianity proffered by the Jesuits. In this chapter, the material life and symbolic significance(s) of Joseph Chihoatenhwa, the paradigmatic convert consistently held up as an exemplary Christian, the Wendat man who most evidently embraced the message of the Jesuits, will be examined. However, it is in exploring the complexity of the figure of Joseph Chihoatenhwa's experience that one may come to see that the lives of this man and of his people cannot be encapsulated merely by clear-cut juxtapositions of conversion and resistance, or of capitulation and autonomy. Rather, Joseph Chihoatenhwa embodies and bears witness to the transformations and new orientations that emerge in the context of colonial encounter. Before meeting Joseph the man, however, we must meet Joseph the symbol, as constructed by the Jesuits, and we must also inquire into the means of his construction: Jesuit writing.

An Economy of Language: The Jesuit Relations

Whereas Brûlé was written and spoken of by explorer and missionary, by European and Native, the life of Joseph Chihoatenhwa was inscribed primarily in the writings of the Jesuit missionaries. Accounts of his life are prominent in the Jesuit Relations, the annual missives composed by the Jesuit missionaries in New France and sent to the provincial of the Society of Jesus at Paris. The Relations are detailed accounts of the establishment and progress of the Jesuit missions among the various Algonquian and Iroquoian groups inhabiting the landmass stretching from the shores of Lake Huron to the Gulf of St. Lawrence. As a general rule, each annual Relation was sent under the formal signature of the Jesuit serving as the superior of the mission to New France in that year. The Relations of the years 1636 through 1641 are the documents in which materials relating to Joseph Chihoatenhwa are found. In these years the Relations were sent under the signature of Father Paul LeJeune. During his tenure as superior in the years 1632 through 1639, he wrote the Relation from Quebec, and continued in this duty during the years 1640 and 1641, despite the fact that during those years Father Vimont had been appointed superior of the mission. However, LeJeune did not compose the whole of every Relation. Beginning in 1635, each of these Relations also contained a detailed annual report from Wendat country, where mission outposts had been established. In these years, the Wendat portion of the Relations were composed by

Fathers Jean de Brébeuf (1635, 1636), François Joseph LeMercier (1637, 1638), and Jérôme Lalemant (1639–44).

Contrary to what one might suspect, these letters were not preserved in the Vatican archives. "According to Father Edmond Lamalle, the Jesuit archivist, after 1600 the Jesuit hierarchy no longer preserved incoming correspondence" (Martin 1988, 2). The *Jesuit Relations* are so readily available at present because in 1632, when LeJeune's first Relation was received in Paris, arrangements were made for its publication. Under the direction of LeJeune's provincial, Father Barthelemy Jacquinot, one Sebastien Cramoisy, printer and bookseller, was licensed to produce annually a vellum-bound duodecimo volume containing the letters from the mission in New France. This arrangement continued throughout LeJeune's tenure as superior, and much beyond, until the year 1673. Reuben Gold Thwaites, the senior editor of the 1896–1901 edition of the *Jesuit Relations*, observed that "[t]he *Relations* at once became popular in the court circles of France; their regular appearance was always awaited with the keenest interest and assisted greatly in creating and fostering the enthusiasm of pious philanthropists, who for many years substantially maintained the missions of New France" (Thwaites 1896–1901, 1:41).

Reading the Relations, then, must be an exercise in caution. In analyzing these letters, several things must be borne in mind. It must be recognized that these documents were intended as propaganda for public consumption, and that their aim was to secure support and funding for the mission. It is also evident, particularly in the case of LeJeune, that the authors of these letters consciously employed the art of rhetoric in which all Jesuits had been educated. The letters sent by the Jesuit missionaries also explicitly dwell on the importance of language to the mission: countless passages, especially in the earliest Relations, detail the necessities and difficulties of learning indigenous languages. Finally, and perhaps most significant for this study, these missives, being the products of seventeenth-century French Jesuits attempting to inscribe indigenous cultures, demonstrate the inability of their authors to understand and value Native cultures on their own terms. In other words, they are exemplary documents in the history of colonial encounters with an opaque "other." Therefore, by reading these colonial texts against their own intentions and limitations, as post-Foucauldian and postcolonial scholarships recommend, it is hoped that these texts shall be recognized as being quite revelatory concerning the very matters that they do not purport to inscribe.

First, the attitude of the Jesuits concerning language must be explored; this may most profitably be done through a brief examination of the life and letters of Father Paul LeJeune. LeJeune was a convert to Roman Catholicism. He entered the novitiate at the Jesuit college at Rouen, pursued further study at the great Jesuit colleges at LaFlèche and Clermont, and was then appointed instructor at the Jesuit colleges at Rennes and Bourges. Following this experience, and most relevant to the subject at hand, LeJeune was named professor of rhetoric. He taught the study of rhetoric at the Jesuit colleges at Nevers and Caen in the years 1626–30. These facts of LeJeune's life point to something that must not be ignored: LeJeune was a product of the Ignatian educational program.

LeJeune was educated under the system of the *Ratio Studiorum*, formally issued to the Society of Jesus by General Aquaviva in 1599 (Farrell 1938). This system divided Jesuit colleges into three academies, two lower and one higher. The first academy was made up of three classes of grammar (lower, middle, and upper). The second academy was composed of a class in humanities and a class in rhetoric. The third academy, that of higher studies, consisted of classes in philosophy and theology. In this examination of the language of the Jesuit Relations, it is the class in rhetoric that is of greatest concern. The *Ratio Studiorum* of 1599 was quite specific in its rules for professors of rhetoric:

> [the class in rhetoric] instructs to perfect eloquence, which embraces the two highest faculties, oratory and poetry (of these two, however, the preference is always given to oratory); nor does it serve only for usefulness, but also nourishes culture. Nevertheless it can be said in general that it is confined to three great fields, the precepts of oratory, style, and erudition. As to the precepts, Quintilian and

Aristotle may be added to Cicero. Although precepts may be looked for and noted in other sources, still in the daily prelections nothing is to be explained except the rhetorical books of Cicero and the rhetoric of Aristotle, and if he likes, the poetics of Aristotle. Style is to be learned only from Cicero (although the most approved historians and poets may be tasted); all of his [Cicero's] books are well adapted for the study of style, but let only his orations be given as prelections, so that the principles of the art may be seen as practiced in the speeches. Let erudition be derived from history and the customs of tribes, from Scriptural authority, and from all doctrine, but in small quantity. (Fitzpatrick, Mayer, and Ball, 1933, 208–9)

The Jesuit course in rhetoric, then, was heavily Ciceronian in orientation. Whereas Aristotle defined rhetoric simply as "the faculty of observing in any given case the available means of persuasion" (Aristotle, *Rhetoric* 1.2), the Roman rhetoricians emphasized in Jesuit education were more concerned with the results of rhetoric. For example, in his *De Inventione*, Cicero stated that "the function of eloquence seems to be to speak in a manner suited to persuade an audience; the end is to persuade by speech" (Cicero, *De Inventione* 1.5.6). The author of *Rhetorica ad Herennium* agreed: the speaker's end is "to secure as far as possible the agreement of his hearers" (*Rhetorica ad Herennium* 1.2.2). For Quintilian, rhetoric was "the science of speaking well" (Quintilianus 2.15.34), and its end was "concerned with action" (Quintilianus 2.18.2). On this point James J. Murphy writes, "Roman rhetoric has such a distinctively homogeneous flavor, and is so traditionally associated with the name of Cicero that it seems fair to describe the works of Cicero, Quintilian, and the author of *Rhetorica ad Herennium* as partaking of a common tradition which could properly be called 'Ciceronian' . . . All make efficiency—that is, the procuring of results—the main criterion of good speech" (Murphy 1974, 8).

The early Jesuit colleges, in subscribing to the teaching of rhetoric in the Ciceronian tradition, revealed themselves as subscribing to that same understanding of the true use and aim of rhetoric: the procuring of results. This particular philosophy of rhetoric precisely conformed with the overarching philosophy of Ignatius. In the *Constitutions of the Society of Jesus*, Ignatius explained that the establishment of colleges was a central concern of the order because education was the means by which his order would produce "the leaders and citizens influential for good who are necessary in ecclesiastical and civil society. To achieve this end, Ignatius encourage[d] students to perfect their Latin style and pronunciation. This was essential in an era when such eloquence was an opening to those who wielded power and influence" (Cesareo 1993, 26). More than once Ignatius revealed his concern with access to temporal power. He advised members of his order "to retain the benevolence . . . of the temporal rulers and noble and powerful persons whose favor or disfavor does much toward opening or closing the gate to the service of God" (Cesareo 1993, 27). It is evident, then, that from the inception of the Society of Jesus, and through its use of the curriculum of the *Ratio Studiorum*, the study and the use of rhetoric were conceived politically: that is, as an avenue to power.

Thus, because LeJeune, in the second of his Relations from New France, observed that "there [was] no place in the world where Rhetoric [was] more powerful" than there, in Canada (Thwaites 1896–1901, 5:195), the import of his statement must not be ignored. His observation was made just after a discussion of the importance of acquiring indigenous languages for the purpose of evangelization. Having witnessed the workings of indigenous communities for a year's time, he gave his opinion on just how conversion should proceed.

> There is no place in the world where Rhetoric is more powerful than Canada, and nevertheless, it has no other garb than that what nature has given it; it is entirely simple and without disguise; and yet it controls all these peoples, as the Captain [headman] is elected for his eloquence alone, and is obeyed in proportion to his use of it, for they have no other law than his word. I think it is Cicero who says that all nations were once vagabond, and that eloquence has brought them together; that it has built villages and cities. If the voice of men has so much power, will the voice of the Spirit of God be powerless? The Savages listen to reason readily—not that they always follow it,

but generally they urge nothing against a reason that carries conviction to their minds. A Captain once asked the Englishman who was here to help them in their wars; the Englishman, wishing to evade him, answered with superficial reasons: that is, that some of his men were sick, and that his people would not get along with the Savages. And this Captain so pertinently refuted all his objections that the Englishman was compelled to say, "I need my men, I am afraid the French will come and attack us." Then the Savage said: "Now you are talking, we understand you well, until now you had said nothing." They acquiesced in this reason. When they are made to see the conformity of the law of God with reason, I do not think that much opposition will be found in their minds. Their will, which is extremely volatile and changeable, when enlightened by the grace of Him who will call them, will at last be brought into the line of duty. (Thwaites 1896–1901, 5:195–97)

Clearly, in this context, LeJeune intended to put his own command of the art of rhetoric to use, to procure the result of conversion.

It should also be noted that in order to sustain the mission to New France, and to finance the Jesuits' efforts toward the conversion of indigenous people, LeJeune's letters contained grateful paeans to past contributors. As has been mentioned, the Relations were published for the consumption of the pious and the curious, and the inevitable result was that the religious-minded (as well as, perhaps, the publicity-minded) were stirred to action in the form of donations to the mission.

LeJeune's rhetoric, then, became a force in the market economy of seventeenth-century France. While his skilled use of rhetoric established his authority, his deployment of that authority brought about the consequences he desired. In a way, his words served as a sort of currency of the colonial mission: certainly his words were just as valuable for sustaining and expanding the mission as were beaver pelts for sustaining and enriching the Company of New France. His words, carrying rhetorical power, were circulated in France, and money and materials were exchanged for mention by him in prayer, but also in print. The irony is, of course, in the fact that the Ciceronian rhetoric of the Jesuit missionaries was directed toward the French, and not toward the Native people who were, ostensibly, the primary object of the mission. Before effective Jesuit rhetoric could be marshaled as a weapon in the battle for the conversion of souls, the Jesuits would have to put aside their Latin and attend to the acquisition of Native languages.

Linguistic Exchanges: Acquiring Language

The quotidian linguistic concern of the Jesuit mission to New France was not the artful deployment of Ciceronian rhetoric; after all, the Relations were composed but annually. On a daily basis, the Jesuit missionaries faced up to the daunting necessity of learning indigenous languages. Luckily, before the Jesuits had arrived, the few Recollet missionaries who had attempted missionization projects had begun to compile dictionaries of indigenous languages. Recollet lay brother Gabriel Sagard's dictionary of the Wendat language (*Dictionnaire de la Langue Huronne*), which he appended to his 1632 work, *Le grand voyage au pays des Hurons*, has already been mentioned. The Recollet Father Joseph LeCaron, who had been in Wendat country from 1615 to 1616, had accompanied Sagard to Wendat country in 1623, where they remained until 1624. During this time Father LeCaron had also composed a dictionary of the Wendat language, as well as dictionaries of the Algonkin and Innu languages; these were presented to King Louis XIII in 1625, but have since been lost.

When in 1632 the Jesuits were given exclusive rights to the mission in New France, they immediately seized upon the dictionaries that had been prepared by the Recollets. However, they seem to have been dissatisfied with these works. In LeJeune's 1633 Relation, he wrote that "Father de Noüe and I concluded that we must find some means of devoting ourselves to the study of the language, without a knowledge of which we cannot help the Savages. I then . . . began to turn over the leaves of a little manuscript Dictionary that had been given to me in France, but it was full of errors" (Thwaites 1896–1901, 5:87). It is impossible to determine whether the manuscript in LeJeune's hand was faulty, or whether the fault lay in his attempt to employ this dictionary in understanding what may have been an entirely different Native language. In any event, LeJeune abandoned the dictionary.

For all of the Jesuits, the road to linguistic competency was long and hard. Father de Nouë, for example, evinced such small ability in acquiring Native languages that eventually, as French colonization began, he was instructed to remain among French settlers, to supervise the colonists in their work and to minister to the ill and dying among them. While de Nouë's linguistic struggles limited him in his ability to contribute to the mission, other Jesuits were much more successful in their quests to acquire languages. Father Brébeuf, Father Chaumonot, and Father Daniel all distinguished themselves. But even these men required time and effort to attain basic linguistic competence. After six months of steady effort, Father Daniel's command of the Wendat language was rudimentary, and after three and a half years in Wendat country, Father Brébeuf still had much to learn (Trigger 1988, 512).

LeJeune was tireless in his dedication to learning languages, but he struggled to discover a profitable method by which to accomplish his task. His 1633 Relation recounted the difficulties he had in persuading French truchements to share their knowledge: "In all the years that we have been in this country no one has ever been able to learn anything from the interpreter named Marsolet, who, for excuse, said that he had sworn that he would never teach the Savage tongue to any one whomsoever" (Thwaites 1896–1901, 5:113). Of course, this merely illustrates the extent to which language and the possessors of linguistic competency had become commodified in New France. Under these conditions, it is quite understandable that Marsolet (Brûlé's erstwhile companion who, with him, was so vilified by Champlain) refused to share his knowledge, given that it was primarily his linguistic abilities that made him, as a truchement, such a valuable commodity in New France.

LeJeune also attempted to learn indigenous languages from another man, Pierre Antoine Pastedechouan. Pastedechouan was a young Innu man who had been taken to France in 1620 by the Recollets. During a six-year stay in Europe, Pastedechouan had learned Latin and French, and LeJeune thought that this young man would be an excellent resource. However, Pastedechouan, having spent his formative years in France, had never acquired the fighting, hunting, and fishing expertise so necessary for the success of a Native man. When he returned to Quebec, he found himself despised, and despised in return both his own people who rejected him and the French people who had so wrongly used him. Although he did promise to assist LeJeune for a brief time, he resisted providing assistance to any French person who, as he saw it, had contributed to the destruction of his life. LeJeune called Pastedechouan "the Apostate," and complained that "contrary to his promise, and notwithstanding the offers I made him, was never willing to teach me,—his disloyalty even going so far as to purposely give me a word of one signification for another" (Thwaites 1896–1901, 7:21). Pastedechouan, suffering terribly from years of alienation from his family of origin and unable to reintegrate himself into Innu culture, starved to death in the winter of 1636, wandering bewildered and alone in his native land.[1]

This unsuccessful attempt to learn an indigenous language did not discourage LeJeune; indeed, LeJeune redoubled his efforts, still convinced that "one who could know the language perfectly, so that he could crush their reasons and promptly refute their absurdities, would be very powerful among them" (Thwaites 1896–1901, 8:37). This statement begins to reveal LeJeune's understanding of the power available to him should he acquire an indigenous language. Not only would his ratiocinations, perfectly expressed, be understood and accepted by Native people, but he would gain the power to accomplish these ends. LeJeune did eventually become competent in some Algonkian languages, but he pinned his greatest hopes on those Jesuits living among the Wendat people, who were not only equipped with the

---

1. Emma Anderson's *The Betrayal of Faith: The Tragic Journey of a Colonial Convert*, a masterful biography of Pastedechouan, vividly portrays and interprets his experiences with Jesuit missionaries in his own country and in France.

older dictionary compiled by LeCaron, but who had the advantage of immersion.

Brébeuf, after demonstrating some gifts at learning the language of the Innu, was sent to Wendat country. "Brébeuf was the first missionary actively to teach an Indian language to his companions and to other Frenchmen who intended to move into the Huron country to trade . . . yet Brébeuf's own knowledge of Huron was still far from satisfactory" (Hanzeli 1969, 48). In his 1635 Relation, he described the daily chore of teaching the Wendat language as he slowly became more competent in it: "As for me, who give lessons therein to our French, if God does not assist me extraordinarily, I shall yet have to go a long time to the school of the Savages, so prolific is their language" (Thwaites 1896–1901, 8:133). The next year he wrote more on the daunting project of acquiring linguistic competency, describing the methods used by the Jesuits during the summer of 1634. "We made a confused memorandum of the words we had learned since our arrival, and then we outlined a Dictionary of the Huron language . . . Finally we busied ourselves in . . . arranging a Grammar" (Thwaites 1896–1901, 10:55). Later in that letter he also gave advice to potential missionaries:

> Instead of being a great master and Great Theologian as in France, you must reckon on being here a humble Scholar, and then, Good God! With what masters!—women, little children, and all the Savages,—and exposed to their laughter. The Huron language will be your saint Thomas and your Aristotle; and clever man as you are, and speaking glibly among learned and capable persons, you must make up your mind to be for a long time mute among the Barbarians. You will have accomplished much, if, at the end of a considerable time, you begin to stammer. (Thwaites 1896–1901, 10:91)

Eventually Brébeuf did become the linguist of the Wendat people, generating a Wendat catechism, a grammar, and a dictionary. As evidence of his growing proficiency, in his Relation of 1636 he included a prayer he had composed in the Wendat language.

It is worth noting that the Jesuits often expressed a desire for divine assistance in learning languages, as did Brébeuf in the 1635 Relation as quoted above. These desires were not merely metaphorical in nature; at times, the priests reported witnessing the hand of God in the bestowal of "extraordinary favors, [such as] a temporary gift for the language, which several have experienced on occasion, understanding and speaking above their range" (Thwaites 1896–1901, 19:129). It was mainly hard work, however, that enabled the Jesuits in Wendat country finally to attain linguistic mastery. They spent hours drilling each other, taking notes on birchbark. "We all work on it diligently," wrote Brébeuf; "it is one of our most common occupations" (Thwaites 1896–1901, 10:55). In 1637 Father LeMercier was finally able to report that

> We have not failed, through his holy grace, to make great progress in the language,—so that now, if there is a question of making little trips to visit and instruct some Savage, the Father Superior [Brébeuf] finds persons all ready to go . . . we gather up all the words from the mouths of the Savages as so many precious stones, that we may use them afterwards to display before their eyes the beauty of our holy mysteries . . . the Father Superior has discovered excellent methods of distinguishing the conjugations of the verbs, in which the whole secret of the language lies; for the greater part of the words are conjugated. (Thwaites 1896–1901, 14:11)

Even with this great advance, the Jesuits still encountered significant difficulties.

Brébeuf himself had soon learned that powerful expression in the languages of the indigenous peoples of New France required more than simple vocabulary and grammar; oratory in particular required the use of metaphor. "Metaphor is largely in use among the People; unless you accustom yourself to it, you will understand nothing in their councils, where they speak almost entirely in metaphors" (Thwaites 1896–1901, 10:219). This attention to Wendat oratory, which included political and ritual speeches (such as the ritualized language of diplomacy, which was employed to condole others for the deaths of kinspersons and thus avoid war), hints at the Jesuit desire to appropriate the language of power and authority. Acquisition of the niceties of the Wendat language was not a mere exercise in the proper conveyance of information, but also involved acquiring a means of expression that would convey authority by means of mastery of sacralized modalities of speech.

Even the mastery of metaphor and the emulation of authoritative speech patterns could not guarantee the reception of the Christian message in the ways the French missionaries intended. The early Recollet missionaries, acting without the greater flexibility of the Jesuits, faced perplexing dilemmas.

> The problem of communication was, in fact, more serious than Sagard, or any of the Recollets, realized. All of the basic teachings of Christianity had, from the earliest days, been tailored for a complex society in which ideas of authority, hierarchy, and punitive justice were taken for granted. To express Christian doctrines in a way that was compatible with the beliefs of people whose whole way of life was founded on exactly the opposite principles required more than linguistic skills which could translate the Christian message. It required the remoulding of Christian teachings to fit a different social code. This was something the Recollets were incapable of perceiving and would have been opposed on principle to doing. (Trigger 1988, 393–94)

The Jesuits were more ready to compromise than their Recollet predecessors. Early instances of the now-famous Jesuit strategy of "inculturation" can be found in the missionaries' struggles to find suitable Wendat terminology with which to express most accurately the content of Catholic theology. Earlier,

> Sagard [had] noted that one of the more serious obstacles to the eventual explanation of Christian beliefs to the Huron was the absence in their language of many necessary theological terms. The Huron had no single words by which it was possible to express concepts such as

sacrament, kingdom of heaven, trinity, holy spirit, angels, resurrection, or hell. Even apparently more universal concepts, such as temptation, faith, and charity, seemed to have no precise equivalents in Huron. The explanation of the simplest religious texts thus required elaborate periphrasis and there was no way of being certain that the intended meaning had been adequately conveyed. (Trigger 1988, 393)

The Jesuits, with their newly acquired linguistic sophistication, attempted to adapt Wendat words to serve their theological ends. For example, the Wendat term for lineage or family, *-hwatsir-* (not incidentally, the same term used to indicate alliance) was used to describe the fellowship of Christians, including those in heaven. An anonymous Jesuit sermon given in the Wendat language, probably written in the 1630s or 1640s and entitled "*Instructions D'un infidel moribund*," speaks of faithfulness after conversion and prayer in these terms: "Have courage, then. Esteem highly that the master adopts you into his lineage. Let it be evident that you valued it when you entered the straight lineage of believers. Let it be that the sky-dwellers know that you love their lineage" (Pomedli 1991, 55). However, this term, *-hwatsir-*, refers to a matrilineage. The Jesuits had found a way to express Christian fellowship and brotherhood, along with the necessity of joining the Jesuits in pursuit of this fellowship, but the term for lineage and alliance was inextricably bound up with the concept of matrilineal kinship. The Jesuits, because of their patriarchal tradition, could not describe God as female, but the term they chose necessarily implied such. "Consequently, the natives generally found it impossible to understand the concept of a male high god" (Pomedli 1991, 55).

The term *oki* (plural *ondaki*) was used in the Wendat language to signify sacred power. For the Wendat people, this power was able to be expressed either positively or negatively. *Oki* could be responsible for any manifestation of power in a person or in nature, and this power, while perceived as extraordinary or marvelous, could also provoke fear and awe. Michael M. Pomedli has observed that before the Jesuits' arrival, Sagard had identified four possible sites of oki. First, "a being possessing supernatural power, generally a demon or devil"; second, "a person so angry and emotionally disturbed that he is regarded as 'out of his mind' or 'possessed by the devil'"; third, Wendat "healers or shamans"; and fourth, "an extraordinary person whose wisdom and ability are exceptional" (Pomedli 1991, 74). Of course, these understandings of oki are profoundly biased. Other than the fourth definition, ondaki are identified with the demonic. Even the third definition is not positive, as Sagard regarded Wendat medicine as chicanery. One might assume that the Jesuits, particularly Brébeuf, would have been perspicacious enough to realize that a word indicating sacred power would have been useful in conveying the power and sacrality of angels or saints, or even of the Holy Spirit, but Brébeuf distanced himself from the use of this word. In his opinion, the term *oki* was too involved with the possibility of the demonic. "The Jesuits were representative of a theological position which could not accept the legitimacy of God's grace flowing . . . in the lives of non-believers. People were either believers or non-believers. If they were non-believers, the devil filled in for the absence of grace. In such a belief system, the Huron reliance on benevolent okis could provide evidence only of the causal power of the devil" (Pomedli 1991, 119).

Further, Brébeuf seems to have decided that the Wendat understanding of manifestations of oki were consistently related to the immanent world, and therefore the word was insufficient for an adequate description of transcendent power. "In Brébeuf's estimation, Huron admiration . . . [of sacred power did] . . . not go beyond the limited wonders of human ingenuity and the beauties of nature" (Pomedli 1991, 75).

Instead, Brébeuf employed the term *ren* when speaking of sacred power. Steckley and Pomedli believe this term originally signified "a spiritual power an individual or group possesses . . . manifest[ed] . . . in chanting, singing, praying, dancing, or in any public ritual . . . [T]he individual or group celebrates his empowerment and invokes or demands that the ren be on his side during some upcoming event" (Pomedli 1991, 121). Brébeuf and other Jesuits employed this term specifically to refer to the power of prayer, and downplayed the negative possibilities of ren. The Jesuit co-optation of this word appears to have been extremely successful. Indeed, "[i]n a later interaction with the Wyandot, Potier [a Jesuit missionary active in the 1740s] writes that the related term for spell-casting, *atren*, was . . . 'non auditur,' meaning it is no longer heard" (Pomedli 1991, 123).

These examples are intended to illustrate the extent to which the Jesuits had to wrench the Wendat language into expressing their theological views. They are also intended to demonstrate that Jesuit intervention into the Wendat language actually seems to have changed the language itself. The Jesuits were unable to make a successful analogy between the Wendat understanding of the sacred and their own. Steckley and Pomedli rightly point out that the Jesuits had their own ondaki, namely angels and saints; the Wendat people noted this resemblance. LeJeune records an instance of Wendat people observing statues of St. Ignatius and St. Xavier in the chapel at Quebec: "they asked if they were *Ondaqui*" (Thwaites 1896–1901, 5:257). The Jesuits, however, were unable to conceive of a concept of sacred power named in other than their own terms as being anything other than demonically inspired (Pomedli 1991, 155–56).

Even more important, the inability of the Jesuits to grasp the complex Wendat understanding of sacred power, indeed, the Jesuit insistence on classifying these manifestations of the sacred as demonic, actually undermines the Jesuit view that their linguistic mastery led to understanding. Because of their inflexibility on certain theological issues, the Jesuits were able to ignore that even their greatest leaps of understanding were undercut by hegemonic theological premises.

Unsurprisingly, Joseph Chihoatenhwa assisted in the translation of the Jesuit's theological concepts into a Wendat framework. In his 1638 Relation, Father LeMercier reported that in the winter of 1637–38, Joseph Chihoatenhwa had asked to learn to read and write.

> [H]e recently asked us if there would be any sin in wishing to know how to write, so that he could set down in writing not only what concerned the progress of his soul, but also the affairs of the country . . . In exchange for this, we have profited greatly, for, in serving him as Instructors in reading, we have made for ourselves a good Master

in the language. When we ask him the initial or final letters of the words, which are sometimes hardly distinguishable, he utters them for us very distinctly; so he will be of great service to us, with the help of God, in the conjugations. (Thwaites 1896–1901, 15:113)

Joseph's inquiry as to whether learning to write might be a sin is of interest because it hints toward other Wendat perceptions of writing. While he surely benefited the Jesuits by embarking upon a course of literacy in French in exchange for instructing the Jesuits in the Wendat language, by learning to read and write he put himself into immediate proximity with what other Wendat considered a mysterious and perhaps dangerous power. He also may have further alienated himself from his people.

Jaenen has opined that "the natives saw some danger in divulging their religious vocabulary to the evangelists of the new religion, therefore they refused to cooperate extensively in the linguistic task of compiling dictionaries and grammars, and of translating religious books" (Jaenen 1974, 277). The Jesuit Relations do not document this phenomenon outright, but they certainly do imply it. One need only examine the case of Carigonan, an Innu medicine man with whom LeJeune spent a fruitless winter, attempting to learn his language. Carigonan responded to LeJeune's continual mockery of his spiritual authority by mocking LeJeune in return: "Wishing to have sport at my expense, he sometimes made me write vulgar things in his language, assuring me there was nothing bad in them, then made me pronounce these shameful words, which I did not understand, in the presence of the Savages" (Thwaites 1896–1901, 7:57). Surely Carigonan, having been so insulted by LeJeune's mockery, would have balked at teaching him any words of power or import. LeJeune did report having learned some insults over the course of this humiliating experience: "Shut up, shut up, thou hast no sense," "He looks like a dog," "He has a head like a pumpkin," and "He is deformed, he is ugly" (Thwaites 1896–1901, 7:63).

Since the arrival of the Jesuits in Wendat country, considerable suspicion had surrounded their ability to communicate with one another by means of the written word. Brébeuf immediately reported that the Wendat were fascinated by many of the objects the French had with them, but "above all the writing, for they could not conceive how, what one of us, being in the village, had said to them, and put down at the same time in writing, another, who meanwhile was in a house far away, could say readily on seeing the writing. I believe they have made a hundred trials of it" (Thwaites 1896–1901, 8:113). A Wendat man named Oëntara was truly suspicious of this ability, and when visiting a neighboring nation,[2] he excoriated the Jesuits, relating that the Jesuits' "writings were only sorceries" (Thwaites 1896–1901, 21:215). The most damning evaluations of the Jesuits' ability to write began as soon as epidemics began to strike the Native people who had been in contact with the French. Father LeJeune wrote in his 1636 Relation that one Native man interrupted a Jesuit conversation about the negative effects of alcohol on the indigenous population with this charge: "[I]t is not these drinks that take away our lives, but your writings; for since you have described our country, our rivers, our lands, and our woods, we are all dying" (Thwaites 1896–1901, 9:207). Father Jérôme Lalemant, enumerating the ways in which the Jesuits were blamed for bringing these diseases to Wendat country, wrote that "[i]f we asked the name of some one, in order to write it in the register of our baptized ones, and not lose memory of it, it was (they said) that we might pierce him secretly, and afterward, tearing out this written name, cause the death, by this same act, of him or her who bore that name" (Thwaites 1896–1901, 19:129). And finally, the next year, some Wendat reported having dreams in which the Jesuit priests were seen "unfolding certain books, whence issued sparks of fire which spread everywhere, and no doubt caused this pestilential disease" (Thwaites 1896–1901, 20:33).

This Wendat suspicion of writing is not, as some would have it, simply evidence of an indigenous group being impressed by a superior technology and regarding it as impressive magic. On the contrary, the

---

2. The Neutral Nation, called by the Wendat people "Attiwandaronk," meaning "people who speak a slightly different language."

Wendat indictments of writing are evidence of Wendat resistance to the Jesuit's claims of superiority. Brébeuf's bemusement by the "hundred trials" to which the Wendat people put his writing illustrates his lack of awareness of the level of Wendat resistance to being inscribed. By 1640, by means of the traditional vehicle for communication with sacred powers—the dream—the Wendat explicitly articulated their association of writing with the stealing of their own powers. Their accusations, and the vivid images of their dreams, made clear that the inscription of their names in baptismal rolls hastened their own deaths. And they were opposed to this inscription. "By contesting the authority of writing, Aboriginal people acknowledged its power but denied its hegemonic function as the embodiment of a universal truth; in this way, if only temporarily, they refused the translation of colonial signifying practices and the authority embedded in them" (Blackburn 2000, 110–11). Joseph Chihoatenhwa, however, chose to learn to harness this power of inscription for himself. He wanted this ability not just to record his own religious experience, "the progress of his soul," but also to record "the affairs of the country" (Thwaites 1896–1901, 15:113). Even "The Believer" wanted to inscribe his own understanding of what had transpired in his country since the Jesuits had arrived. He was prepared to write his own testimony.

The Jesuit attitude toward learning indigenous languages presumed the transparency of these languages. They believed they could master these languages, and translate their doctrine into these languages. When indigenous languages failed to have immediately apparent cognate concepts, the languages and cultures themselves were seen as lacking. LeJeune himself, on arriving in New France, wrote that the Innu language was "full of abundance, and full of scarcity . . . all words for piety, devotion, virtue, all terms which are used to express the things of the other life; the language of Theologians, Philosophers, Mathematicians, and Physicians, in a word, of all learned men . . . all that concerns justice, reward, and punishment . . . all these things are never found either in the thoughts or upon the lips of the Savages" (Thwaites 1896–1901, 7:21). LeJeune then proceeded, at great length, to articulate the matters in which the language was rich, including grammar and syntax: "an infinite number of proper nouns ... different verbs to signify an action toward an animate or toward an inanimate object ... [and} all these adjectives, and even all the nouns, are conjugated like Latin impersonal Verbs" (Thwaites 1896–1901, 7:21–29). In this respect, LeJeune was not at all unlike other colonialists of their period. Steven Jay Greenblatt has recorded many instances of such ambivalent observations on the part of diverse explorers and travelers from a century before (Greenblatt 1990, 23). The absence and yet the abundance of speech is one of the key dualistic themes in the European imagination of the Americas.[3]

Writing later, from Wendat country, Father Jérôme Lalemant was much less ambivalent and much more negative as he complained in reference to the Wendat people, "Not only do words fail them to express the sanctity of our mysteries, but even the parables and the more familiar discourses of Jesus Christ are inexplicable to them. They know not what is salt, leaven, stronghold, pearl, prison, mustard seed, casks of wine, lamp, candlestick, torch; they have no idea of Kingdoms, Kings, and their majesty; not even of shepherds, flocks, and a sheepfold,—in a word, their ignorance of the things of the earth seems to close for them the way to heaven" (Thwaites 1896–1901, 20:71). His negative valuation of the language belied the Jesuits' very desire for it, their acquisitiveness in wanting to master this language and use it for their own ends.

As Long has observed, "Specific empirical languages are not transparent; they are opaque ... When opacity (the specific meaning and value of another culture and/or language) is denied, the meaning of that culture as a human value is denied" (Long 1995, 107). By regarding these Native languages as acquirable commodities with use-value,

---

3. Cervantes (1990), Todorov (1984), Greene (1993), Pagden (1993; 1995), and Long (1995) have each examined, in various ways, the European production of discourses that describe (and inscribe) the Americas and their inhabitants simultaneously as utopian and barbarian, paradisiacal and hellish. LeJeune's description of both the richness and the poverty of Native languages is a fine example of this ambivalence or multiple consciousness.

the Jesuits engaged in a type of mercantile activity they had otherwise rejected. While they refused to engage in overt trade in pelts and liquor, they employed every means at their disposal to acquire language, which was the scythe with which they might reap their harvest of souls. After discovering that the language was "rich," after discovering that it could be parsed, the Jesuits explored every avenue of gaining that which they desired.

In exploring every avenue by which to gain linguistic competency and oratorical authority, they were unable to admit (or even to perceive) that the language of the Wendat people was indeed opaque; it contained ideas about power, about the sacred, about relationships that the Jesuits could never comprehend because of the colonial and missionary discourses in which they were embedded. In valuing the uses to which command of the Wendat language could be put, rather than valuing the cultural context of the language, the Jesuits involved themselves in yet another set of lopsided, nonreciprocal exchanges. They were unable to value Wendat culture as a human value; they could only regard it as a field from which a harvest might be taken.

Exchanges: Disease, Death, Sacred Power, and Conversion

To the Jesuits, converts were the tangible fruits of their harvest of souls. But how could they most effectively reap such a harvest? Father Paul LeJeune, the first superior of the mission, observed early in his career in New France that "mind is not lacking among savages, but education and instruction" (Thwaites 1896–1901, 5:33). At first the Jesuits conceived of conversion as a goal to be attained through intellectual appeal, and thus aimed to educate and instruct through reason. In the initial stages of the Jesuit mission, the priests leaned on the adage *fides ex auditu* (Thwaites 1896–1901, 5:191), and carefully constructed rational arguments for the Christian faith. In 1633 LeJeune opined that "when [Native people] are made to see the conformity of the law of God with reason, I do not think much opposition will be found in their minds" (Thwaites 1896–1901, 5:195). However, the Jesuits were soon surprised to learn that their rational presentations of Christian theology were not immediately embraced. This was not because the Native people had no respect for rational argument; on the contrary, the Jesuits continued to observe the respect that Natives had for the ability to persuade an audience through the use of rhetoric or "fine speech." Yet the Gospel message of the Jesuit missionaries most often went unheeded by healthy adults, who had world views perfectly adequate to their lives.

Very often, Jesuit rational arguments regarding the Christian faith were immediately rebutted by Native hearers. As previously mentioned, Natives often replied from a position of cultural relativism. Brébeuf's 1635 Relation from Wendat country indicated that he encountered relativistic attitudes with regularity: "And when we preach to them of one God, Creator of Heaven and earth, and of all things, and even when we talk to them of Hell and Paradise and of our other mysteries, the headstrong savages reply that this is good for our Country and not for theirs; that every Country has its own fashions" (Thwaites 1896–1901, 8:119). In 1637 Jesuit Father François Joseph LeMercier recorded an occasion on which Aenons, a Wendat chief, commented that "we have our own ways of doing things, and you yours, as well as other nations . . . Your ancestors assembled in earlier times, and held a council, where they resolved to take as their God him whom you honor, and ordained all the ceremonies you observe; as for us, we have learned others from our own Fathers" (Thwaites 1896–1901, 13:171–73).

Instead, then, of the anticipated harvest of mature adults actively choosing to embrace Christianity, the first "converts" made by the Jesuits were dying members of various Native nations. Jesuit missionaries chose to baptize these persons in accordance with Roman Catholic Canon Law (865 §2), which states that "an adult in danger of death may be baptised if, with some knowledge of the principal truths of the faith, he or she has in some manner manifested the intention to receive baptism and promises to observe the requirements of the christian religion." Missionaries would thus inquire of Native people on their deathbeds as to whether they desired the sacrament of baptism; if willingness was articulated, the priests proceeded with the sacrament. The Jesuits in New France also baptized dying infants, again, in accordance with Canon Law (868 §2), which states that "an infant of catholic parents, indeed even of non-catholic parents, may in danger of death be baptised even if the parents are opposed to it."

Many scholars have observed that because in the early stages of their mission the Jesuits performed the sacrament of baptism primarily upon the dying, some Natives made an entirely logical association between the sacrament of baptism and the hastening of death. Kenneth Morrison investigated the phenomenon of Jesuit baptism of Innu people, who, in the 1630s, were suffering the ravages of European diseases and negotiating the problematic presence of the French. The Innu "were grappling with ultimate issues, particularly the increasing pain of postcontact life and the meaning of death . . . There was a widespread awareness that the mounting numbers of deaths correlated with French settlement, and the Jesuits were therefore distrusted. But . . . Thinking in terms of the vital symbols of traditional power, the [Innu] concluded that if baptism could kill, it might also cure" (Morrison 1990, 420). Morrison is here referring to what he labels one of the central existential categories of the Innu (and of other Algonquian-speaking nations): that of sacred power. Morrison describes power as being "cosmologically central" and observes that "power could be abused as well as extended in affirmations of solidarity" (Morrison 1990, 418, 432). Thus rituals of baptism were understood by the Innu as manifestations of sacred power that could produce either positive or negative results.

Perhaps just as important, the sacrament of baptism was sometimes perceived to be a ritual performance in which a Native person was made a member of the French community. The Jesuits admitted as much, describing baptism in no uncertain terms as a means by which to ally with the French. In Father Jean Brébeuf's portion of the 1636 Relation from Wendat country, he reported that

> Monsieur de Champlain and Monsieur the General du Plessis rendered us a great service last year, by exhorting the Hurons in full council to embrace the Christian religion, and by telling them that

it was the only means not only of being some day truly happy in heaven, but also of cementing in the future a very close alliance with the French, who if this were done, would readily come into their country, marry their daughters, teach them different arts and trades, and assist them against their enemies. (Thwaites 1896–1901, 10:27)

As further evidence of this, the Jesuits, when administering baptism to infants, often promised that if these infants should live, the Jesuits would take these children to be educated among the French. "In other instances, prominent French people became the godparents of baptized [Innu], effectively demonstrating that baptism extended the bonds of social solidarity. Baptism thus operated like many traditional native rituals which aimed to create and maintain alliances" (Morrison 1990, 421). Baptism, then, was viewed by some Native people as a means by which to establish bonds of fictive kinship and thus to lay the groundwork for other relationships of alliance, including that of intermarriage, cooperation in warfare, and trade. In this view, the experience of the Wendat closely mirrored that of the Innu. The Jesuits record, over a period of years, examples of Wendat attitudes in regard to baptism. Wendat evaluations of the desirability of baptism constantly invoke factors such as the effect of baptism upon disease (as cause or cure), the effect of baptism upon alliances (with the French and with other Native nations), and the effect of baptism upon the maintenance or severance of kinship ties.

Among the perceived potentially positive results of baptism was a cure of the baptized person's illness. Like the Innu about whom Morrison writes, the Wendat also sought healing through the ritual power of baptism. And like the Innu, in the 1630s the Wendat were also suffering from the devastation of waves of epidemics, which seem to have consisted of a type of measles, followed by influenza and then smallpox. Bruce Trigger conservatively estimates that the epidemics of 1634, 1636, 1637, and 1639 had reduced the Wendat population from approximately eighteen thousand to nine thousand (Trigger 1988, 589). The Jesuits recorded, with dismay, numerous instances of members of the Wendat confederacy seeking baptism solely as a cure for these diseases.

During the fall and winter of 1634, Jesuit Fathers Jean de Brébeuf, Antoine Daniel, and Ambroise Davost, who had just established a residence on the outskirts of the northern Attignawantan village of Ihonatiria, performed thirteen baptisms during the first wave of epidemic in Wendat country (Thwaites 1896–1901, 8:133). Ten of these took place in Ihonatiria itself. The first two were infants struck by illness, each of whom died shortly after the administration of the sacrament. The third was Oquiaendis, the mother of the village headman, who lived to recommend the virtues of baptism to others. The fourth was a young man whose life seemed to be prolonged for a time by the ritual, and the fifth, sixth, seventh, and eighth were men who succumbed to illness despite baptism. The ninth and tenth were young children who recovered. At this early stage of the Jesuit presence in Wendat country, opinion was divided between those who regarded baptism as a hastening of illness and those who regarded it as a potential cure. At this point, despite positive or negative outcomes and evaluations of the ritual, the Wendat were clearly articulating their understanding of the Jesuit priests as embodiments and/or manipulators of ondaki, sacred powers (Thwaites 1896–1901, 8:109).

Prior to the second wave of illnesses in the autumn and winter of 1636, Jesuit actions had effected an important change in the Wendat interpretation of baptism. In 1635 the Jesuits had decided to baptize a large number of healthy children and only a very few ill adults. Because so few of the eighty-six Wendat adults and children baptized from summer 1635 through the summer of 1636 had died, it was possible for an observant Wendat person to conclude that the ritual had succeeded in protecting those baptized from illness and even from death (Trigger 1988, 516). By the time the influenza epidemic of late 1636 began, many Wendat had begun to seek out baptism specifically for its potentially curative properties. During that epidemic, six priests (including Father Jean de Brébeuf) and four Frenchmen were in residence at Ihonatiria; all of them survived and thus served as positive examples of the efficacy of being French, Catholic, and baptized. It is conservatively estimated, however, that the Attignawantan alone suffered the death of approximately five hundred of their kinspeople (Trigger 1988, 528). In addition, during this epidemic, Father Brébeuf had declared to the Wendat people that their villages would not recover unless they converted to Christianity. He also made it clear to the Wendat that if a member of their kinship group had been baptized, that person was going to heaven. Because of this doctrine, a new concern arose among the Wendat: how to remain within their kinship groups in the afterlife.

During the epidemic of 1636, many Wendat were again suspicious that baptism did not cure, but rather killed. The power of the ritual was not questioned, but the effects of the ritual were up for debate. The argument that baptism was lethal was reinforced by the fact that between the fall of 1636 and the spring of 1637, the Jesuits had resumed baptizing ill persons (mostly children) at an astonishing rate. Father François LeMercier proudly reported 250 baptisms over that period (Thwaites 1896–1901, 14:107). The Jesuits performed many of the infant baptisms included in this number surreptitiously; Wendat antipathy toward the suspected death-rite was too high for many parents to allow the Jesuits to perform the ritual. However, some adults did choose baptism, and this was for the newly emerging reason mentioned above: concern for joining family members in the afterlife. The Jesuits recorded several instances of this rationalization of baptism. One woman was quoted as seeking baptism so that she might "go to find [her] brother . . . who was baptized and died two years ago" (Thwaites 1896–1901, 13:29). Conversely, others rejected baptism because they feared that if sent to heaven, they would be separated from their deceased kinspeople. On one occasion recorded by Father LeMercier, a woman dissuaded her husband from baptism by "representing to him that it would not be proper for him to go to heaven, since none of his relatives were there" (Thwaites 1896–1901, 13:127). Yet another man was quoted as stating unequivocally that "for my part, I have no desire to go to heaven; I have no acquaintances there, and the French who are there would not care to give me anything to eat" (Thwaites 1896–1901, 13:127).

Lest the impression be given that this debate over the result of baptism was merely intellectual, let us note that an incident recorded in Father LeMercier's 1638 Relation from Wendat country poignantly illustrates the frustration of the Wendat people in ascertaining the cause of the diseases that continued to plague them. A council of men from the Bear nation formally called the Jesuits to attend a council at the village of Angoutenc, delivering solemn speeches and reporting the devastation of their villages by disease; "they spoke only in sighs," reported LeMercier, "each one undertaking the enumeration of the dead and sick of his family" (Thwaites 1896–1901, 15:47). These men importuned the priests to explain themselves and their role in regard to death and disease. One unnamed man finally confronted the priests, saying, "[I]f thou wilt only tell us what makes us die" (Thwaites 1896–1901, 15:47).

The epidemics returned during the winters of 1637–38 and 1638–39. Ritual innovations were noted by the Jesuits in the Relations outlining the events of these years. In January 1638 a medicine man named Tehorenhaegnon had undergone a ritual fast by the shores of the great lake, and introduced a curative ritual for ailing Wendat that involved "a kettle filled with mysterious water with which he sprinkled the sick" (Thwaites 1896–1901, 13:241). In the winter of 1639–40, a new ritual, explicitly critical of the Jesuit program, emerged. A man of Ossossané reported having a vision in which Iouskeha appeared and urged the performance of this new rite. In this vision, Iouskeha (the mythological creative force, twin of Tawiscaron) indicated that the French wrongly called him Jesus because they did not know him well. Iouskeha confirmed that it was the Jesuits who were the cause of sickness among the Wendat and recommended that the Jesuits be expelled. He instructed his people to prepare lake water in a certain way and distribute it to the sick, all the while conducting a ritualized mimesis of warfare. As the Jesuits recorded this curative ritual, feasts were held for several consecutive nights, and "a great kettle full of that diabolical water," evidently specially sacralized for the occasion, was distributed by the elders of the village. At the same time, "all the youth and the War Captains [went about] acting like madmen through all the cabins . . . [e]verywhere were heard only howlings, nothing but agitation and madness" (Thwaites 1896–1901, 20:29–31). This ritual is of obvious importance, as it clearly constituted a hybrid strategy of resistance. In Tehorenhaegnon's ritual, water was sprinkled on the sick; this ritual action reasserted Wendat sacred power and reclaimed the power of medicine men to cure, but deployed this power in a form extremely similar to the Christian baptismal ritual. The ritualized mimesis of a war raid made clear the Wendat intention to fight against and defeat the disease by directing traditional religio-cultural resources against this new enemy. The new dreams reported, including the image of Jesuits with books from which the disease was spread, directly critiqued the Jesuit presence and articulated suspicion of the textual orientation of those priests. While the French origin of the "great kettle" can be suggested but not proven, the use of water to cure again borrowed from baptismal rites. However, in the Wendat ritual, the water was taken from the lake, the central water of Wendat geographic orientation.

The Jesuits were not unaware of the Wendat appropriation of Christian ritual and, predictably, were outraged. They referred to these rituals as "learned from the demons themselves" (Thwaites 1896–1901, 13:237) and to the practitioners of these rituals as "masqueraders" and "physicians of hell" whose souls were "possessed by the demon" (Thwaites 1896–1901, 20:31). But it was Joseph Chihoatenhwa who eventually arrived and, speaking in council, "passe[d] more than two entire hours in discoursing on the mysteries of our Faith" (Thwaites 1896–1901, 20:35). While he did not convince the chiefs in council to join him in working for the Jesuits, he did seem to defend the Jesuits sufficiently to prevent them from being expelled from Wendat country. Father Lalemant documented the effect of Joseph's speech, writing that "this assembly and its result, which was favorable to us, appeased their minds somewhat; the grievances they had against us, greatly diminished; they began to receive our Fathers quite peaceably in most of the cabins" (Thwaites 1896–1901, 20:37).

Ironically, it may be observed that at this juncture, the Wendat had indeed listened to Joseph Chihoatenhwa, but not in the way the

Jesuits had intended. Instead of ceasing their critique of Christianity and of the Jesuits, instead of embracing baptism and identifying themselves as converts, some Wendat had appropriated Jesuit sacred power by incorporating "being struck with water" into their own curative rituals. It may not have been Joseph's eloquent defense of the faith that moved Wendat medicine men to action, but another of his exhortations seems to have had an effect. In 1639 Father Lalemant wrote that Joseph Chihoatenhwa had often lectured his people on the topic of their cultural relativism and enjoined them to consider embracing the ways of the French.

> "You are disheartened, my Brothers" (he sometimes said to them), "because the matters of your salvation that the French propose to you are new things, and customs of their own which overthrow ours. You tell them that every country has its own ways of doing things; that, as you do not urge them to adopt ours, so you are surprised at their urging us to adopt theirs in this matter, and to acknowledge with them the same Creator of Heaven and of Earth, and the universal Lord of all things. I ask you, when at first you saw their hatchets and kettles, after having discovered that they were incomparably better and more convenient that our stone hatchets and our wooden and earthen vessels, did you reject their hatchets and kettles, because they were new things in your country, and because it was the custom of France to use them and not yours?" (Thwaites 1896–1901, 17:47–49)

Evidently, although most Wendat were not yet inclined to acknowledge the same Creator, they were indeed ready to embrace the Jesuit custom of "striking with water."

Morrison's conclusion in his analysis of Innu responses to the Jesuit program was that the value of alliance with Jesuit power overrode traditional cultural solidarity, and the Innu were moved to "forge a new symbolic cultural order" and reconstitute society through baptismal initiation of all willing persons, and, most non-traditionally, through expulsion of all those unwilling to restructure the religious and social order (Morrison 1990, 430–31). The Wendat experience with baptism was a bit different. Certainly, like the Innu, most Wendat saw the wisdom of establishing relationships with sacred power. However, Wendat appropriation and transformation of baptismal ritual practices remained within a traditional Wendat framework. Wendat spirits (here, Iouskeha) provided counsel through the traditional vehicle of dreams, Wendat medicine men performed the rituals, and the community of young men and war chiefs enacted the symbolic warfare against the disease. At least through 1640, the majority of the Wendat, facing the same devastation as the Innu, did not convert to Christianity as the Jesuits advised. Instead, they attempted to incorporate the sacred power wielded by the Jesuits into their own curative ritual actions. In so transforming baptism, they maintained their own cultural integrity a bit longer.

This is not to say that some Wendat did not accept the baptism performed by the Jesuits. Some did indeed treat baptism as a potentially healing ritual, even though the Jesuits tried to convey the meaning of baptism as a medicine not for the body but for the soul (Thwaites 1896–1901, 13:189). There was also at least one way for a Wendat person to appear to acquiesce to baptism through polite evasion. One Wendat man, Joachim Annieouton, eventually confessed to the Jesuit priests that for years he had intentionally deceived Fathers Ragueneau and LeMercier about his desire for baptism, and thereafter about his official status as a believing Christian. When he was asked to accept baptism, he responded by uttering the Wendat word *aaao*, which is "a sort of long-drawn and languid" pronunciation of the Wendat word for "yes" (*ao*) that actually means, because of its distinctive pronunciation, "I will do nothing of the sort" (Thwaites 1896–1901, 30:297). Annieouton thus escaped further attentions from the priests, who regarded him thereafter as fully Christian and bothered him no more about baptism.

Conversion: Joseph

Joseph Chihoatenhwa first appeared in Father François Joseph LeMercier's Relation of 1638. LeMercier wrote this letter in Ossossané, the primary mission in Wendat country (called *La Conception*—the Immaculate Conception—by the Jesuits) and forwarded it to his superior, Father Paul LeJeune in Quebec. As was usual, LeJeune included the report from Wendat country in his Relation of that year, which was sent on to Estienne Binet, provincial of the Society of Jesus in France, who forwarded it to be published by Cramoisy. LeMercier devoted nearly four of the ten chapters of his Relation that year to an account of the background, conversion, baptism, and demonstrated piety of Joseph Chihoatenhwa. Ossossané, Joseph Chihoatenhwa's village, was an important settlement of the Attignawantan (Bear People).

While the major event of 1638 for LeMercier appears to be the conversion of Joseph Chihoatenhwa, for the Wendat people the 1630s were characterized by the horrors of communicable disease. The course of these epidemics has been examined above; let it suffice to say that the villages of Ossossané and Ihonatiria were hardest hit. These villages were, of course, the places wherein the primary missions of the Jesuits were located. Ihonatiria in 1637 has been described as "a ruined village" (Trigger 1988, 538), and in that spring the Jesuits relocated back to Ossossané.

In the summer of 1637, Chihoatenhwa was one of those Wendat stricken with disease. It is impossible to ascertain whether his disease was measles or influenza, but it is certain that Joseph was in fear of death. He decided to reject the traditional cures offered by Wendat medicine and to take a chance on the medicine of the Jesuits. The priests, however, did not baptize him right away, because they did not believe he was in imminent danger of death. Instead, they visited him often, catechized him, and ministered to his illness as well as they could. For example, the Jesuit priests covered Joseph with hot blankets in hopes that he would sweat out the illness.

By August 1637 it looked as though Chihoatenhwa would die. When the imminence of his death became evident, Father Jean de Brébeuf decided to baptize him. At baptism, the name Joseph was bestowed upon Chihoatenhwa. And after his baptism, he began to show signs of recovery. He genuinely seemed to believe that his cure was owing to his baptism. His words are recorded in a letter the Jesuits sent to their superiors in France. Joseph is quoted as saying, "no doubt God has had regard to my submission . . . and now since it has pleased him to restore me to health, I am resolved to be very faithful to him all my life; I will so act that the others will know it" (Thwaites 1896–1901, 15:87). Soon thereafter Joseph arranged baptisms for his nephew and his nieces, promising to see to their upbringing in the Catholic faith. A year later his partner, Marie Aonetta, was baptized, and the two were married in the Catholic Church that same day.

What was remarkable about Joseph was that unlike many Wendat who chose baptism, he did not soon renounce his new status as a full member of the Roman Catholic Church. Many Wendat men and women who accepted baptism in order to be healed, but then survived, apostasized in the eyes of the Jesuits. That is to say, most baptized Wendat seem to have believed that they had had a disease, were cured of that disease by the sacred powers invoked in the ritual of "being struck with water," and saw no reason to keep taking that medicine, or to keep invoking those sacred powers after they were well again. They also saw no real contradiction between being People of the Peninsula, which involved participating in Wendat religio-cultural ways, and being baptized. Baptism was just another form of medicine, a way in which a sacred power could be invoked and used to enhance one's life.

Joseph, unlike the great majority of baptized Wendat, seems to have taken his baptism quite seriously, and immediately set to work assisting the Jesuits in their work of proselytization. There are several possible arguments that might explain Joseph Chihoatenhwa's evidently sincere conversion. It might be argued that he chose baptism because those who converted to Catholicism were then perceived as being in close relationship, or alliance, or "brotherhood" with the French, who could then be called upon for their assistance in trade, in warfare, or in times of material hardship, such as famines and winters. In fact, Joseph Chihoatenhwa's position in the village of Ossossané was not a particularly notable one. He was from a prominent family; he was the nephew of Hannenkiriondik, "protruding fir tree," the principal chief of Ossossané. However, he was rather young and unimportant at the time and had not particularly distinguished himself as a warrior, healer, orator, or title-holder. Joseph does seem to have engaged in some level of trade, however. Therefore, it is possible that he converted in order to gain some sort of prestige and to use the French to enhance his trading abilities and reputation.

On the other hand, Joseph may have converted because of his survival of the deadly illness that afflicted him. While he was ill, the Jesuits ministered to him, catechized him, and baptized him. Perhaps he was impressed by the effective healing ritual of baptism. Perhaps this rite had introduced him to a sacred power, the power that Jesuits named "God," and this power had worked on him and within him. Because this sacred power was mediated by the Jesuits and symbolized by the "cure" of baptism, he would then have been placed in relationship with this source of power, and with the people who had introduced this power to him. Perhaps this new relationship enabled him to interpret the great crises of disease and death among the Wendat; perhaps now, he could say that although traditional Wendat medicine did nothing to avert this catastrophe, the Jesuit's ritual did seem to work, and moreover, he had emerged from his near-death experience with more sacred power than he had before.

The Jesuits reported that before his acceptance of baptism, Joseph Chihoatenhwa had been more interested than most in the Jesuits and their mission. His first approach of the Jesuits, wrote LeMercier, was after the Feast of the Dead, during which he heard Brébeuf address a council of headmen. "[N]ot long afterwards, he presented one of his little sons to the Father Superior, 'to be baptized, and consequently,' as he said, 'to go to Heaven'" (Thwaites 1896–1901, 15:81). This request took place during a particularly vicious wave of disease, "when the Father was consoling the people of his village during the malady, which was increasing from day to day, and was revealing to them the most efficacious means for appeasing God" (Thwaites 1896–1901, 15:81). It seems, then, that Chihoatenhwa's interest in the Jesuit program for the aversion or survival of epidemics was quite strong. When he was taken with disease, "he ran to our house and begged us to instruct him as to how he should act during his sickness . . . and what kind of remedies he was permitted to use" (Thwaites 1896–1901, 15:81). "'My brothers,' said he, 'if you tell me that this medicine displeases God, I renounce it from this moment, and would not use it for anything in the world'" (Thwaites 1896–1901, 15:83). Chihoatenhwa then obeyed the Jesuits' every instruction "not only as to the guidance of his soul, but even as to the care of his health" (Thwaites 1896–1901, 15:83). Evidently Chihoatenhwa perceived great power in the Jesuits' abilities to deal with disease; LeMercier recorded an incident during which the Jesuits visited Chihoatenhwa's longhouse, and finding him feverish, covered him with a blanket. "He remained so all day, with considerable discomfort, until our return; and then he made us blush, asking us with his natural frankness if he might give himself a little more air" (Thwaites 1896–1901, 15:83). Chihoatenhwa obviously took excruciating care to follow their instructions religiously; he attended to each detail as if performing ritual action, and perhaps indeed he was. The careful adherence to every aspect of a ritual was crucial to the Wendat: "these peoples dread to fall short in the least detail of all their wretched ceremonies,—for there would follow from this omission, not only the privation of what they were expecting, but even physical punishment, which the devil for this reason exercises upon these poor wretches" (Thwaites 1896–1901, 15:161). The Jesuits, perceiving Chihoatenhwa's illness to be serious, eventually asked him about baptism. "'It is not for me to speak of that,' he said, 'no, it is not for me . . . I have often testified to you that I believed, I have asked you a hundred times for Baptism; and during the time of my sickness you have never come to see me when I have not said to myself, 'Ah, why do they not baptize me? It is for them to arrange that, for they know too well that I shall accept it gladly'" (Thwaites 1896–1901, 15:83). In this statement, Chihoatenhwa had clearly expressed his submission to the authority of the Jesuits. And he was then baptized with the name of Joseph.

After his baptism, he began to recover. LeMercier wrote that "we attributed his recovery to his Patron saint, for he seemed to be out of danger two days after we had supplicated the latter with all our hearts" (Thwaites 1896–1901, 15:83). The Jesuits' construction of agency here is interesting. They attributed Joseph's recovery to the intervention of St. Joseph, but even St. Joseph's actions were to some degree contingent upon the Jesuits' intercessory prayers. The Jesuits' efficacy of prayer, their language of approaching and entreating sacred power, had brought them a soul to harvest. And this convert was extremely grateful for the effects of the Jesuits' role in the manipulation of sacred power. In his gratitude Joseph announced that "No doubt God has had regard to my submission. . . . And now, since it has pleased him to restore me to health, I am resolved to be very faithful to him all my life; I will so act that the others will know it" (Thwaites 1896–1901, 15:85). It seems by this speech that Joseph had attributed his recovery to his own evidently satisfactory relationship with sacred power, and in this speech, he vowed to keep propitiating this sacred power in the manner the Jesuits recommended.

In the years after his baptism, Joseph remained closely associated with the Jesuits, assisting them in translating prayers and doctrinal concepts into the Wendat language, and actually preaching among the Wendat, exhorting them to follow his example and to embrace the ways of the Jesuits. His family was hit particularly hard by disease, and the Jesuits commented that "in less than a month, his cabin and that of his Brother were filled with sick people; he lost a great many of his relatives, and, above all, the last of his children, who was the heart of his heart . . . his first care for the sick was to have them baptized, without awaiting their last hours" (Thwaites 1896–1901, 15:89). He seems to have remained hopeful that the ritual of baptism would prevent death, even in the face of its failure to do so. His actions in convincing members of his family to receive baptism were largely successful. Father LeMercier mentioned the names of his three nieces, Agathe, Cecilia, and Thérèse, and his sister-in-law Anne. In this lengthy account of Joseph's conduct during this catastrophic time in Wendat country, Joseph is said to have "special communication with God, begging him every day, with tears in his eyes, that it may please him to look with pity on his poor country" (Thwaites 1896–1901, 15:95). Although there is but little scholarly exploration of Joseph Chihoatenhwa's experiences and conversion, there has been scant attention paid to Joseph's evident and constant concern for his community. His concern for his family was demonstrated in his attempts to have them healed through baptism, but even in his prayers, he articulated his care for all People of the Peninsula. As was mentioned above, when asking to learn to write, he desired "to record the affairs of the Country" (Thwaites 1896–1901, 15:113). Other Wendat, still opposed to the Jesuit presence, castigated Joseph Chihoatenhwa for choosing the medicine of the Jesuits over that of his own people. LeMercier noted that "[t]here were many who reproached him for the danger in which he placed himself and his relatives by not consenting to use the remedies of the whole country. In short, the report was almost universal that these good Christians were possibly associated with us to ruin their entire nation by the disease" (Thwaites 1896–1901, 15:99). The irony here is heavy, but understandable. Joseph Chihoatenhwa had chosen to affiliate with the sacred power of the Jesuits, importuning this power to save his people. However, other Wendat saw his actions not only as neglecting to practice traditional medicine and to invoke sacred powers with which the Wendat were familiar, but also as possible involvement with the Jesuits' negative use of power against the Wendat community. In other words, by acting independently of Wendat tradition and associating with those Jesuits who were under suspicion of destroying Wendat society, Joseph Chihoatenhwa placed himself in a position of being accused of witchcraft, or more accurately, in Wendat religious terms, using one's relationship with sacred power selfishly, rather than using it to help one's community.

Joseph did not waver in his chosen affiliation. He defended the Jesuits from verbal attacks by others, even family members, and even in council. LeMercier described a council meeting in which Joseph "courageously reproved one of his cousins, who maliciously complained that not one of the French had died during the contagion. 'The remedy which they use,' said he, 'is to believe in him who has made all; it only depends upon thee to avail thyself of this'" (Thwaites 1896–1901, 15:115). Joseph not only took the side of the strangers over his family, he remained steadfast in his allegiance to the medicine of the Jesuits. Joseph soon began to preach in assemblies, and seems to have persuaded some Wendat of the wisdom of Jesuit medicine. He was particularly effective in serving as an interlocutor when the Jesuits would catechize. LeMercier commented on this ability: "Our Joseph does wonders, for acting sometimes as objector, sometimes as ignoramus, and anon the Doctor, he gives opportunity to Our Catechist to explain by Dialogue, and with more clearness, what otherwise would be only half understood. It is hardly credible how much these questions and answers please them, and hold their attention" (Thwaites 1896–1901, 15:123). What is remarkable here is the extent to which Joseph seems to have transmuted what would have been individual oratory on the part of a Jesuit into a participatory conversational form. He appears to have undermined the Jesuits' adoption of ritualized authoritative speech, only to revalorize the content of such speech by creating a form of rhetorical exchange in which inquiry, reason, and persuasion are employed. Moreover, Joseph seems to have purposely and conscientiously provided the Jesuits with the opportunity to clarify points of doctrine especially strange to Wendat culture. As to the effectiveness of Joseph's assistance, suffice it to say that the next year the number of catechumens who were baptized had risen to forty-nine, with "nearly a hundred in the country making the same profession, to whose conversion he had contributed not a little" (Thwaites 1896–1901, 17:25, 53).

In 1639 the Jesuits moved from their headquarters in Ossossané (La Conception) and mission station in Teanaostaiaé (St. Joseph) to a new place in the land of the Ataronchronon. This new headquarters was modeled after the Paraguayan *reducciònes* and after Sillery, the réserve established by Father LeJeune outside of Quebec. They named this residence Ste. Marie. This new residence was not in an established village, but rather was to constitute a new settlement whence converted Wendat might relocate. The building, on the model of a longhouse but modified in some respects, was also "to serve, among other things, for the retreat and meditation of our evangelistic laborers" (Thwaites 1896–1901, 19:137). Joseph Chihoatenhwa assisted in the relocation, having made a trip to Quebec, where he met Marie de L'Incarnation and secured some saints' relics. Evidently Joseph had transported these relics back to Ste. Marie for its consecration (Thwaites 1896–1901, 19:143). The Jesuits were surprised and delighted when, as soon as it was built, Joseph was its first retreatant, staying there during a period of eight days to perform the Spiritual Exercises recommended by Ignatius Loyola. One of the insights expressed by Joseph during his retreat was this: "I do no longer fear death at all, and I would thank God if I saw myself at the end of my life, in the firm hope that I have, that I should go to heaven: in like manner, I no longer apprehend the death of any of my relatives, provided that they die in the grace of God" (Thwaites 1896–1901, 19:147). It seems that still the death of his kinspeople was much on his mind. However, Joseph still found time during this retreat to make a fellow convert of one of a group of Wendat who visited the new residence, and after his retreat he stopped, with LeMercier, to visit some kinspeople in a nearby village. He preached to these people, notably on two topics in particular: the hostilities toward the Jesuits and those affiliated with them, and Joseph's own redefinition of kinship.

> They will soon assure you quite afresh,—what they have often assailed your ears with,—that I am one of the causes of the ruin of the country; that the French have taught me the secret, and that I am past master in the matter of spells. Others will come to tell you that the resolution to kill me is already adopted, or even that they have already split my head. (Thwaites 1896–1901, 19:153)

> [A]s long as thou shalt be the devil's slave, I will not regard thee as my brother, but as a stranger from whom I am to be separated forever . . . Those who have taught me properly are my brothers, and I regard as my relatives only those who have renounced the devil, and received holy Baptism. Those are the ones with whom I shall live eternally in Heaven; those are the ones whom I truly call my brothers. (Thwaites 1896–1901, 19:159)

Joseph's awareness of the suspicion in which he was held will be addressed shortly; his recognition that he is a site of contestation is important. What is of greatest significance here is his redefinition of kinship to exclude unconverted kin, and to include all those who are baptized as Christians. This was a highly nontraditional utterance and demonstrated the extent to which he had reoriented himself. Joseph

Chihoatenhwa had adopted the Jesuits' language of Christian fictive kinship and made it into his own practice. He had been displaced from his own originary network of meaning in several ways. First, because of the decimation of his countrymen and the deaths of many of his own family members, his kinship networks had been disrupted. Second, by embracing the medicine of the Jesuits and rejecting traditional medicine, he had been further distanced from his community. Third, by bringing actual kin along with him into his new way of being, he set in motion a larger rupture of his community. Fourth, by teaching the Wendat language to the Jesuits, he compromised the opacity of his own culture. Fifth, by practicing the rituals of the Jesuits and overtly rejecting traditional Wendat ritual, his actions bespoke his new orientation. Finally, by leaving his kinspeople in what was left of Ossossané in order to perform the Spiritual Exercises in this new structure intended to serve as a réserve, he physically abandoned his originary milieu and enacted an embrace of a new geography, one defined by the Jesuits.

Upon his return to Ossossané, he was persecuted more than ever, and was compelled to announce, "I do not fear to die; let them kill me for this cause" (Thwaites 1896–1901, 19:247). Despite persecutions, his wife, Marie, also fearlessly joined him in his mission; in the letter of that year, Father Lalemant relates a story told by Father Ragueneau, who witnessed Marie Aonetta taking great risks to catechize her dying cousin and announcing that she would also take great pains to see her cousin's brothers baptized as well, averring that "we shall be but one family in heaven, as we constitute but one on earth" (Thwaites 1896–1901, 19:251). Later that year, Joseph Chihoatenhwa, assisting the Jesuits in establishing a mission station in Contarea, known as St. Jean-Baptiste, defended the Jesuits in council, and is described by Lalemant as spending "more than two hours in discoursing on the mysteries of our Faith. Those old Captains are greatly surprised to see a young man speak like a master, in a new language" (Thwaites 1896–1901, 20:35). This new language had become Joseph's most powerful asset. Because of his ability to express himself in this language, a hybrid of Wendat words and Jesuit theology, he had placed himself in a precarious position in Wendat society. However, the new form of rhetoric that he constructed for himself had given him a place in diplomacy and thus an opportunity to speak in the councils of villages all over Wendat country.

Treason: The Murder of Joseph

Joseph Chihoatenhwa also attempted to secure permission for the Jesuits to visit the people to the south of Wendat country, called by the French the Tobacco Nation because of their trade in tobacco, and called by the Wendat "Etionnontateronnon," or "people who live where there is a hill." Joseph left five seriously ill children in order to accompany the priests, and replied to his wife's entreaties to stay with "As for our family, [God] will take care of it, if he please" (Thwaites 1896–1901, 20:57). Because of the devastation that the Jesuits had appeared to have brought to the Wendat confederacy, other nations were loath to admit the Jesuits into their territories, and the villages of the Etionnontateronnon were adamantly opposed to a Jesuit presence. The priests were chased from villages and barred from longhouses. But accompanying Fathers Charles Garnier and Isaac Jogues to nine villages of the Tobacco Nation, Joseph sometimes prevailed upon their ethic of hospitality. On other occasions, he reviled their lack of hospitality. Castigating the headman of one village whose young men chased the Jesuits away, hatchets in hand, Joseph delivered a speech in which he said, "You drive out those who love you more than themselves. . . . Our ancestors have been in some sort excusable if they have not adored this great master who has created the world, for no one taught them; but you will be a hundred thousand times more severely punished than they, since you choose to remain in your misery" (Thwaites 1896–1901, 20:65).

Soon after his return from Etionnontateronnon country, toward noon on the second day of August in the year 1640, Joseph Chihoatenhwa went out walking with three of his nieces in the fields of corn, beans, and squash that surrounded his village. He led them in a prayer of thanksgiving for the harvest, told them to go and pick some squash, and after they retrieved it, he told his nieces to go home, because it was not very safe in that area. He remained outside the village, going into the woods to cut some cedar in order to build the ribs of a canoe. Suddenly, as Father Lalemant related the incident, two men jumped out of the woods and ambushed him, piercing him with a long javelin-like weapon. The men struggled, but in the end, Joseph was assaulted twice with a hatchet as well as scalped. The men ran off, leaving Joseph's dead body outstretched there in the woods, covered in blood (Thwaites 1896–1901, 20:79).

Lalemant told this story in an addendum to that year's Relation from Wendat country. "I was preparing to write Your Reverence [Father Vimont] for the last time in this current year, by the hand of Joseph Chihouatenhoua, our good Christian; and now the same paper of which he should have been the bearer is used to carry to Your Reverence the news of his death" (Thwaites 1896–1901, 20:79). Lalemant wrote that he was told by some Wendat people that the murder was done by two Haudenosaunee, likely Seneca, warriors from the south. The Jesuits reported that story back to their superiors in France. The Jesuits had no problem with that account of events; they and the Wendat were in the midst of great conflict with the Haudenosaunee at the time. Traditional hostilities between the Haudenosaunee and Wendat confederacies had been exacerbated by the presence of French, Dutch, and English colonials attempting to gain access to material resources through the exploitation of traditional Native trade networks. Thus the Haudenosaunee were viewed by the French as threats to their various enterprises. Exacerbating tensions, the people of the Haudenosaunee confederacy were, at this time, generally opposed to Jesuit attempts at conversion. Even given this situation, however, it has been argued that the Jesuits' explanation of the circumstances of Joseph's death is questionable.

Joseph Chihoatenhwa was killed while alone in the woods surrounding his village. No one else was reported to have been bothered or killed that day. He may have perceived some sort of danger beforehand; he did send his nieces home. It does seem unlikely that two lone Haudenosaunee warriors would travel all the way to Wendat country just to kill one man. Both Trigger and Steckley have opined that Joseph Chihoatenhwa was killed by his own people. Steckley's argument proceeds in this fashion: During the summer of 1640, another epidemic, this time smallpox, had hit Ossossané. Joseph had been told by his brother, Tehondechoren, that other Wendat people were again blaming the Jesuits for the disease and were also speaking ill of Joseph. However, the point was also made that if the Wendat killed the Jesuits in retaliation for their evil works, Wendat trade with the French would be in jeopardy; therefore, killing the Jesuits was rejected. That is to say, although the Jesuits may have been adjudged guilty of witchcraft, it did not seem practical to carry out the punishment. Therefore, Joseph Chihoatenhwa was killed by his kinspeople because he was perceived by the Wendat as guilty of using his relationship with sacred power in a selfish way. Chihoatenhwa had survived the illness that was caused by French Jesuits, and then had allied himself and his household with those same death-dealing Jesuits (Steckley 1981, 11–14).

Further, Joseph Chihoatenhwa's accompaniment of the Jesuits on missions to the Etionnontateronnon may have appeared potentially treasonous to the Wendat, especially if he was suspected of attempting to forge an unmediated trading alliance between the French and the Etionnontateronnon. Individuals were not allowed to facilitate alliances between nations. Moreover, the Wendat confederacy already had established kinship/trading alliances with the Etionnontateronnon and with the French. The proper establishment of an alliance between the French and the Etionnontateronnon would have had to have been ritually accomplished by duly appointed representatives of the Wendat confederacy. There would have to be a feast in which gifts were exchanged, and both groups would have to present the Wendat representatives with a great deal of gifts in gratitude for the introduction. However, that alliance would never have been attempted, because it was not in the interest of the Wendat confederacy at that time. In the late 1630s Wendat prestige and success depended on their prominence as middlemen, as facilitators of trade. If a trading alliance were to have been made between the French and the Etionnontateronnon, the Wendat would have compromised this position. Accordingly, any person who tried to mediate such an alliance, ostensibly in order to enhance his own trade apart from that of the entire confederacy, would have been adjudged treasonous. Among the Wendat, treason was grounds for murder. It might be objected that the Wendat council informed the Jesuits that Joseph was killed by Haudenosaunee men. However, members of the council had good reason to misrepresent the facts. All People of the Peninsula knew in what high regard the Jesuits held Joseph Chihoatenhwa, and the Wendat would not desire to jeopardize their relationship with the French: regard their great reluctance to kill the French priests, despite their growing suspicions of Jesuit misuse of relationships with sacred power.

Steckley has taken this argument further and has ventured that Joseph Chihoatenhwa may have desired martyrdom, and therefore may have actively courted his own death by entering the woods alone that day (Steckley 1981, 13). While this theory cannot be substantiated, neither can it be ruled out. Surely Joseph Chihoatenhwa had been exposed to the Jesuits' beliefs regarding the desirability of martyrdom. However, although Joseph was aware of the danger to his life posed by Wendat traditionalists and had articulated this awareness on many occasions (see Thwaites 1896–1901, 19:53 above, for one example), this does not necessarily imply that he embraced the concept of martyrdom and sought it that day.

One other issue yet remains to be explored. In the Relation of 1641, Father Lalemant included reference to an incident reported to him by a convert by the name of René Tsondihwane.

> René, a short time after his baptism, was fishing with our late Christian Joseph Chihoatenhwa, and the latter happened to dream all that really befell him about fourteen months afterward, —namely, that three or four Iroquois attacked him; that having defended himself, he was thrown to the ground; that they took off his scalp, and gave him a blow with a hatchet on the head from which they had removed it. The late Christian awaking after this dream, spoke to René his

companion. "Ah, my comrade," said he, "it is now if we were not Christians, that we should be obliged to have recourse to our songs and feasts, in order to efface the calamity of my dream. But it is not that which is the master of our lives,—it is he of whom they have taught us, and in whom we believe, who alone disposes of it according to his good pleasure." We have reason to think that this same dream returned to him several times afterward; for members of his family declared that often in the morning they heard him speak on awaking, and say, *Art thou the master of it? No, no, it is only God who shall dispose of it.* (Thwaites 1896–1901, 21:161–63)

Dreams were central to Wendat life. "The very heart of their culture [was] a belief in the intercommunion of beings and this [took] place preeminently in the dream world" (Pomedli 1991, 87). Dreams were arenas in which the desires of the soul were revealed, future events were disclosed, diseases were diagnosed, and medicines were prescribed. In other words, they were sites from which extremely valuable information could be derived. Sometimes, the content of the dream was obvious, and the person who had the dream need only act upon it. Other times, specialists were consulted in determining the meaning of and the appropriate response to the dream. As Brébeuf marveled,

> They have a faith in dreams which surpasses all belief . . . They look upon their dreams as ordinances and irrevocable decrees, the execution of which it is not permitted without crime to delay . . . The dream is the oracle that all these poor Peoples consult and listen to, the Prophet which predicts to them future events, the Cassandra which warns them of misfortunes that threaten them, the usual Physician in their sicknesses, the Esculapius and Galen of the whole Country,—the most absolute master they have . . . It is their Mercury in their journeys, their domestic Economy in their families. The dream often presides in their councils; traffic, fishing and hunting are undertaken usually under its sanction, and almost as if only to satisfy it. They hold nothing so precious that they would not readily deprive themselves of it for the sake of a dream . . . It prescribes their feasts, their dances, their songs, their games, in a word,

the dream does everything and is in truth the principal God of the Hurons. (Thwaites 1896–1901, 10:169–71)

Dreams were the sites where one's internal oki could commune with external oki (Pomedli 1991, 87), and where these sacred powers revealed truths to the dreamer.

Jesuits responded to this valuation of Wendat dreams by denigrating both their form and their content. They understood that dreams were competing sources of religious authority, so they characterized the dreams in various negative ways. Pomedli has analyzed the various Jesuit reactions to dreams and has schematized these responses as follows: demonically inspired, completely illusionary, a form of madness or non-sense, and barbaric (in the sense of linguistically confused) (Pomedli 1991, 94–104). Interestingly, the Jesuits did not condemn the dream that Joseph reported. Because Joseph was Christian, and because the Jesuits were engaged in composing a hagiography of sorts in relating the events of his life, his rejection of the dream was emphasized. They lauded his triumph over the temptations the dream presented. According to Father Lalemant, Joseph acted virtuously by refusing to discern the means of subverting the destiny revealed in his dream by consulting a Wendat person of power. In this case, Lalemant did not take the occasion to describe Joseph's dream as demonically inspired, as illusionary, as madness, or as barbarism, nor did he care to speculate on the possible source of this dream. Instead, Lalemant used this story to demonstrate that Joseph's refusal to "have recourse to songs and feasts" to avert the fate his dream foretold inspired another convert, René Tsondihwane, who was also struggling with a dream.

Lalemant's interpretation of the religious challenges Joseph faced notwithstanding, dreams remained a foundational and formidable resource for Wendat people; it was in dreams that various sacred powers revealed themselves, and it was in dreams that Wendat people could establish and maintain relationships with these sacred powers. Despite all colonial and missionary attempts to control the waking lives of Native people, dreams remained powerful potential sites of Native resistance to Jesuit missionization.

Symbol: Joseph Chihoatenhwa

The Jesuit treatment of Joseph Chihoatenhwa in the published Relations was, both before and after his death, hagiographic in nature. His virtues were recounted. Stories were told of his progress in the faith, and demonstrations were presented of the grace of God at work in his apprehension of doctrine, his assistance of the missionaries in linguistic and evangelistic endeavors, his horror of sin, his dedication to the salvation of his family, and his passionate and effective preaching. He was at once the "first fruits" of the mission and a symbol of the success of the mission. Moreover, the stories of Joseph reached a devoted public; pious readers of the Relations were encouraged by the example of Joseph that their donations would have good effect and would contribute directly to the growing harvest of souls in New France. Joseph was transformed by his Jesuit biographers into a sort of commodity that would be reproduced again and again, if only the reading public would invest in him. Moreover, Joseph is portrayed as participating and succeeding in the effort to reproduce himself.

But of course there is more to the story than the production of a commodity by the Jesuits for the French reading public. There was the Joseph that Joseph himself constructed. The true creativity of Joseph resided in the novelty of his way of being in the world. Unlike most traditional Wendat persons, Joseph Chihoatenhwa acted independently. He was cured of his disease, and he kept taking his medicine long after his recovery. He converted to Catholicism, he went around preaching to others that they should convert. He acted as the head of his household in a culture in which women were traditionally heads of households, matriarchs of longhouses and clans. Because he acted in this fashion, he was upheld by the Jesuits as a paragon of virtue and the future of the Wendat people. Also because he did so, he was considered by the Wendat to be a disruptive element. He not only refused to participate in traditional ritual activity, he actually recommended innovation. He allied himself with a new and dangerous power, wielded by the Jesuit interlopers, and encouraged others to follow him in this alliance. Worst of all, he betrayed his people.

By breaking with tradition, by establishing a relationship with a suspicious foreign power without the consent of his people, he loosed himself from his moorings, and he was a central participant in the crisis that would damage Wendat society terribly, and perhaps irreparably. Yet Joseph was also on the side of the preservation of kinship and of the survival of his people. His choices were made in order to keep himself, his family, and his people alive. Joseph Chihoatenhwa constructed his own intercultural and interreligious space, and in that sense, he was an innovator in religio-cultural hybridity.

The colonial encounters of early New France were characterized by their use of a certain language: the language of exchange. Certain persons, namely translators and converts, in being exchanged between cultures, were displaced from their original sites of meaning and placed into new sites of meaning. They were given (or forced into) the very strange and very new opportunity to create whole new lives, whole new selves. In so doing, they became sites of religious contestation. Other people fought over them, fought about their status, fought about their validity as persons, fought about their meaning, fought about their value. And of course, value was assigned very differently by French and by Wendat people.

Joseph Chihoatenhwa created his own sense of value: that of survival of the most critical period in Wendat history. He attempted in every way to ensure that he and his family, he and his people, survived. In no way can it be said that Joseph Chihoatenhwa became a French person. He certainly assisted the French in numerous ways. He was the ultimate fruit of their harvest of souls, their key into the language of the Wendat relationships with the sacred, and their apostle to the Wendat people. Given the manner of his death, however, it is evident that the Wendat rejected his hybridity and dismissed his strategy. Embraced by strangers, rejected by family, Joseph Chihoatenhwa, by virtue of cultural displacement and dislocation, by means of creativity and innovation, created a new hybrid orientation.

Traditional Wendat society had a solution for coping with a dislocated member of the culture. If a Wendat acted against the interest of the social body, he or she had acted treasonously and required careful removal. As in the case of Étienne Brûlé, a force determined to be acting as a detriment to the integrity of the social body and its relationships was eliminated. On the other hand, the French Jesuits actually worked to produce dislocated members of indigenous cultural bodies. Their program included giving this dislocated subject a hagiographic frame, and using this subject as a template for producing more dislocated subjects. Joseph was fictionalized by the Jesuits in order to demonstrate the integrity and efficacy of their mission, to preserve and extend their boundaries. If he were killed by his own people, he could have been portrayed as having been martyred by intransigent barbarians. As it was, the Wendat produced a fiction of their own: Joseph was killed by a threatening other. As it happened, this threatening other was being demonized by the Jesuits as well, and the fiction of Joseph's murder by Seneca warriors was accepted and presented as further evidence of the necessity of the extension of the Jesuit mission.

Joseph Chihoatenhwa was used by the Jesuits as a rhetorical device, a pedagogical lesson, and was displayed as a self-replicating commodity. The final use of Joseph Chihoatenhwa in the Jesuit Relations was the inclusion of a prayer he had composed. At the very end of his 1641 Relation, Lalemant wrote, "Certain persons have desired to see a specimen of the Huron language, in order to ascertain its structure and their methods of expression. I cannot select anything better here than one of the most ordinary communions which Joseph Chihoatenhwa, that excellent Christian whom we have mentioned, had with God toward the end of his days; by the same means can be recognized the Spirit of God which animated him" (Thwaites 1896–1901, 20:251). In this prayer, rendered in the Relation of 1641 in parallel in both the French and Wendat languages, Joseph invoked his understanding of the sacred power with which he chose to enter into relationship (see appendix 2). In certain of his phrases, the creative hybridity of his language is apparent. Throughout his prayer, the crises facing the Wendat in general, and Joseph Chihoatenhwa and his kinspeople in particular, are viscerally rendered. Steckley, the preeminent scholar of the Wendat language, has translated this prayer.

> Just as we are the masters of the canoes and the longhouses we have made, so you are our master because you made us. It is a matter of little importance that we are the masters of all that we possess as it is for a short time only that we are the masters of the canoes and the longhouses that we have made. It is for a short time that we are masters. As for you, you have become the permanent master of we who are called human beings. While it would not be a trifling matter that you are master when we are still living, it is principally at the moment that we die that you are master. (Steckley 1981, 16)

In this passage Joseph employs the material of daily life among the Wendat in order to convey the createdness of humanity. Just as Wendat people crafted their dwellings and conveyances, the "one who made all" (the Jesuit-created Wendat locution for the deity) created human beings. Analogically, as the Wendat people had use and ownership of the objects they created, so does the deity have use and ownership of human beings. To further explain, the term used for "master" in Joseph's prayer is the term *awendio*, which translates as "great voice, great word" (Pomedli 1991, 54). "The verb, *-io*, refers to political masters or leaders and, when combined with the noun, *-wend-*, means voice, word; in combination, *-wendio-* refers to those who controlled, probably for trading purposes, rivers, paths, and lakes" (Pomedli 1991, 54). God, then, is one who has ownership or control over the use of human beings.[4]

> Behold, I am now offering myself to you; I who am located here. Behold, I now choose you for my master. You are the principal master of I who am located here. Use your wisdom when you are thinking about I who am located here. (Steckley 1981, 16)

Joseph's choice to enter into relationship with this deity is here articulated, but the locution of identification of self is of special interest.

---

4. The phenomenon of trade route ownership is further explored, especially as it has to do with issues of gender, in chapter 4.

In the Wendat language, expression of specific selfhood (not, for example, self-in-relation, as in "uncle" or "sister") contains a locative element, rendered by Steckley as "I-who-am-located-here." This traditional locative understanding of self is preserved in Joseph's choice of the word of self-reference.

> You have all of us in my family within your sphere of influence. If I am not present when something happens to my family, I will think that he who most assuredly has us within his sphere of influence is watching. As for me, I am not of such a stature. It will be of little import if I am present, as my family will die even if I am there. (Steckley 1981, 16)

The expression "sphere of influence" puts one in mind of relationships of alliance as configured by the Wendat. After relationships were ritually established, the persons exchanged were now "within the sphere of influence" of the chosen kin. The importance of family to Joseph is palpable here; it is also indicative of the critical state of the Wendat confederacy that when Joseph speaks of family, he immediately invokes death and absence.

> And if my soul wishes to become rich, I will think that he does not think of God. I will greatly fear this and take care as to how I live. For it is easy for one who is rich to be one who offends, as, unknown to him, he is accompanied by a bad spirit. Alas, those people who are rich brag in vain. For, either rich or poor, we do not surpass one another. You love us equally; both those who are rich and those who are poor. (Steckley 1981, 16)

The mention of the "soul wish[ing]" to become rich is a clear reference to the desires articulated in dreams. Joseph personified this internal oki, noting that if this oki desired prosperity, "he does not think of God," and wishes to live in a state that is itself an occasion of sin. (The term "offends," used in this portion of the prayer, is the Wendat word chosen by the Jesuits to approximate the notion of sin.) The juxtaposition of rich and poor appears to have some import given the context of the Wendat economy during Joseph's lifetime; Wendat trade route owners' rise to economic prominence will be examined in the next chapter.

> I completely abandon myself to you, I who am located here. Behold, as we now cast away from us all kinds of things that we value while we are still living. Behold, they are no longer valued. Just you alone are valued. Apply your wisdom, great master, with respect to I who am located here. (Steckley 1981, 16–17)

Joseph here expresses his rejection of "all kinds of things that we value while we are still living . . ." He has truly forsaken many things traditionally valued in Wendat society. For example, back in 1637, LeMercier wrote that Joseph "does not use tobacco" and had "never indulged in the diabolical feasts" (Thwaites 1896–1901, 15:79). At the same time, LeMercier noted that Joseph had never used a powerful charm he had inherited from his father, "although he could have taken it as his own" (Thwaites 1896–1901, 15:79). Joseph renounces traditional medicine when he takes ill and ignores the import of his dream, the traditional vehicle of communication with sacred power. However, he has held on to that which he centrally values: his family, and optimally their survival—barring that, their unity in the afterlife. Through his preaching he has attempted to reconstitute Wendat society by uniting them in this new orientation. However, in Christian fashion, he acknowledges that God's wisdom will prevail in this matter.

> Truly, it is likely that we might suffer while we are living. There will be great cause for our rejoicing in the sky, and people will no longer cling tenaciously to life when they are sick. It is no longer a difficult thing to die. It is in vain that we fear to die while we are living. We are foolish. For at the moment of death, when one goes to heaven, one should be very happy. (Steckley 1981, 17)

Joseph's return to the theme of death should not be surprising, given the context of his life. In this passage, he most clearly articulates his new orientation to sickness and death. "It is no longer a difficult thing

. . ." and "it is in vain that we fear to die . . ." He knows well the inevitability of death, even given the medicines of the Jesuits. Here he hints toward a world to come in which this suffering will end. Joseph may be located here, but he has set his sights on the hereafter.

> These are my thoughts, God, the master. I now no longer fear death. I will express satisfaction when I am at the point of death. I will not suffer or be sad when relatives of mine die. I will think that God deliberated on it and willed that he loves them very much, for he willed that people would depart for a place where they will be very happy. (Steckley 1981, 17)

Death is the final thought in his prayer. He also speaks of the place described by the Jesuits, which he does not completely understand and about which many Wendat have a tendency to be skeptical. "I should not examine [the sky] for faults as things are quite perfect in the sky. I would have overestimated my ability if I thought that I could examine it, for I am not of such a stature" (Steckley 1981, 17). However, despite not comprehending the mystery of heaven, he accepts that unlike his present location, it is a place where his people will be happy. There, that which he truly values will be present.

4
Thérèse Oionhaton

Women: Displacement, Resistance, and Conversion

After Joseph Chihoatenhwa's death, his wife, Marie Aonetta, remained a faithful Catholic and continued to evangelize in Ossossané. She sent her daughter, Thérèse Oionhaton, to Quebec, accompanied by her recently converted brother-in-law, Joseph Teondichoren. For two years Thérèse remained in Quebec in the convent of the Ursuline sisters, led by Marie de L'Incarnation. She was tutored in reading, writing, and Christian doctrine. Like her father, she became a favorite of the French. A Jesuit priest wrote of her that "[s]he is . . . so steadfast, so well taught, so beloved, so fervent in the Faith, that on seeing her, one would not take her for a Huron. She will be the greatest mind among the Hurons when she shall return" (Thwaites 1896–1901, 22:195). When her uncle retrieved her from Quebec in 1642, on their way home to Wendat country their party was attacked and the young woman was taken captive by the Mohawk raiders. She became the wife of the Mohawk man who adopted her upon her arrival in his village; although the Jesuit Isaac Jogues attempted to negotiate her release, Thérèse Oionhaton remained with her new kinspeople. Years later, in 1654, the Jesuit Simon LeMoyne encountered Joseph Chihoatenhwa's and Marie Aonetta's daughter, who had retained her Catholic faith. Thérèse Oionhaton spoke to LeMoyne about her own evangelization of a woman of the Neutral Nation who also had been taken captive by a Mohawk war party. LeMoyne baptized her. Marie Aonetta's legacy was, then, a line of female Catholic converts, godmothers and goddaughters.

It is significant, however, that Thérèse Oionhaton was not in her village of origin when she catechized the woman of the Neutral Nation. Her experience, in many ways, mirrored that of her people. Just as she had spent years in Quebec, in the final three years of the Wendat confederacy many Wendat had spent time in various locations along the St. Lawrence Valley. Some Wendat "had come either to trade or to help the Algonkin and [Innu] wage war on the Mohawk and were prevented, either by the winter or by Iroquois blockades, from returning home. Some . . . joined the [Innu] in their winter hunts south of the St. Lawrence River. Others appear to have hunted by themselves in the same area. Still other Huron wintered among the French at Quebec or Montreal, or with the Algonquian-speaking Indians who lived under French protection at Three Rivers" (Trigger 1988, 797–99). Still others wintered with the Innu and a few members of other Native groups at Sillery, a réserve established in 1637 by the Jesuits, after which Ste. Marie in Wendat country had been modeled. There had been a seminary for Wendat young men established at Three Rivers, but that experiment began with difficulty (mothers refusing to hand over their children) and ended in abject failure in 1644, with five of the six students and Father Bressani captured and later killed by a Haudenosaunee raiding party (Thwaites 1896–1901, 26:19–53). The only other Wendat girl to undergo Catholic instruction in a residential environment during this period was a young woman brought in 1646 to the Ursulines by Michel Ekouandaé, a Christian convert. She remained with the Ursuline sisters until 1648, unable to return to Wendat country because of the danger of travel owing to the growing number of Haudenosaunee raids on Wendat travelers to and from Quebec. While there is no documentation of the young woman after her return to Wendat country, the man who brought her to the Ursulines returned to them after the fall of the Wendat confederacy and served the sisters until his death in 1651 (Thwaites 1896–1901, 31:175–79, 32:215, 36:205). This does not mean that there were no Wendat in Quebec; on the contrary, many, especially converts, are recorded in the *Jesuit Relations* and in the writings of Marie de L'Incarnation as having visited Quebec for reasons of trade. None, however, appeared to have taken up residence until after the Wendat dispersion. Just as Thérèse had been integrated into the Mohawk nation by adoption, by 1650 the entire Wendat confederacy had scattered, and many of its members had been absorbed into other nations. Others had followed the remaining Jesuits to Quebec, eventually forming a new community at Ancienne Lorette. Here follows a brief outline of the events that brought about the end of the Wendat confederacy.

Dispersion: The End of the Wendat Confederacy

After 1646 the Mohawk nation had ritually exchanged gifts with the other nations of the Haudenosaunee confederacy in order to affirm their alliance in warfare "and to invite them to join in an attack on the French and their allies" (Trigger 1988, 725). "Possibly after discussions with the Mohawk in the summer of 1646, the Seneca adopted what seems to have been a radically new policy towards the Huron. Hitherto, they had been content to raid them for furs . . . Now the Seneca decided to destroy the Huron confederacy and disperse the Huron people" (Trigger 1988, 726). Trigger also notes that this new policy was not only in response to Mohawk overtures, but also reflected a continuation of the tradition of mourning wars between the Mohawk nation and the Wendat confederacy. Their other motive was economic: "This strategy aimed to provide the Seneca and other western Iroquois tribes with a northern hinterland in which they could hunt and rob furs, as the Mohawk were already accustomed to do further east" (Trigger 1988, 729).

The Wendat were divided in their response to elevated Seneca hostilities. Traditionalists were in favor of negotiations, and perhaps in favor of creating alliances with the Haudenosaunee league. "It is not unlikely that in their efforts to support the French-Huron alliance, the Jesuits encouraged their converts to oppose any discussion of peace with the Iroquois" (Trigger 1988, 731). Although overtures to the Onondaga nation were eventually made, this only stayed the fate of the Wendat confederacy for a short while. The Jesuits responded to escalating crises in the Wendat confederacy by relaxing their catechistic requirements. A new superior of the mission to Wendat country, Father Paul Ragueneau, allowed converts to continue to practice traditional rituals. "Having worked until then to segregate Christians from traditionalists in order to protect their converts' faith, the Jesuits now judged Christianity to be well-enough established that their converts could be trusted again to participate in community activities, and even to assume a leading role in them" (Trigger 1988, 739). The result was a huge expansion of the baptismal rolls.

> These new regulations and the growing sense of dependence on the Jesuits as the Iroquois became more menacing, resulted in many more conversions. We have estimated that by the spring of 1646, about 500 Huron considered themselves to be Christians. The following year over 500 were baptized and in 1647–48, another 800. There were approximately 1700 baptisms in 1648–49 ... From July 1648 to March 1649, about 1500 people were baptized ... By the summer of 1648 about one Huron in five was a Christian and as the crisis deepened, this figure rose to almost one in two. (Trigger 1988, 739)

In 1648, again six Wendat representatives were sent as an envoy to the Onondaga nation to present gifts to reaffirm the alliance. They were captured, and four of them were killed by Mohawk warriors. After this setback, Seneca attacks continued to escalate, and the Wendat confederacy was in serious crisis. Certain traditionalists, although becoming a minority among the Wendat, met in secret and planned to raid Ste. Marie and kill the first French person they saw (Thwaites 1896–1901, 33:231). "Those who had secretly been the instigators of the murder ... [said] that the doors of the villages should be closed to [the Jesuits], and that we should be driven from the country. Some even added that all the Christians should be banished from it, and their number be prevented from increasing" (Thwaites 1896–1901, 33:231). The person they killed was a *donné* named Douart living at Ste. Marie.[1] This action had immense repercussions. Headmen

---

1. *Donnés* were lay assistants who contracted to serve Jesuit missionaries without pay for a certain period of time. The terms of their contracts included the promises

representing all the villages of the entire confederacy held a three-day meeting to discuss the murder, and it appears that although there was sizable opposition (arguing that continuing to tolerate the French presence and maintaining that alliance was far less desirable even than entering into a relationship of dependence upon the Haudenosaunee confederacy), consensus was reached. A decision was made to make reparations to the French. Traditional reparations (a condolence ceremony including prestations of wampum with various symbolic referents) were accepted by Father Ragueneau, and he reciprocated with gifts that symbolized the abatement of the anger of the French (Thwaites 1896–1901, 33:325–49). Afterward there came into being a split in the traditionalist faction between those wishing to approach the Haudenosaunee confederacy and surrounding nations and plead for incorporation, and those who wished to continue to rely on French protection (Trigger 1988, 750).

In the 1647 trading season, the Wendat did not even travel to meet with the French because of the dangers of Haudenosaunee raids; this produced further privation in Wendat communities. Also in that year, the village of Teanaostaiaé, "one of the largest and best fortified settlements" (Trigger 1988, 751), was destroyed and dispersed by Haudenosaunee warriors. "While more Huron escaped from Teanaostaiaé than were lost there, the destruction of this one community cost the Huron about one-tenth of their remaining population" (Trigger 1988, 753). In 1648 trade resumed, and about 250 of the Wendat made the journey to Three Rivers to meet the French. Governor Montmagny was present and ritually reaffirmed the Wendat-French alliance, which also implied continued French protection from the Haudenosaunee (Trigger 1988, 755).

In the spring of 1649, the Haudenosaunee raids on Wendat country resumed. An army of more than one thousand Haudenosaunee warriors attacked the Wendat village of Taenhatentaron and occupied

---

to practice poverty, chastity, and obedience while in the Jesuits' employ, but they did not take any formal or permanent vows.

it. From there, several other raids were launched, including one on Ste. Marie. At Ste. Marie, Fathers Jean de Brébeuf and Gabriel Lalemant (nephew of Fathers Charles and Jérôme Lalemant) were captured and brought back to Taenhatentaron, where they were ritually tortured and killed. Evidently some of the Wendat who had been captured and adopted by the Haudenosaunee people were part of this war party, and these men participated in the ritual torture of the priests. The usual procedures of ritual torture were carried out, but at least one special hybrid ritual was invented by a Wendat man who had himself been baptized by Brébeuf. This man,

> hearing [Brébeuf] speak of Paradise and Holy Baptism, was irritated, and said to him, "Echon," that is Father de Brébeuf's name in Huron, "thou sayest that Baptism and the sufferings of this life lead straight to Paradise; thou wilt go soon, for I am going to baptize thee, and to make thee suffer well, in order to go the sooner to thy Paradise." The [man], having said that, took a kettle full of boiling water, which he poured over his body three different times, in derision of Holy Baptism. And each time that he baptized him in this manner, the [man] said to him, with bitter sarcasm, "Go to heaven, for thou art well baptized." (Thwaites 1896–1901, 34:29)

This raid on the mission at Ste. Marie led to the end of the Wendat confederacy. The priests the Wendat had relied upon for protection had been killed. "Within less than two weeks, all of the Huron villages had been deserted and burned by their inhabitants, lest they should be used by the Iroquois, as Taenhatentaron had been" (Trigger 1988, 767).

The Wendat scattered. Some went south to join the Tionnontaté nation, others joined the Neutral Nation. Still others fled to Gahoendoe, now called Christian Island. This last group held a council at Gahoendoe, wherein it was decided that all among them would become Christians and invite the Jesuits remaining in Wendat country to join them (Thwaites 1896–1901, 34:209–35). There the Jesuits, along with the approximately three hundred Wendat families on the island, established Ste. Marie II. Unfortunately, there were not sufficient supplies to sustain this group, and many perished of starvation, exposure, and disease in the winter of 1649–50. Conditions were horrific; people died pitifully, corpses were robbed of their clothing, and some seem to have resorted to eating the flesh of the dead (Thwaites 1896–1901, 35:19–29, 79–105, 183–97). Some few who fled the island were killed by Haudenosaunee warriors who were patrolling the former country of the Wendat to make sure they did not return.

Eventually the remaining people held a council, and the decision was made to leave the island en masse, dispersing in whatever directions they might find, including toward the Haudenosaunee warriors who awaited them. The Jesuits were approached and asked if they would accompany some three hundred Wendat on a journey to Quebec, where they would take refuge with the French. The priests agreed. The journey was undertaken, and most survived the difficult and dangerous trek. Some three hundred others remained on the island, planning to wait and leave for Quebec after corn could be harvested so that they would have some provisions for their journey. These remaining Wendat were soon approached by representatives of the Onondaga nation, who offered to incorporate them into their clans. The Wendat pretended to agree, but upon departure, killed the Onondaga men escorting them, fled to Manitoulin Island, and soon thereafter proceeded toward Quebec, where they joined the people who had fled with the Jesuits (Thwaites 1896–1901, 36:177–91). The Wendat were settled on Ile d'Orléans; events transpired in which some of the Wendat on Ile d'Orléans were taken and incorporated into the Mohawk nation, which was maneuvering to have some French people (and, by extension, Natives protected by the French) in its territory. In this period, some Wendat relocated to Sillery. The Wendat people remaining were eventually resettled in 1673 in Ancienne Lorette, a village outside of Quebec. In 1697 they were removed to Jeune Lorette, where many of their descendants still dwell.

Observations: Champlain and Gender

Because the major sources for investigation of Wendat culture during the colonial period are French sources, it should be clear by this point that of necessity a particular method of interpreting the textual sources has been formulated. This method, as should be clear at this juncture, involves beginning at the boundaries (Wendat-French contact) and working toward the center (Wendat culture and social structures). This method of investigation, as it has been employed in the first two chapters, has been especially fruitful in its illumination of a concept and practice central to the Wendat people: the association of trade with kinship ties. For the Wendat, economic activities and social relationships were closely interwoven. Upon entering into trading relationships with the French, the Wendat inevitably made overtures toward the performance of kin exchange. Therefore, because trade with the French altered traditional Wendat economic structures, it is not unreasonable to seek evidence of ways in which contact with the French altered Wendat social structures. As ethnohistorical scholarship (particularly that of Trigger) has shown, French contact did not eradicate traditional Wendat trade networks, but altered their meaning and importance. Likewise, French contact did not eradicate traditional Wendat social structures, but forced the Wendat to change them in various ways.

Champlain's first sojourn into Wendat country has been outlined, but his encounters with women have been omitted—not because he was unconcerned with matters of gender, but because Champlain records no encounters with Wendat women until his return to Wendat country in 1615. When Champlain arrived, he spent the night in a longhouse in the village of Toanché, but wandered alone outside after dark "to escape the fleas," when "a shameless girl came boldly up to me, offering to keep me company, which I declined with thanks, sending her away with gentle remonstrances" (Champlain 1971, 3:47). Although Champlain clearly did not understand that in the context of Wendat cultural practices, by walking out alone at night he was making himself available for such a proposition, he soon put himself to the work of observing Wendat culture. During the winter of 1615–16 spent in Wendat country, he chronicled detailed observations of Wendat life and social organization. He described Wendat longhouses, each of which he believed contained twelve fires, and thus twenty-four "*ménages*" (households). He detailed the contents of the Wendat diet, which mostly comprised various mixtures of corn and beans, infrequently supplemented by deer and fish. He made much of the fact that

> [a]mong these tribes are found powerful women of extraordinary stature; for it is they who have almost the whole care of the house and the work; for they till the soil, sow the Indian corn, fetch wood for the winter, strip the hemp and spin it, and with the threads make fishing-nets . . . likewise they have the labor of harvesting the corn, storing it, preparing food, and attending to the house, and besides . . . accompany their husbands from place to place, in the fields, where they . . . carry the baggage . . . As to the men, they do nothing but hunt deer and other animals, fish, build lodges and go on the warpath. Having done this, they visit other tribes, where they have access and acquaintance, to trade and exchange what they have for what they have not, and on their return do not cease from feasting and dancing, with which they entertain one another, and afterwards they go to sleep, which is their finest exertion. (Champlain 1971, 3:136–37)

Champlain noted that when the men did go hunting or fishing, the game they caught was saved for eating at ceremonial occasions. He also described the intricacies of courtship among the Wendat young people. The women were courted and offered gifts, and if they accepted them, "the lover will come and sleep with her three or four nights." Women were allowed to engage in successive liaisons, retaining the gifts from each suitor, "until a satisfactory union." Even after this union was achieved, the partnership could be easily dissolved, "leaving all to the wishes of the woman." Only after children were born did monogamy prevail, and Champlain noted that when a young woman was visibly pregnant, all her previous suitors vied over fatherhood. "It is the woman's choice and option to take and accept whoever pleases her most, having in these courtships and amours gained much wampum and, besides, this choice of a husband." Further, he observed, "the children never succeed to the property and honors of the fathers . . . but indeed they make their successors and heirs the children of their sisters" (Champlain 1971, 3:136–40). These were the last records left by Champlain testifying to the conditions of Wendat society and culture. After his trip back to Quebec in April 1616, he never returned to Wendat country.

Champlain's journals are certainly biased, and therefore the information to be gleaned from them is limited in some respects. Champlain had no understanding of clans or of matriliny; therefore, he cannot be expected to testify to the form, or indeed the existence, of such things. But some details of his observations, in concert with certain of his experiences, can serve as data on the state of Wendat society at the time of Champlain's 1615–16 sojourn.

Champlain observed a gendered division of labor. Men, according to Champlain, built the longhouses. Archaeological data reveals that every eight to twelve years, villages would relocate because of the depletion of the soil, and hence new longhouses would be built in the new locations selected for settlement (Heidenreich 1971, 180–89). The men also fished and hunted, but as Champlain stated, the meat from fish and game was consumed infrequently, generally being kept for ceremonial consumption. Wendat men were also warriors. It appears, from Champlain's account, that the Wendat conducted warfare for two reasons: first, to demonstrate alliance (as the Arendarhonon nation did by accompanying the Onontchataronon people in their raids upon the Mohawk nation), and second, to avenge the deaths of their own people in raids upon them (as the Wendat people did in their raid upon the Onondaga or Oneida in 1616). Implicit in Champlain's record is the fact that the men sat on governing councils. When Champlain first arrived in Wendat country, he was brought to the governing councils of several villages and introduced to many of the most prominent local chiefs. He observed that there were several chiefs in each village (this may signify representation of each clan), that these chiefs came together in council to discuss all sorts of affairs, and that among these chiefs, some, "the eldest and bravest," were held in higher regard than others, according to "honor and respect" (Champlain 1971, 3:157). Champlain also noted that "they have general assemblies . . . from which every year comes a representative of each province, and they assemble in a town they appoint . . . and there they renew friendship, deciding and ordering what they think fit for the preservation of their country, and there also they give one another fine presents" (Champlain 1971, 3:159–60). The Wendat men left their villages in summer for other reasons, to "visit other tribes, where they have access and acquaintance, to trade and exchange" (Champlain 1971, 3:137).

The women impressed Champlain with their power and stature, as well as with their hard work; next to them, the men seemed lazy to Champlain. The women had charge of all the agricultural labor, from planting seeds to reaping harvests, from storing food to preparing food. Their domain was also the home and its upkeep, including securing the necessary supply of wood for fires. They also made clothing and pottery, and wove the nets for fishing. Although Champlain did note the importance of the industry of Wendat women, he did not explore the lines of descent or clan structures of Wendat society, and thus did not mention the centrality of these things to Wendat kinship structures. However, he did acknowledge the sexual autonomy of women, the ability of women to choose the socially acknowledged fathers of their children, and the fact that property and position is inherited not through the paternal line, but through the agnatic line. It is this last point that establishes matriliny as an active social system among the Wendat people at the time of Champlain's visit.

(Ex)Changes: Trade

Although the Arendarhonon Wendat had initial control of all Wendat dealings with the French (through Ochasteguin's contact with Champlain and Tregouaroti's exchange of his brother Savignon for Étienne Brûlé), by bringing the fifty beaver pelts and four wampum belts to Champlain, and by inviting him and his men to live in Wendat country, the Attignawantan, Ataronchronon, and Attigneenongnahac nations were also brought into this relationship. It was not merely the potential scope of the trade that compelled the Arendarhonon to include the other confederated nations, but also the prestige that this sharing would accord them. The value the Wendat placed upon sharing and redistributing goods was eventually compromised, however, by the practice of permitting families to control specific trading routes.

> The rights to a particular route were said to belong to the family of the man who had discovered it. No other Huron was supposed to trade along such a route without first receiving permission from the head of the family that had legal title to it, and such permission was normally granted only in return for valuable presents . . . Although most trading was done by ordinary men in the prime of life, all of the major trading routes were under the control of the leading headmen. Such control must have provided the headmen with an important means of acquiring wealth, which in turn could be used to validate their high status within their tribes. (Trigger 1988, 65)

Thus, as trade expanded, the wealth and importance of men who traded also expanded. Wendat society began to lean toward an increasing emphasis upon trade, and in the years between 1617 and 1634 the men who most successfully profited from this trade gained more and more prestige.

Observations: Brébeuf, Women, and Trade

Father Jean de Brébeuf had preceded Champlain to Wendat country in 1616 and had left in 1617, only to return in 1623, accompanied by Recollet Fathers Nicolas Viel and Gabriel Sagard. LeCaron and Sagard left in 1624, and Viel was drowned on his journey back to Quebec in 1625. Fathers de Noüe, Daillon, and Brébeuf resided in Wendat country from 1626 to 1627, 1626 to 1628, and 1626 to 1629, respectively. In 1634, after much negotiation between Champlain and the Wendat people, Fathers Brébeuf, Daniel, and Davost were taken to Wendat country and settled in the Attignawantan village of Ihonatiria. Father LeJeune, back in Quebec, received reports from Brébeuf and included them in his Relations.

In Brébeuf's missive of 1635, he described his journey to and arrival in Wendat country. He reported that the priests also began to catechize a dozen young boys whom they planned to take back with them to Quebec to be further educated by the Jesuits. However, the women of these boys' families raised such heated objections that the Jesuits' plans were thwarted, and only three boys were permitted to go to Quebec (Thwaites 1896–1901, 9:283–85). "The departures of these boys was a matter of vital concern to their extended families, and in family matters Huron women had a strong voice. The key role ascribed to the grandmothers, or head women, of these households clearly indicates that matrilineal and matrilocal principles remained important to the Huron" (Trigger 1988, 523). Here is clear evidence of resistance on the part of Wendat women to Jesuit activity that would undermine Wendat social structures.

In Brébeuf's 1636 missive to LeJeune, he submitted his most detailed observations of Wendat life. The second half of his letter contained chapters purporting to deal with the following: their myths of origin; their ideas regarding the soul; their gods, superstitions, and faith in dreams; their feasts, dances, games, and the practices of Ononharoia; their sorcerers; the form of their government and polity; the order of their councils; their burial and mourning rituals; their Feast of the Dead (Thwaites 1896–1901, 10:125–317). This taxonomy of Wendat life was clearly composed in a manner more reflective of European Catholic classificatory categories than of Wendat modalities of thought, but these chapters remain the richest available textual source describing Wendat society and culture as it was during that time.

In the chapter on polity and government, Brébeuf made two remarkable statements. The first was in regard to a perceived change in Wendat governance: "Formerly, only worthy men were Captains, and so they were called Enondecha, the same name by which they called the Country, Nation, district—as if a good chief and the Country were one and the same thing. But today they do not pay so much attention to the selection of their Captains, and so they no longer give them that name" (Thwaites 1896–1901, 10:232). Following this statement, Brébeuf then corroborated Champlain's observations of matrilineal inheritance, but only to a certain extent, and also implied that there had been a degree of change since 1616. Brébeuf wrote that chiefs "reach this degree of honor partly through election; their children do not usually succeed them, but properly their nephews and grandsons" (Thwaites 1896–1901, 10:233). Brébeuf also mentioned an additional requisite for accession to position: these nephews and grandsons are appointed "only in so far as they have suitable qualifications, and accept the position, and are accepted by the whole Country" (Thwaites 1896–1901, 10:233). According to Brébeuf, "there are even Captains to whom . . . matters of government are referred on account of their intellectual superiority, popularity, wealth, or other qualities which render them influential in the Country" (Thwaites 1896–1901, 10:231). These observations all support Wallis Smith's opinion that by the 1630s Wendat social structures had been affected by contact with the French. Regarding Brébeuf's description of Wendat governance, Smith writes,

> These statements certainly do not prove the absence of an operative kinship principle in the succession to political office, but they do indicate the intervention of non-kinship factors beyond what the Huron considered—or Champlain indicated—to be common or traditional in the functioning of their system . . . I would suggest that under the impact of the fur trade . . . the matrilineal system of succession had to a degree broken down and exogenous political contingencies were beginning to override the dictates of kinship . . . That is, there are indications that the strength of the matrilineal principles was waning. (Smith 1970, 195)

When discussing rights to trading routes, Brébeuf also wrote that "it is in this that most of their riches consist" (Thwaites 1896–1901, 10:225). This may be read as an indication of the possibility of individual male-headed family accumulation of wealth, as well as the social power and prestige associated with wealth. Because of the increasing importance of trade for the Wendat, this may imply an ascendance in the cultural and societal significance of agnatic inheritance in general.

This is not to say that individual profits derived from trade were not subject to redistribution. Brébeuf's description of the 1636 performance of the Feast of the Dead revealed that this ritual remained a significant site of the redistribution of wealth. The Feast of the Dead dates from the middle Iroquoian period, and initially served as a method of uniting clan segments in their own ossuaries (Trigger 1988, 147). As time went on, the Feast of the Dead was elaborated, becoming a reinterment ritual that served as an important site of the redistribution of goods through feasting and gift exchange, but also as a recognition of trade alliances through the affirmation of kin relationships. This affirmation of relationship was articulated by burying the dead of several nations (including, in 1636, some people who were not of the Wendat confederacy (presumably fictive kin who were allies in trade and warfare) in a common ossuary, marked by elaborate ceremony. Archaeological findings demonstrate that in the colonial period, as trade with the French escalated, the proportion of trade goods interred with the bones of the dead dramatically increased (Trigger 1988, 426–27). Brébeuf's 1636 letter reported that some twelve hundred gifts were brought to this feast, and of these gifts, "forty-eight robes were used in adorning the [burial] pit. Each whole body had its robe, and some had two or three" (Thwaites 1896–1901, 10:303). Trigger states that the ossuary at which Brébeuf was present contained, besides the robes and in addition to indigenous objects such as shell beads and pipes, a large percentage of European-manufactured goods, such as glass beads, knives, rings, kettles, iron axes, metal arrowheads, and iron cups (Trigger 1988, 417). It is clear that much of the elaboration of the Feast of the Dead was owing to European influence. Although Trigger interprets this elaboration as "the florescence of a traditional feature of Huron culture rather than a radical departure from it" (Trigger 1988, 427), Brébeuf makes an observation in the context of this ritual that testifies to the extent to which Wendat culture had been affected by the influx of European goods. This effect was expressed in terms of wealth differential. "The Old Men and the notables of the Country, who had the administration and the management of the feast, took possession secretly of a considerable quantity [of beaver pelts]; and the rest was cut in pieces . . . and ostentatiously thrown into the midst of the crowd . . . It is only the rich who lose nothing, or very little, in this feast. The middle classes and the poor bring and leave there whatever they have most valuable, and suffer much, in order not to appear less liberal than the others in this celebration" (Thwaites 1896–1901, 10:304–5). It appears that "the Old Men and the notables" were the men who profited most from trade, and even in their participation in the ritual of redistribution managed to preserve their own wealth. This phenomenon only supports the conclusion that by 1636 Wendat society had undergone economic and cultural change, in that trade, always highly valued by the Wendat, had become a route to maintainable wealth and prestige, and thus the power of certain men had risen above the power of others.

Further, the ability of a Wendat man to accumulate wealth affected the processes of the governing councils. Brébeuf reported that by 1636, in councils, the Old Men (principal chiefs) held sway. These men appear to have been selected increasingly on the basis of their wealth and prominence in trade. Brébeuf himself stated that the economic position of Old Men was such that "in short, if they are successful in trading, they are richer than the others" (Thwaites 1896–1901, 10:253).

He goes on to say that "when someone, be he Citizen or Stranger, wishes to obtain something from the Country, the custom is to grease the palms of the principal Captains . . . The regret that some private individuals have for such irregularities, and the envy of the other Captains who have not been called upon to share the booty, discourage the practice more than they like; they decry one another, and the mere suspicion of these secret presents stirs up sometimes great debates and divisions" (Thwaites 1896–1901, 10:253).

The escalation in Wendat trade with the French enabled the accumulation of individual wealth by some leading Wendat men. Some Wendat resisted this concentration of wealth in the hands of a few, as seen in their protestations against such "irregularities" as acquisition without sufficient redistribution. However, this opposition did not alter the course of cultural change. From the first encounter with the French, despite traditional methods of assuring reciprocity, Wendat participation in French mercantile structures enabled a few male leaders to accumulate and retain a larger share of wealth and status. The balance in Wendat society was shifting toward a greater degree of status differentiation on the basis of wealth, perhaps also toward the greater valuation of male contributions to Wendat life.

Trigger disagrees with Smith and others who argue that Brébeuf's records indicate a shift toward the devaluation of female labor in Wendat society as trade increased in importance. Trigger asserts that a rise in trade could only have come about if supported by a concomitant rise in agricultural production, the province of women. "If men had formerly been dependent on women for most of the food they are, they were now also dependent on them for their key item of trade . . . the power of women should have increased under such conditions" (Trigger 1988, 420).

However, it is not a lessening of valuation of the female role among the Wendat that is most significant here—it is rather the increased differential in status between people with a stake in ownership of trade routes and those without. More to the point, the most important dimension of this shift is the new orientations acquired by these Old Men. Evident in these Old Men who are accumulating wealth is the expression of a new orientation toward the material, as vividly illustrated by their reclamation of pelts from the pit of the Feast of the Dead. It includes a new orientation toward other Wendat, because the Old Men chose not to evenly redistribute wealth among the community. It also demonstrates a new orientation toward the sacred, and in particular toward one of the things centrally sacred to the Wendat: kinship. In taking those beaver pelts, the Wendat Old Men reappropriated the gifts meant for their deceased kin, furs intended to wrap together the deceased of many nations and make of them one people.

Dreams: Some Wendat Women Speak

In May 1646 Father Paul Ragueneau, the French Jesuit in charge of the mission in Wendat country, sent his annual report on the condition of that mission to his superior in Quebec. In this letter, Father Ragueneau complained that terrible rumors had been sweeping through Wendat country that winter. These rumors, Ragueneau averred, were invented by Native traditionalists hostile to Christianity. "In order . . . to sap the foundations of our faith," wrote Ragueneau, "they have tried to shake them by falsehoods that they invent, and with which they fill the whole country" (Thwaites 1896–1901, 30:25). One particular rumor was most bothersome to Ragueneau. "This it is," he wrote, "which has found most credit, which has most awed the simple, and which has constituted the most powerful rhetoric of the enemies of our faith" (Thwaites 1896–1901, 30:29). Ragueneau's account of this terrible rumor read as follows:

> It was said that a Huron Christian woman, of those who are buried in our cemetery, had risen again; that she had said that her soul, having left the body, had actually been taken to Heaven; that the French had welcomed it there, but in the manner in which an Iroquois captive is received at the entrance to their Villages,—with firebrands and burning torches, with cruelties and torments inconceivable. She had related that all Heaven is nothing but fire, and that there the satisfaction of the French is to burn now some, now others; and that, in order to possess many of these captive souls, which are the object of their pleasures, they cross the seas, and come into these regions as into a land of conquest, just as a Huron exposes himself with joy to the fatigues and dangers of war, in the hope of bringing back some captive. It was further said that those who are thus burned in Heaven, as captives of war, are the Huron, Algonquin, and Montagnais [Innu] Christians, and that those who have not been willing in this world to render themselves slaves of the French, or to receive their laws, go after this life into a place of delights, where everything good abounds, and whence all evil is banished. This risen woman added, they said, that, after having been thus tormented in Heaven a whole day,—which seemed to her longer than our years,—the night having come, she had felt herself roused, near the beginning of her sleep; that a certain person, moved with compassion for her, had broken her bonds and chains, and had shown her, at one side, a deep valley which descended into the earth, and which led into that place of delights whither the souls of the infidel Hurons go; that from afar she had seen their villages and their fields, and had heard their voices, as of people who dance and who are feasting. But she had chosen to return into her body, as long as was necessary to warn those who

were there present of such terrible news, and of that great misfortune which awaited them at death, if they continued to believe the impostures of the French. This news was soon spread everywhere; it was believed in the country without gainsaying. At [S]aint Joseph, it was made to come from the Christians at [L]a Conception; in the Village of [L]a Conception, it was said to come from St. Jean Baptiste; and there it was reported that the Christians of [S]aint Michel had discovered this secret, but that we had corrupted, by many presents, those who had seen it with their own eyes, and that they had not dared to tell it except to some of their intimates. In a word, it was an article of faith for all the infidels, and even some of the Christians almost half believed it. (Thwaites 1896–1901, 30:29–31)

The rumor that so troubled Father Ragueneau was another instantiation of a religiously creative Native response to the notions of heaven and hell proffered by the Jesuits. There are recorded in the Jesuit Relations many other creative responses to and reappropriations of these notions. This instance, however, is particularly rich in both form and content.

In form, this account was articulated as a message carried back to the living by a Wendat woman who was recently deceased. The attributed source of this "rumor" was a woman who had been converted by the Jesuits and therefore had been buried in their consecrated cemetery. The explicit identification of her place of burial is quite significant. As far back as 1637 Jesuits had been attempting to institute the practice of separate burials for converts to Christianity. With this push for separate interments in ritually bounded sacred ground, serious problems had arisen. Among the Wendat, death was an occasion of great sorrow and mourning. The loss of a kinsperson was of such great import that all relatives had to be condoled through the ritual distribution of gifts; consequently, burial practices were highly elaborated. This solemn ceremony, known as the Feast of the Dead, has been outlined in the previous chapter. This ritual of common reburial, so essential to Wendat culture, manifested the importance of interment in common ground. As Trigger has written,

"The significance of the mingling of the bones of the dead . . . cannot be overstressed. The Huron [people] said that because their dead relatives were united in this way, it was necessary for the living to cooperate and be friends with one another" (Trigger 1988, 87). Because the Feast of the Dead was "the key ritual for expressing solidarity" (Trigger 1988, 427), the Jesuits were undermining the very fabric of social cohesion by insisting on separate burials for converts. A Feast of the Dead for members of the northern Attignawantan nation had taken place the year before the emergence of this "rumor," and on that occasion, the Jesuits had attempted, and failed, to secure separate Christian reburial for the exhumed bodies of converts. Thus the rumor's ascription to a woman buried in Christian consecrated ground is central to the story. It is quite possible that the content of the message she delivered also served as a commentary on her separate interment in the Jesuit cemetery. Separate burials, insisted upon by the Jesuits, would have appeared to the Wendat to be a refusal to participate in community and a repudiation of the symbolic articulation of kinship enacted by the Feast of the Dead.

A bit of background on Wendat concepts of the self should clarify at least some of the images present in the message delivered by the woman who had returned from the dead. The "rumor" asserted that this woman's "soul" (*âme* in French) had left her deceased body and had been taken to heaven. John Steckley and Michael Pomedli, linguists with expertise in the Wendat language, have shown that it is not as easy as one might think to identify the way that this aspect of the deceased woman's self would have been articulated in the Wendat language. Pomedli notes that in the Wendat language, the verb root *-sken-* can be understood as "to be a manifestation of a person who has died" (Pomedli 1991, 127). The root is used in the word *hatisken*, which signifies the (plural) bones that are reburied during the Feast of the Dead (Steckley 2004, 31). The French word used by Rageneau in this context is *âme*, or "soul." Steckley contends that although Brébeuf may have used the term "esken" to refer to "soul" early in his mission, he later chose the Wendat word *onywennonkwat* (from the verb root -(e)nnonkwat-), which Steckley translates as "our medicine." Steckley also notes that "another of the terms for the soul that Brébeuf mentioned was *khiondhecwi*, which was used 'in so far as it merely animates the body and gives it life'" (Steckley 2004, 36). Significantly, this latter term is also the name for the spirit of the corn, beans, and squash, the Three Sisters that sprang from the body of Aataentsic, the grandmother of the Wendat people, at the time of the creation of the world. Khiondhecwi is the force that gives life to the people (Steckley 2004, 36).

In Wendat cosmology, upon death, a constitutive part of the deceased person would embark upon the path of souls ("le chemin des âmes," as the French called it), and if its journey was not interrupted, it would join its kinspeople and live with them in the Village of the Dead, where dancing and feasting would be the order of the day. Indeed, in the "rumor" repeated by Ragueneau, this is precisely how the Wendat woman described the scene she saw from afar. However, the woman's tale revealed that the anticipated journey to the Village of the Dead would never occur if one accepted and lived by the teachings of the Jesuit priests. Rather than journeying to the Village of the Dead, "that place of delights" (Thwaites 1896–1901, 30:29), the convert would be held captive for eternity in a hot place near to the sun, called heaven, to be tortured mercilessly by the French.

The concepts of torture and captivity, as invoked by the "rumor" in question, are explicated elsewhere in the Jesuit Relations, most clearly in numerous instances of Wendat resistance to Christian evangelization particularly because of the Jesuit use of images (often actual illustrations) of hell. Early in the mission to New France, Father LeJeune noted that in regard to successful conversion of the Native population, "fear is the forerunner of faith in these barbarous minds" (Thwaites 1896–1901, 11:9). LeJeune, noting the difficulties of communicating the idea of hell to people whose cosmologies contained no such place, requested that the readers of his letters send him vivid pictures of hell with which to evangelize. He went so far as to ask for custom-made representations: "If some one would depict three, four, or five demons tormenting one soul with different kinds of tortures,— one applying to it the torch, another serpents, another pinching it with red-hot tongs, another holding it bound with chains,—it would have a good effect, especially if everything were very distinct, and if rage and sadness appeared plainly on the face of the lost soul" (Thwaites 1896–1901, 11:89).

Putting aside the artistic challenge of simultaneously depicting rage and sadness, it is clear that LeJeune's idea of effecting conversion through the use of pictures of hell presented unanticipated theoretical difficulties, and even may have opened up a new symbolic space in which the Jesuits' potential converts might express their opposition to the Jesuit program.

For example, in Lalemant's 1642 Relation from Wendat country, he reported that some people were so resistant to his preaching that they ordered him from their homes:

> "If [you wish] to speak to me of Hell," they sometimes say, "go out of my Cabin at once. Such thoughts disturb my rest, and cause me uneasiness amidst my pleasures." "I see very well that there is a God," another will say, "but I cannot endure that he should punish our crimes." A certain man, who one day found himself pressed too hard, said to [the Jesuit Father] who came to instruct him, "I am content to be damned," while dealing him a blow with a knife, which, however, merely cut his cassock. In another village, a woman who would not listen to God's word, and had closed her ears, threw live coals in the face of one of the Fathers who spoke to her, calling out that she became crazy when she heard his discourse. "No," said an impious man . . ."no, I will not listen to what they preach to us about Hell. It is these impostors, who because they have no other defense in this country than the fear of an imaginary fire of Hell, intimidate us by such penalties, in order to save their own lives, and to arrest the blow that we would have already struck, had we any resolution." (Thwaites 1896–1901, 23:189–91)

For many Wendat, the Jesuits' (verbal or figural) representations of hell were disturbing. Some, as the man above, went so far as to accuse the Jesuits of making up these stories in order to keep them in fear and thus prevent the Wendat from attacking them outright. But consider the knife-wielding man mentioned by Father Lalemant, the man who said that he was content to be damned. In the above context, Lalemant presented this man as simply one of many whose "hearts [were] hardened in their impiety" (Thwaites 1896–1901, 23:19). Compare that man's reaction to threats of damnation to hell with another Wendat man's reaction, this one documented by Lalemant two years earlier. In this instance, Lalemant had come to offer baptism to a dying man. The man refused. Lalemant asked him if he were then ready to be damned to hell. "'Certainly, I am fully resolved,' he said, 'to suffer the fires and flames of hell. I have prepared from my youth to be cruelly burned; I will show my courage therein'" (Thwaites 1896–1901, 19:229–31).

This Wendat man was referring to the warrior complex that served as an essential underpinning of his culture and of his self-understanding. The primary aim of warfare among Iroquoian cultures in general and Wendat culture in particular was the taking of captives, not the murder of enemies. Mourning wars were conducted in order to assuage the grief of those who had recently suffered the death of family members. The capture of prisoners was often the aim, because they could be taken as replacements for the deceased kinsperson and adopted into the bereaved families, thus easing the family's suffering over the loss of a beloved relative (Thwaites 1896–1901, 6:259, 17:65, etc.; Trigger 1988, 68–75; see appendix 1). Warfare, then, may be understood as a locus of reciprocity through which lost kinspeople might be replaced. Further, given the warrior complex that comprised the Wendat understanding of proper male behavior, prisoners, as warriors, were expected to conduct themselves with stoicism and to demonstrate their strength while bearing torture. This torture was conducted while ritually addressing the captive as a respected kinsperson (Trigger 1988, 73–75; Thwaites 1896–1901, 1:271–73, 4:199–201, 5:29–31). Therefore, quite naturally, a Wendat adult male would have prepared for the possibility of capture during warfare. The men described above reacted to Jesuit threats of hell by recontextualizing within Wendat cultural practices the Jesuits' threats of torture by fire. These reactions may be viewed as instances of locative re-situations of these transcendent or "imaginary" images into the Huron people's actual cultural space.

This locative re-situation is well illustrated in the rumor of the returned dead woman recorded by Ragueneau in 1646. This rumor stated that the woman was said to have returned from Heaven, where she had been "welcomed" by the French "in the manner in which an Iroquois captive is received at the entrance to their [Wendat] Villages— with firebrands and burning torches, with cruelties and torments inconceivable" (Thwaites 1896–1901, 4:29). In other words, in Heaven the French were treating the Wendat just as the Wendat treated war captives. The woman had visited this place called Heaven, which was not at all like the Jesuits' description, but was like a place known to the Wendat: the entrance to a village, the setting of the ritual torture of captives. Conversion, then, was problematized not only because of the consequences (torture, and in this case, torture of women rather than of trained warriors), but also because of the imbalance of reciprocity it demonstrates. The Wendat had not been engaging in warfare with the French—indeed, they had welcomed the Jesuits into their villages, despite their odd ways and their refusal to participate in many of the rituals constitutive of community. The Wendat did not capture and torture the French, but apparently the French were engaged in the capture and torture of the People of the Peninsula—after they died. Moreover, by taking them captive, the French seemed to be ensuring that the Wendat would never rejoin their relations in the traditional land of the dead. In sum, the rumor indicted the Jesuit missionaries for their refusal to integrate themselves into Wendat society, for their outright rejection of normative expressions of reciprocity and exchange (including the traditional ritualized institutions of warfare and the torture of captives), and consequently for their undermining of traditional Wendat cultural practices.

Reinforcing this interpretation is the final portion of the rumor, which asserted that Jesuits had "corrupted, by many presents, those who had seen [the woman returned from the dead] with their own eyes . . . [so that] they had not dared to tell" (Thwaites 1896–1901, 30:31). Here the Jesuits were being accused of overt improprieties in practices of exchange. In Wendat culture, the exchange of gifts did not "corrupt," but established relationship, even kinship. The rumor itself imputed to the Jesuits a malicious undermining of the gift-giving process.

This rumor reported by Father Ragueneau was, in one obvious respect, an incisive critique of Christian theology and missiology. The Christian heaven was revealed as being a literal hell for the Wendat. In a second respect, this "rumor" served as a deeper indictment: a condemnation of Jesuit refusals to enter into reciprocal relationships, into community, with the Wendat. Not only did the Jesuits want their dead to be buried separately, but they also declined mutuality in other exchanges: those of warfare, captivity, and torture, and by extension those of adoption and the creation of kinship ties. Because of Jesuit reluctance to enter into true mutuality of relationship as it was defined by the Wendat, the Jesuits' images of heaven and of hell were rejected, reimagined, and redeployed by some Wendat, in service of their own end, which was, of course, the maintenance of their own community and their own cultural practices.

Charles Long has characterized certain movements within so-called "religions of the oppressed" in light of Kenelm Burridge's expression "myth-dreams." Although Burridge defines the "myth-dream" as a sort of community daydream, in which mythico-religious histories are constructed and articulated, in Long's usage, myth-dreams may perhaps be better understood by correlating them with Miguel Leon-Portilla's term "visions of the vanquished." In myth-dreams, subjugated people respond to having been defined solely by the categories of thought and language used by their enslavers and colonizers. In myth-dreams, vanquished people articulate their visions of the cosmos, and of themselves. Long identifies the construction of myth-dreams as constituting one modality of expression of what W. E. B. DuBois termed "double-consciousness," a way of seeing things in which colonized people "long for or imagine the meaning of their existence as human beings prior to the definitions imputed to them . . . through the hegemony of Western languages" (Long 1995, 121).

Long also employs the terms "transparency" and "opacity" in his analysis of the power relationships between colonizer and colonized. In short, the colonized people are assumed by their oppressors to be transparent—easily categorized, explained, and understood. The colonized people, on the other hand, are invested in maintaining a certain level of opacity, a place "behind the veil" in which they may simultaneously critique the presumption of their transparency and create alternative visions of themselves and their world. Long has characterized the intentionally opaque myth-dreams or visions of the vanquished as "attempt[s] to create a new humanity out of the chaos of a cultural disequilibrium" (Long 1995, 135).

Telling dreams and repeating rumors without fear of Jesuit reprisal actually reinforced the self-preserving opacity of the vanquished. Although Jesuits may have assumed that the popularity of the rumors was evidence of the transparency of the creators of the myth-dream, clearly influenced as they were by Satan, and while the Jesuits certainly ridiculed the content of the rumors and dreams, they remained unable to decode the categories of thought employed in the myth-dream. They remained unable to realize that in the myth-dream, their definitions of the people they had subjected were not simply critiqued, but dismissed. While the Jesuits were more easily able to dismiss the myth-dreams because their content was judged to be nonrational, non-Christian, and probably demonically inspired, in truth the myth-dreams actually and actively employed categories of thought unavailable to them. In these categories of thought, the very identities of the Wendat and of their increasingly unwelcome guests, the Jesuits, were being recreated. In the myth-dreams, the indigenous people were not victims facing cultural (and even literal) genocide; they were the People of the Peninsula, with the ability to communicate with the spirit world, with the sensibility to reject missionary propaganda; they were also having their own self-understandings verified. In their proper afterlife, things were always as they had been: game was abundant, vegetation lush; this world was expressly for and about them. Despite the missionary messages, and because of the apparent transparency of the myth-dream, the veil was not torn asunder; the self-preserving opacity of the vanquished remained intact. In the proper Wendat afterworld, which was confirmed in the here and now, the Wendat were able to define themselves.

Réserve: Gender and Sexuality at Sillery

For several obvious reasons, the Jesuits neglected to record substantial information about the daily lives and concerns of women in Wendat country. The missionaries' pedagogical practices and evangelical techniques had been shaped in the European Jesuit tradition of educating boys and young men. Their initial attempts to establish seminaries for Native youth in New France were thwarted, however, because of the disinclination of Native families to part with their children in situations that were not clear, ritually governed establishments of alliance. Moreover, when some few young men eventually were sent to study with the Jesuits, they were often unruly, resistant, and disinclined to stay. The Jesuits were also inextricably bound up in the patriarchal traditions of the Roman Catholic Church and of seventeenth-century European society. Therefore, after seminary experiments failed, their subsequent plans were to catechize males, assuming that as heads of households, their families would follow their example. The Jesuits persisted in seeing males as heads of households even when faced, in Wendat country, with overwhelming evidence to the contrary. However, the economic shifts outlined above that enabled males with ownership of trade routes to secure a higher and more stable social status also enabled the Jesuits to keep to their program of evangelizing males. As demonstrated in the case of Joseph Chihoatenhwa, some men with fewer routes to social status and with great desires for effective medicine found conversion to be means toward establishing a significant relationship with sacred power. This missionary focus on Wendat men, coupled with the inability of Jesuit priests to cross traditional Wendat gender boundaries and access the sphere of women, resulted in glaring omissions in the Jesuits' writings.

The presence of women in Wendat country is only acknowledged under certain circumstances. When women were on their deathbeds, and therefore possible candidates for baptism, the symptoms and gravity of their illnesses were sometimes recorded. These same women's reactions to the Jesuits' desire to baptize them were sometimes documented. Objection or acquiescence to the baptism of a kinsperson was generally noted, particularly when an objection was strong, or when baptism of a kinsperson was actively sought. But most often in the *Jesuit Relations*, women's words were heard indirectly, when their voices rose in protest of the Jesuit presence, in "rumors" and dreams. Because of this tendency toward omission in the writings of the Jesuits in Wendat country, it can be helpful to explore the acknowledged presence of women in other mission contexts, such as at the réserve established by Father Paul LeJeune at Sillery.

While Brébeuf and the other priests were establishing missions in Wendat country, the Jesuits in Quebec had established the réserve at Sillery in 1637. This mission was specifically intended to serve the Innu and other Algonquian-speaking people of the area. The foundational idea behind Sillery was that it would encourage Native people to become permanent settlers and to adopt agriculture as their primary means of subsistence. This obviously assumed a causal connection between a sedentary agricultural way of life and the development of Christianity. It also echoed Champlain's assumption that a sedentary French peasantry would model Christianity to the Native population, and along with intermarriage would produce the ideal habitations he hoped to establish in New France. This is perhaps the clearest evidence of the beginnings of what would later become the intentionally land-acquisitive and genocidal structure of settler colonialism. At the time, however, while LeJeune was aware that the mere implantation of French farming families would not be enough to bring about the conversion of Native peoples, he did believe that with assistance, the goal could be reached (Thwaites 1896–1901, 5:151). The establishment of Sillery also had an economic impetus. Beaver had been overhunted in the area, and the local Native population was suffering privation; their new state of dependence became more than just a problem for the local Natives; it also became a drain on the French trading company (Trigger 1988, 577). The profit motive convinced the trading company to support the establishment of Sillery. LeJeune was quite aware of the trading company's position and addressed it in this way: "If they are sedentary, and if they cultivate the land, they will not die of hunger . . . we shall be able to instruct them easily, and Beavers will greatly multiply" (Thwaites 1896–1901, 8:57). The local Innu people had their own agenda. They had indeed overhunted the beaver, and their traditional enemies, the nations of the Haudenosaunee confederacy, were posing a threat to their welfare and livelihood. In 1636 an Innu headman named Makheabichtichiou who had been attempting to ally with the French, going so far as to request baptism on numerous occasions, approached LeJeune with a request. Makheabichtichiou asked LeJeune and Governor Montmagny for assistance in constructing a settlement near Three Rivers, in which his band would agree to live. LeJeune insisted that such an undertaking need necessarily include capitulation to instruction by the Jesuits. The Innu people balked at this condition. "All the elders favored French aid, but there was a nearly uniform rejection of any moves toward accepting Christianity" (Ronda 1979, 4).

Although this first attempt at establishing a village failed, LeJeune soon accomplished his goal. He successfully solicited a substantial donation from Nöel Brûlart de Sillery, a former ambassador, commander of the Order of Malta, knight of St. John, member of the Compagnie de Cent-Associés, and avid friend and supporter of St. Vincent DePaul. In 1637 Sillery furnished the funds for the establishment of a village, and François Derré de Gand donated land suitable for the enterprise. LeJeune even located two willing Innu families, headed by converts named Nöel Negabamat and François Xavier Nenaskoumat, who agreed to set up household in the village, named St. Joseph de Sillery. The settlement was built and Jesuit control over the réserve was established. LeJeune even went so far as to make an arrangement with the Compagnie de la Nouvelle-France to grant the same privileges to Sillery residents as they did to the French (Thwaites 1896–1901, 16:33). The first families moved into the village, which at first consisted of only one house. Unfortunately, they fell ill, several children died, and the settlement was disbanded in 1639 because of a smallpox epidemic (Thwaites 1896–1901, 16:103). Sillery was reconstituted in 1640 when a number of families, only a minority among them having been baptized, arrived and were greeted by Governor Montmagny and Father LeJeune.

The remarkable event of their assemblage and decisions regarding the administration of Sillery was recorded by LeJeune. At first, as LeJeune reported it, those baptized among them wished to "get the Savages together and offer them strong inducements to believe; if any one showed himself an open enemy to the faith, they resolved to drive him away from the village they are beginning" (Thwaites 1896–1901, 18:95). One recent convert, Étienne Pigarouich, "said that they must banish the devil from their new residence, and that the unbelievers retained him with them, especially those who wished to have two wives; and consequently, that it was necessary either to believe or to separate" (Thwaites 1896–1901, 18:95). Pigarouich had had a long journey toward his own baptism, being refused numerous times until he gave up all but one of his wives; evidently he wished all to conform to his conduct. The group of Christian men then approached the governor to appoint a headman, but he "recommended to the Christians constancy in their marriages" and "gave them to understand that it would be well if they should elect some chiefs to govern them" (Thwaites 1896–1901, 18:101). The assembled men were then told about the secret ballot by the priests, and they employed it, each coming alone to tell the priest of their vote for headman.

> After the votes were counted by the missionaries, it was declared that four men—three Christians and one Traditionalist—had been elected village magistrates. To these posts were added two men—one Christian and one Traditionalist—who would enforce proper moral conduct among Montagnais [Innu] young men. Finally, one man was selected as Captain of Prayers to act as a lay teacher at Sillery. These seven men were to serve for one year after which a new election would be held. What emerged from all these events was a village government dominated by the Christian minority, supported by powerful outside allies, and bent on imposing new values and beliefs on a reluctant and often hostile majority. (Ronda 1979, 11)

What also emerged was a patriarchal government, without the benefit of women's voices for guidance or advice. The first action of the

Christian men in power was to assemble all the women and to exhort them to be baptized. The following day, some of these women sought out the priests, asking to be baptized and explaining that

> [y]esterday the men summoned us to a Council, the first time that women have ever entered one; but they treated us so rudely that we were greatly astonished. "It is you women," they said to us, "who are the cause of all our misfortunes,—it is you who keep the demons among us. You do not urge to be baptized; you must not be satisfied to ask this favor only once from the Father, you must importune them. You are lazy about going to prayers; when you pass before the cross, you never salute it; you wish to be independent. Now know that you will obey your husbands; and you young people, you will obey your parents and our Captains; and, if any fail to do so, we have concluded to give them nothing to eat." (Thwaites 1896–1901, 18:107)

Immediately after this gathering, one woman, "not wishing to obey her husband," fled Sillery. When she was captured by the headmen, they "came to ask [the Jesuits] if, having found her, it would not be well to chain her by one foot; and if it would be enough to make her pass four days and four nights without eating, as penance for her fault" (Thwaites 1896–1901, 18:107). Given this new state of harsh punishment for the transgression of disobedience, some women fell immediately into line. Two blind women had a very difficult time in determining the exact location of the cross before which they were supposed to bow, but persisted, and finally located it with the help of staffs they carried. They bowed reverently (Thwaites 1896–1901, 18:107–9). The majority of the rest of LeJeune's Relation of 1640 regarding the conduct of the people at Sillery addressed issues of gendered behavior, particularly marriage and courting. The priests promoted especial adherence to "the law which forbids the Christian to ally himself to the unbeliever," and related several incidents of young women refusing men who were yet to be baptized. The Jesuits also heavily ritualized and thereby rewarded the establishment of approved marriages between Christians. Governor Montmagny and pious French women were critical in this process.

> [Montmagny] saw the importance of authorizing this Sacrament, and of making it reverenced among these peoples, and he desired that the ceremony for three marriages that we had published at Sillery should take place at Kebec, and wished himself to make a magnificent feast for all those invited to the nuptials. Madame de Pelletrie and some other French Ladies took charge of dressing the brides; and as for the men, we had them richly clothed . . . The Savages, when they saw this ceremoniousness, were enraptured . . . some Montagnais [Innu] and Algonquins, not invited to the wedding, regarded these ceremonies with astonishment; and their wives, seeing the young girls and women who were about to be married arrayed in the small treasures of the country, which they greatly value, said to one another, "one could easily tell that these brides are not orphans, that their fathers are not dead; that they would not be so fine if they did not have good parents," praising by this admiration the care that is taken of these new plants in the garden of the Church. (Thwaites 1896–1901, 18:127–29)

The Jesuits were also regarded as matchmakers, and were approached by men and women alike for this service (Thwaites 1896–1901, 18:131). One match that seems to have been made by the Jesuits was unwelcome by the woman in question, but it does not appear that there was an acceptable way to protest her objection. She attempted to hang herself, and a Christian reported this to the Jesuits. LeJeune, on approaching the woman and asking her if she were not afraid of damnation, was given the reply that she "was not thinking of that . . . but only of freeing [herself] from the annoyance of that man" (Thwaites 1896–1901, 18:165). LeJeune did not report the outcome of that arranged marriage. The Jesuits' gender role enforcement was effective in many ways. Women were careful to confess the slightest deviations from these roles, including disobedience to their husbands (Thwaites 1896–1901, 18:135).

The Jesuits were by no means the only enforcers of gender role adherence. The Christian community policed itself by reporting possible transgressors and was less merciful than the Jesuits. A young woman who was seen speaking to a traditionalist young man "so scandalized the Christians that [the missionaries] were immediately informed of it" (Thwaites 1896–1901, 18:141). Although the priest found no fault in her, as she had only told the young man to go and speak to the Jesuits if he wished to court her, the community was so upset that "she was made to understand so clearly the harm there was in scandalizing her neighbor" (Thwaites 1896–1901, 18:143). A young man who lived for a brief time with a traditionalist young woman was condemned by the Christians of Sillery, who decided "that he should be driven away and forbidden ever to live again with the Christians, for having been guilty of so bad an action" (Thwaites 1896–1901, 18:175). In this case the Jesuits counseled mercy, so the Christians "decreed that he should publicly entreat God for mercy upon his sin," which he did, prostrating himself in public worship. Afterward, the Jesuits discovered that he had had no sexual contact with the woman and were amazed at his penitence although he was "so little guilty before God" (Thwaites 1896–1901, 18:173–77). When a young Christian man beat his wife, members of the community complained to the Jesuits and brought the couple to them so that the priests could admonish them. It is illustrative of the Jesuits' construction of gender that the man was not held to be of sole responsibility; his wife "had insolently provoked him . . . [and] was more guilty than her husband" (Thwaites 1896–1901, 18:155). In a similar instance, a man confessed striking his wife for ignoring his request to accompany him to Mass. The wife did not hesitate to confess and repent her disobedience, even though she had not heard her husband ask (Thwaites 1896–1901, 20:149). Anecdotes like these make one wonder about the true motivation of the woman who believed herself to be dying in childbirth and vowed that her child "should always be a virgin . . . —that is, that they would make her a Nun when she was grown up, if she wished to be one" (Thwaites 1896–1901, 20:181).

The least explored and yet perhaps most significant gendered act described above was the participation of the French women in arraying the indigenous brides prior to their marriage ceremonies. Although the French men made a matching effort to provide appropriate clothing to the Native men, it was the bridal display of wealth that earned the approval of the onlooking Native women. Marriage is, of course, a central ritual in establishing kinship. The French women, familiar with the necessity of properly clothing a bride, dressed the Native women in such a way that the women witnessing the marriages could approvingly comment that these brides were "not orphans." In other words, French women made it obvious that the brides had "families," fictive or otherwise, who valued them. The French women provided the necessary and visible evidence of that value.

James Ronda and Kenneth Morrison have each explored the establishment of Sillery and its effects on the primarily Innu residents. Ronda concluded that Jesuit civilization planning was disastrous for the Innu, as "Indians who agreed to settle in permanent villages were made easy targets for both their own enemies and unscrupulous Europeans" (Ronda 1972, 395). Ronda also observed that the mission station served as a concentrated site of an attempt at massive social change that ultimately divided its occupants into two opposing groups: zealous converts and persistent traditionalists (Ronda 1979, 14–15). Central to this rift were issues surrounding the practice of traditional rituals, as well as the proper expression of gender and sexuality. The abolition of polygamy and the institutionalization of courting behavior acceptable to Christians were obviously central to the Jesuits' (and converts') agenda.

However, as Ronda rightly notes, the traditionalist majority at Sillery did indeed display overt resistance to these Jesuit demands. In 1640 there seems to have been sufficient resistance to the rule of the Christian minority that the Christian men resolved to imprison and deprive of food "he who should fall into any error" (Thwaites 1896–1901, 20:143). In one case, a traditionalist woman chided her recently baptized husband, saying, "Dost thou not see that we are all dying since they told us to pray to God? Where are thy relatives, where are mine? The most of them are dead" (Thwaites 1896–1901, 20:197). In 1642 the decision was made by the Christian leaders to lock up baptized women who left their husbands, and in 1643 a prison was built in the village for this purpose, so that women would not have to be transported to Quebec. A woman facing imprisonment fled, but was caught and taken by force. "Some Pagan young men, observing this violence, —of which Savages have a horror, and which is more remote from their customs than Heaven is from earth,— made use of threats, declaring that they would kill anyone who laid a hand on the woman. But the Captain and his people, who were Christians, boldly replied that there was nothing that they would not do or endure, in order to secure obedience to God" (Thwaites 1896–1901, 22:83). Several other women were imprisoned in the cell at Sillery, without covering, food, or water. When Jesuits attempted to relieve the prisoners, the men objected. A young woman who spent time with a traditionalist young man who wished to court her was publicly flogged (Thwaites 1896–1901, 22:115–21). "Yet the intensified moral Puritanism of the Christian minority, employing even the most extreme measures, failed to alter old habits and customs" (Ronda 1979, 13). While Ronda is correct in perceiving that a traditionalist majority persisted despite informants and harsh punishments, and that these traditionalists maintained their ways because abandoning them would have been "cultural suicide," he does not explore further the traditionalists' critique of the gender roles demanded by the Jesuits and the zealous converts, nor does he sufficiently explore the concept of conversion. His analysis is confined to an exploration of the failure of the community despite the intentions of the Jesuits and the zeal of the converts.

Morrison's more nuanced analysis attends to the conflict between the individualism of Jesuit Catholicism and the goals of solidarity sought by the Innu residents of Sillery (Morrison 1990, 417). Morrison also argues that Native ideas about sacred power were not altered by the conversion experience, but that the Innu took symbolic action in response to an imbalance in their relationships with sacred power, as evidenced by the alarming rates of death by disease. Morrison contends that baptism served as the vehicle by which Innu traditions were transmuted into Christian practices (including the incorporation of heaven, hell, and purgatory into their cosmology and the internalization of a sense of sinfulness), but that in the end, "the integration of Montagnais [Innu] and Catholic symbolism did not work" (Morrison 1990, 433). Morrison perceptively notes that in policing themselves to such a degree, the converts "created a political system which mixed the techniques of achieving the traditional goal of consensus with the coercive measures of French society" (Morrison 1990, 430). The Innu and other Algonkian-speaking inhabitants of Sillery were indeed interested in maintaining a social consensus, and in maintaining a relationship with the sacred power revealed to them by the Jesuits. They took great pains to remain in a state of reciprocal relationship with this sacred power, and this fact is the key to understanding the behavior of the converts. In addition to the punishments inflicted on disobedient women, punishments, particularly prostrations and flagellations, were inflicted by converts upon themselves. The converts had discovered that the sacred power spoken of by the Jesuits operated on a system of relationship; sacrifice was the means by which a damaged relationship was restored. If this relationship was less than perfectly attended to, if a person in relationship with sacred power failed to act in the proper manner, that person must perform humiliating acts of sacrifice and penance in order to be restored to relationship. Moreover, individual errors jeopardized the entire group. If a person offended this sacred power, he or she endangered the relationship of all with that power. While the Jesuits perceived dedicated Christians, observant to a fault, they could not perceive that the converts had not at all abandoned their traditional values. They valued the survival of their communities, which appeared to require the protection of the French. The sacred power to which the French required obeisance demanded a reciprocal relationship. Reciprocity was a traditional value and was closely adhered to in the relationship with this sacred power. The only traditional value abandoned at Sillery was the value of women's autonomy.

Carol Devens makes a similar observation in her analysis of the experiences of several groups of Native women in contact zones in the Great Lakes area. While she only briefly touches on Sillery, her work contributes to this conversation in that she has documented a great deal of resistance to Christian conversion on the part of the women of these traditional societies. She attributes women's resistance to several factors. First, the dependence on French goods and on trade diminished women's economic importance. Clothing and foodstuffs traditionally made and prepared by women were gradually replaced by French goods. Although women still contributed to the new dominance of trade in Native economies, their activities shifted from production of the staples of existence to production of items auxiliary to the trapping and trading process (Devens 1992, 17). In the case of the Wendat, this could be said to imply that although women still raised corn, the value of corn shifted from being the nutritive basis of life to being a commodity necessary for continued and expanding trade. For example, as Wendat country was overhunted, corn remained important, but less for consumption than for exchange with northern nations, such as the Ottawa, for pelts. A second reason for women's resistance explored by Devens is the reluctance of Jesuits to focus directly on them as potential converts (Devens 1992, 20). The Jesuits were loath to catechize women; LeJeune himself wrote that "it is not becoming for us to receive them into our houses" (Thwaites 1896–1901, 6:143). He also documented an instance in which a woman took him to task for not instructing women; remarkably, he heeded her advice, but he soon regretted it. "I told her she was right, and that we would have them come in their turn, which we did, but we soon had to dismiss them, for they brought their little children, who made a great deal of noise" (Thwaites 1896–1901, 12:141). A third of Devens's reasons for women remaining resistant to conversion is the Jesuit prohibition of courting and marriage customs that were favorable to women (Devens 1992, 25). In the case of Sillery, this has been amply documented.

It seems, then, that the recurring phenomenon of women's resistance to conversion can be found throughout the texts of the Jesuits, even though they chose not to have close contact with women. While Ronda is correct in noting that Sillery remained a divided community, he does not explore the resistance of women as central to this division. Morrison's recognition of the fact that converts were maintaining traditional values even in their conversion is important, but he does not attend to the persistence of the traditional values of women. Devens outlines some important issues in women's resistance to the Jesuit program, but she does not adequately explore the reasons and underlying motivations for women's conversion.

Kinship: Women in the Diaspora

For women in Wendat country, conversion was often perceived as a direct threat to kinship ties. LeMercier wrote of a man who considered conversion, "but his wife . . . diverted him from his purpose, representing to him that it would not be proper for him to go to heaven, since none of his relatives were there" (Thwaites 1896–1901, 13:127). Another woman, on her deathbed, pretended not to hear the Jesuits as they preached heaven and hell to her. Her only words in reference to the Jesuits were "Drive them from me." Her sister defended her so-called "obduracy," stating that "she will decide [where she will go] when she is dead" (Thwaites 1896–1901, 13:135). One woman rejected baptism outright, stating, "I do not wish it"; this sentence was uttered when she learned that if baptized, she must remain with her husband throughout her lifetime (Thwaites 1896–1901, 13:141). Although this woman was not interested in maintaining that particular relationship for eternity, other women voiced the importance of kinship ties in their various ways of dismissing the Jesuit priests. A woman who had declined baptism seemed to have died, and upon recovery reported the experience she had in death. She went to the Village of the Dead and met her departed relatives, who counseled her to remain alive because without her, "there would be no more relatives to prepare food for the souls thereafter" (Thwaites 1896–1901, 13:153). A woman who did finally consent to baptism begged the priests, "do not give me a new name" (Thwaites 1896–1901, 13:183). Evidently, the name she bore was the only one by which her relatives knew her. A mother refused baptism because her child had died without being baptized, and "she desired only to go where [he] was" (Thwaites 1896–1901, 13:209). There are countless anecdotes like this in the Relations from Wendat country, with the common theme of women rejecting baptism because it would mean separation from kinspeople in the afterlife.

During the horrific events of the Wendat defeat and dispersion, the Jesuits recorded numerous heartrending stories of the suffering of women. The deaths of mothers and their children together are duly reported in these Relations. Ragueneau, the author of these Relations, took care to include the dying words of one mother: "I firmly believe that, being companions in death, we shall all rise together" (Thwaites 1896–1901, 35:92–93). The story of an old woman's near death while stranded overnight on the ice was also recounted (Thwaites 1896–1901, 35:185–87). These few stories are significant in that for the first time, the Jesuits were recording events in the daily lives of women, not just baptisms or objections to baptisms. In these dire circumstances, the Jesuits observed the women suffering and dying alongside the men.

In the letters describing the arrival of the Wendat in Quebec, more detail was given about the experiences of women and girls than ever before. This is partly owing to the fact that the Ursuline sisters took a number of Wendat girls into their school. "They [the Ursulines] took immediate charge of a very numerous family . . . they threw open their seminary to some little girls . . . their classes were opened to a number of day-scholars, whom they instructed in the Catechism, [in] the Huron tongue, and to whom they gave food" (Thwaites 1896–1901, 35:209). The Jesuits were now in communication with local women and with the Ursuline sisters, so that, given the segregation along gender lines that prevailed at that time among the Wendat people (and among French religious), they were finally able to include a greater amount of information about women.

The event of a terrible fire at the Ursuline convent enabled the Jesuits to include even more information about these Wendat women. They related a story of a Wendat girl thought lost in the fire; the girl was later found, and after her recovery, appeared to have wished to pursue a life among religious women: "The girl is now in the house of the Hospital mothers; it seems as if God has chosen her for Religion" (Thwaites 1896–1901, 36:213). The story of other survivors of the fire, a Wendat woman and her daughter, was also written; this widowed woman, Cecile Arenhatsi, had found work as a servant in the Ursuline convent, and her daughter attended the seminary. "She has an excellent mind, a very gentle disposition, and a much better will . . . When she was in the Huron country she heard of 'the holy virgins' (thus the Hurons call the nuns), and her whole heart and her purest love turned toward them . . . She waits, patiently and lovingly, until the good Mothers have rebuilt their house; and hopes that she will not die elsewhere than with them" (Thwaites 1896–1901, 36:213–15). Sparse as this record is, it provides evidence that at least some Wendat women, having lost their kinspeople and having been bereft of the communities of women to which they belonged, sought out and integrated themselves into alternative female kinship structures such as the communities of the Ursulines and the Hospitalières.

In a particularly notable incident, the Wendat as a whole expressed gratitude toward the charity the Ursulines had shown them since their arrival in a clearly hybridized condolence ceremony by presenting the sisters with their few remaining objects of importance: two large wampum belts. A headman, Louis Taiaeronk, delivered an oration in which he invoked both the dislocation of his own people and that of the Ursulines, as well as their reconstitution. Kinship is the central trope employed in his rhetoric, kinship is the issue he recommends the Ursulines attend to, just as kinship was the means by which the Wendat people allied with the French and, indeed, survived the dispersion.

> Holy virgins, you see before you miserable carcasses, the remnant of a country that once was flourishing and that is no more, the country of the Hurons. We have been devoured and gnawed to the very bones, by war and famine . . . you see to what misery we are reduced. Look at us on all sides and see whether there is anything in us that does not compel us to weep for ourselves, and to shed unceasing torrents of tears. Alas! This sad accident that has happened to you increases our woes and renews our tears, which had commenced to dry. The sight of that beautiful house of Jesus, that house of charity, reduced to ashes in an instant; the sight of the flames raging there

... all this has brought back to our minds the universal destruction by fire of all our houses, of all our villages, and of the whole of our country ... Let us weep, let us weep, my beloved countrymen; yes, let us weep for our misfortunes which were solely ours before, but which we now share in common ... We have come here for the purpose of consoling you; and, before coming here, we have entered into your hearts, to see what might afflict you still more since your fire, so as to apply some remedy to it ... If we had to deal with persons like ourselves, the custom of our country would have been to make you a present to dry your tears, and another to strengthen your courage ... we seek no remedy in that respect ... We fear that, when the news of the accident that has happened to you reaches France, it will affect your relatives ... we fear that they will recall you and that you will be moved by their tears. How can a mother read, without weeping, letters telling her that her daughter is without clothes, without food, without a bed ... ? The first thought that nature will inspire in those disconsolate mothers will be to recall you to them ... A brother would do the same for his sister; an uncle and an aunt for their niece; and afterward we would be in danger of losing you, and of losing in your persons the assistance for which we had hoped in the instruction of our daughters in the faith ... do not allow yourselves to be persuaded by love of kindred ... To strengthen you in these resolutions, here is a present of twelve hundred porcelain beads which will root your feet so deeply in the soil of this country that no love for your kindred or for your own country can withdraw them from it. The second present, which we beg you to accept, is a similar collar of twelve hundred porcelain beads, to lay the foundation of an entirely new building wherein ... classes shall be held, in which you may teach our little Huron girls. Such are our desires; they are likewise yours, for doubtless you could not die happy if, when dying, this reproach could be cast at you that, through too tender a love for your relatives, you had not contributed to the salvation of so many souls which you have loved for the sake of God, and which will be your crown in heaven. (Thwaites 1896–1901, 36:219–21)

Father Ragueneau, remarking on the eloquence of this ritual, was careful to note that "I have added nothing to it; and in fact, I cannot add the charm imparted to it by the tone of his voice and the expression of his countenance" (Thwaites 1896–1901, 36:221).

Although this ritual was performed by a man, there are several notable dimensions of the speech delivered by Louis Taiaeronk, including that of gender. First, the adaptation of a mourning ritual to these altered circumstances is a brilliant innovation. This oration has been made into a site in which the Wendat people are able to articulate their relation to the Ursulines in several ways. As in traditional Wendat condolence ceremonies, kinship is established from the outset. Through this speaker, the Wendat voice their identification with the circumstances of the displaced Ursuline sisters; their situations and bereavements are paralleled. The actual kinspeople of the Ursuline sisters are mentioned, and despite their great cultural differences, Louis Taiaeronk is able to express his understanding of the feelings of these kinspeople in France. By identifying with the feelings of the relatives of the nuns, the Wendat orator demonstrates his own humanity, as well as that of his people. Indication of the matrilineal structure of Wendat society is also present; the mention of mothers, brothers, and uncles and aunts (rather than fathers) reveals the speaker's perception of the nearest kin of the Ursuline women. His enumeration of the roles in this kinship structure illustrates the extent to which the Wendat were able to identify with the Ursuline society of religious women. Like Wendat women, and like Wendat society as a whole, the Ursuline sisters employed (fictive) kinship structures as a means of constituting relationship. The prestations are described not as traditional prestations to dry tears and strengthen courage in bereavement, but as prestations intended to redraw kinship lines. The Ursulines are told to "root [their] feet deeply in the soil of this country," to be persons who are located here, in this village on the St. Lawrence River, among their relations, the Wendat. The second prestation is intended to serve as a strong foundation for the rebuilding of the Ursuline house, wherein the sisters will resume their pedagogical relationships with the Wendat girls. These relationships, of course, were also articulated in terms of kinship, as the girls addressed the Ursulines as "sister" and "mother." Finally, like the Wendat themselves, the Ursulines are counseled to take comfort in the fact that at their death, their sacrifice of their love for their kin in France in favor of their love for "so many [Wendat] souls" will "be [their] crown in Heaven." It is important to note that even the fact that no one has actually died does not prevent the Wendat orator from mentioning death. His hopes for happiness at death and in the afterlife reflect not only Jesuit theology, but, poignantly, the magnitude of the recent bereavements of his people.

Lay women in Quebec were also able to provide the Jesuits with inspirational tales of their encounters with Wendat women. "Some highly virtuous and devout French Ladies informed me that a Christian Huron woman inspired them with devotion, for she prayed to God every day before the blessed sacrament, with a tenderness that showed on her countenance, and inspired them with higher sentiments toward God than they usually had" (Thwaites 1896–1901, 36:207). It seems that even in the absence of the mediatory rhetoric of the Jesuits, the People of the Peninsula served as inspirational examples to the pious. Even with the numerous reasons Native women would have to resist the Jesuit program, some women are still described as having embraced Christianity. The question of which values women were articulating as they made their choices and recreated their orientations remains to be explored.

Gendered Symbols and Reoriented Women

The women of Wendat country were rarely described by the Jesuits in positive terms. The few who accepted baptism on their deathbeds were certainly not given undue praise. Marie Aonetta seems to be an exception to this rule, but even in her case, when described by LeMercier, his rhetoric is less than florid. "Now one word about Marie Aonetta, his wife. She is only too fortunate in having encountered so good a Father in so faithful a husband. She confesses often; what makes us hope that she will persevere is that she goes on frankly and heartily" (Thwaites 1896—1901, 15:107). As has been mentioned, the Jesuits' patriarchal and often misogynistic model, coupled with their culture-bound convictions, prevented them from seeing the virtues of these women. One Wendat man, castigating the Jesuits' attitudes toward women, pointed out that "[t]he French teach . . . that the first woman who ever lived brought death into the world" (Thwaites 1896–1901, 16:39).[2] Given the Jesuits' negative construction of female gender, it is remarkable that some women did convert.

But did they convert? Did anyone? As Kenneth Morrison has observed, the women who converted may not have been orienting themselves in the manner the Jesuits desired or believed. As Morrison asserts, "any argument for or against conversion must be made within Native American understandings of reality" (Morrison 2002, 155). These "understandings of reality" may be better described as orientations. The term "conversion" is itself interrogated by Morrison.

> The concept of conversion is a dehumanizing reification that overlooks, denies, and dismisses [Native] historical agency. Conversion claims that Native Americans came to agree with pervasive and aggressive critiques of their lifeways. Conversion denies that either pre- or post-contact Native American life had or has systematic and intellectual integrity. Conversion contends that Native Americans themselves perceived the superior truth claims of Christianity as a series of overarching theological and cultural propositions about reality. Conversion claims that Native Americans repudiated their religious traditions, and thus their ways of perceiving, thinking, valuing, and acting . . . As an ethnocentrically charged but multivalent category, conversion fails utterly to understand the distinctive and integral character of Native American life both before and after contact. (Morrison 2002, 161)

There is, then, ample documentation of women's responses to Jesuit efforts to produce converts. Native women acted in response

---

2. This man's interpretation of this doctrine was quite singular, however; because the Jesuits had told him of the Ursuline sisters' presence at Quebec, he insisted that it was the arrival of French women that precipitated the epidemics in his country. His critique of the French presence implies that the only rationale for associating women with death would be intimate knowledge of women of this sort.

to the Jesuits' presence in various ways. Some dismissed the Jesuits, others interrogated and explored the Jesuits' relationship with sacred power. Some capitulated to undergoing the ritual of baptism, others rejected outright this sacrament. Some wished the Jesuits to leave their homes and villages, others desired French alliance and Jesuit protection. In the context of the Wendat diaspora, some chose to affiliate with enemy nations rather than depend upon the Jesuits; others followed the Jesuits to the shelter of Quebec. When there, many of these women, displaced from their families of origin, rapidly found ways to integrate themselves into networks of women, creatively establishing kinship relationships in order to sustain themselves.

The women of Wendat country were not converts as the French priests would understand the term. They were women struggling through disease, displacement, warfare, famine, missionization, mercantilization, dispossession, captivity, adoption, and bereavement. These women were not capitulating to European desires for and projections of themselves. They were agents in maintaining that which they valued, such as traditional kinship structures. They creatively responded to the cultural disequilibrium in which they found themselves by drawing upon traditional modalities of life. They survived, and in some cases they even flourished, by establishing new orientations, new religious networks of meaning, for themselves. These women dedicated themselves to the maintenance of connections, the preservation of that which is valued, even in the face of the bereavements, displacements, and disequilibriums of colonial contact and exchange.

Mythic Possibilities of New Orientations

Like kinship structure, myth was also a dimension of the orientation of the Native peoples of the colonial period in New France. As Long has argued, myths "emphasize the primordial and *a priori* forms of the world. But myth at the same time defines the locus of the rupture between humanity and the world" (Long 1995, 34). By this he means that in the very recitation of myths, human beings distance themselves from the ground of being; the stories told mark human beings' expressions of the fact that they are removed from this primordium. The use of the myth-dream as the language of the formulation of new orientations has already been explored. The following consists of the raising of the possibility of a second type of iteration of new orientation in the colonial context.

Brébeuf documented a myth he heard recited by the Wendat in 1636 that may itself most eloquently testify to the experiences of women during the crises generated by French incursion into Wendat country. In this myth, a Wendat man had lost one of his sisters to death. He mourned her for some time, but was so devastated by her loss that he resolved to go to the Village of the Dead to reclaim her. On his agonizing three-month journey, she appeared to him every night, giving him food and sustenance, but disappeared every time he reached out to her. He came to a river, crossed it, and there met a man in a dwelling who gave him the information that all the inhabitants of the Village of the Dead were then gathering in a longhouse, dancing to heal Aataentsic, the Grandmother, who is sick. This man, who revealed himself to be the keeper of the brains of the dead, gave the mourning brother a pumpkin, and told him that within this pumpkin he might retrieve his sister. The brother continued on his journey with the pumpkin, and finally arrived at the longhouse of Aataentsic. The dead, upon seeing him, disappeared, but he sat by the fire in the longhouse until they returned in the evening to continue their dance. When they appeared, he tried to seize his sister and failed, but succeeded a second time. As he wrestled with his sister she became smaller and smaller, and finally small enough to put inside the pumpkin. He left the longhouse with the pumpkin, stopped at the man's house by the river to retrieve his sister's brains, which he put inside another pumpkin. The man gave the brother instructions as to how to revive his sister's body. He was to disinter her remains, and to give a great feast for all of the people in his home village to attend. When all were assembled, he was to bring in the two pumpkins, along with his sister's body, ordering all present to avert their eyes. When he returned to his seating place in the longhouse with the pumpkins, his sister would come back to life. When the brother returned to his village, he followed the man's instructions to the letter. When he entered his longhouse with the pumpkins, he felt his sister's lifeless body begin to stir. But when he was only a few steps from his seating place, one curious person raised his eyes, and at that moment his sister's life force escaped from the pumpkin, and he could only return his sister's body to the grave (Thwaites 1896–1901, 10:149–51).

This myth surely contains what Long has identified as a "nostalgia for wholeness and completeness" and the "drive toward human autonomy" that he finds in mythic language, which expresses an acknowledgment of dependence on ontological reality (Long 1995, 35). However, the context in which this myth was recited to Brébeuf may provide an additional insight into the means by which the new orientations of the Wendat were being constituted.

In a theological spirit, Brébeuf had inquired of a number of the People of the Peninsula about their ideas regarding the existence and operations of the soul. He was appalled to discover that they had a complex understanding of the concept, which was revealed by the fact that "they give it different names according to its different conditions or different occupations" (Thwaites 1896–1901, 10:141). When he asked how they received their ideas about the persistence of a soul after death, and about the existence of a Village of the Dead in which these beings dwelt, they offered as evidence the myth of the lost sister described above. Brébeuf, in relating this myth, pronounced it "most stupid," although he admitted it was told to him by a person "of intelligence and judgment" (Thwaites 1896–1901, 10:149). Somewhat ironically, Brébeuf's characterization of the narrator may possibly indicate that this person was receptive to Jesuit evangelization.

Although the opacity of myth-dreams must be acknowledged, it may be beneficial to attempt an alternative reading of this situation: Brébeuf, in the midst of an epidemic in Wendat country, inquired about matters having to do with death. In response to his inquiries, he was told an important story that elucidated the orientation of the Wendat in relation to death. He was told that the Village of the Dead was toward the west, and that upon death, part of a person separates from that person's body and abides near the burial ground, sometimes wandering into its home village and eating leftovers from kettles. After the Feast of the Dead, the deceased leave the burial grounds, and they begin together a journey to the Village of the Dead. Children and very old people have difficulty making this journey, so they sometimes stay together and form their own villages not far from their original homes. They till the fields the living people have abandoned, and also retrieve burned corn when fires strike the fields of the living. Those who have died in warfare or by their own hands are feared, and are not admitted to the Village of the Dead (Thwaites 1896–1901, 10:143–45).

There are several things indicative of the precontact orientations of the Wendat people in this myth: the very existence of the Village of the Dead, and the great loss experienced at the death of a beloved sister, for example. But the context in which this myth was recited may reveal some evidence of the emergent orientations of the Wendat as they experienced epidemics and death on an unprecedented scale as the Jesuits established their missions. In this myth, Aataentsic, the grandmother of all the Wendat, is ill. All of the women in the myth are in peril, and all the actions of the men (and even of the deceased, for the success of the curative dance for Aataentsic is not mentioned) do not bring the women back to health and life. It is possible that this myth, given its 1636 telling, is indicative of great mourning for the loss of powerful women. They have been taken away, and they cannot be retrieved. The most powerful woman of all, Aataentsic—the mother of Tawiscaron and Iouskeha; the grandmother of all living beings; the mythic ancestress from whose dead body sprang the Three Sisters, the corn, the beans, and the squash—is ill. Despite the medicine of the pumpkins, the beloved sister cannot be retrieved, and the grandmother, the source of that which nourishes all life, languishes. The khiondhecwi, that which gives life to the people, is in danger, and everyone waits to see whether the curative ritual will take effect.

5

Marie Rollet Hébert

Marie Rollet Hébert: La Première Habitante

While seventeenth-century source materials relating to Marie Rollet Hébert and her husband, Louis Hébert, are sparse, the symbolic significance of the couple remains palpable, particularly in Quebec history, French-Canadian genealogy, and Francophone Canadian self-understanding. Louis Hébert and his wife, Marie Rollet Hébert, were the first French couple to establish a household in the newly established colony of New France. While Louis Hébert had visited the colony with Champlain and Jean Biencourt de Poutrincourt as early as 1604, again in 1606–7, and had lived in the colony from 1610 to 1613, he did not bring his wife and family to settle there until their voyage together in 1617.[1]

Louis Hébert was related by marriage to Jean Biencourt de Poutrincourt, who had been granted the lands then containing Port-Royal

---

Much of the material in this chapter is based on my 2004 article "Godmothers and Goddaughters: Catholic Women in Colonial New France and New England," in *Encyclopedia of Women and Religion in North America*, ed. Rosemary Skinner Keller and Rosemary Radford Ruether (Indianapolis: Indiana Univ. Press).

1. Some secondary sources have asserted that Marie Rollet accompanied her husband to Port-Royal in 1610, solely on the basis of one employment of the phrase "Louis Hébert et son compagnon" in Lescarbot's *Nova Francia* (1928). In my estimation, there is no evidence that Marie Rollet Hébert was the companion here mentioned, especially given that Lescarbot would have had every reason to make specific mention of the presence of French women in New France at that time.

(Nova Scotia). During his second visit to the colony at Port-Royal, Hébert, an apothecary by trade, had ministered to many, both French and Native, including the notable Mi'kmaq chief Membertou during what would be a fatal illness.[2] Having returned to France in 1613, Hébert arranged to accompany Champlain on his next voyage. Louis Hébert was completely in accord with Champlain's desire to settle and farm the land. Champlain promised him a contract for his service as apothecary, which granted him six hundred livres annually and ten arpents of land, as well as lodging and support for his family while he cleared that land for their home and farm. Hébert and his wife sold their house and garden in Paris, and took their three children, Anne, Guillemette, and Guillaume, as well as a servant named Henri, to settle in New France in 1617. To Hébert's dismay, upon arrival in Honfleur, the port from which his family was to sail, the promised contract was unilaterally revised by the Compagnie du Canada, and Hébert learned that he was to receive only half of the promised salary and only six arpents of land, and his family was to be in the employ of the company without payment. He was offered only a three-year contract, was required to provide medical services to any employee of the company, was enjoined from engaging in trade in furs, and was required to sell to the company any surplus in agricultural production. This contract revision was imposed because the current monopolists were interested more in the fur trade than they were in settlement and did not wish to encourage agricultural colonization any more than was necessary.

Few details of the perilous voyage are available to us, but there is one story provided by the Recollet priest Gabriel Sagard, who wrote of this journey in his *Histoire du Canada et voyages que les Frères mineurs recollects y ont faicts pour la conversion des infidèles depuis l'an 1615*. Sagard was interested in telling of this particular voyage because the Recollet

---

2. Membertou had been the first Native man baptized in New France—the priest Jessé Fléché had performed the ritual in 1610, naming him after King Henri and naming his wife after Queen Marie.

priest Joseph LeCaron was aboard. He related that during the crossing of the Atlantic, a storm arose. Father LeCaron was hearing the confessions of passengers readying themselves to meet their maker. While the priest was pronouncing his benedictions, Marie Rollet Hébert, discontent with the fact that only adults were being ministered to, lifted through the hatchway her two youngest children so that they too might receive the necessary blessings (Sagard 1866, 1:45).

The ship survived the storm, and all arrived safely. Upon arrival, Louis Hébert immediately began working toward situating his family in a permanent dwelling at Quebec, Champlain's trade depot and habitation, and began to clear his land. Hébert, like Champlain, was committed to the establishment of an agricultural colony. After clearing land, which was itself backbreaking work, especially without a plow, Hébert built a stone house for himself and his family—likely the first stone dwelling in the colony, but certainly the first stone single-family home. This house was thirty-eight feet long and nineteen feet wide. He had brought grain with him from France, and he immediately set to farming the land he was granted. Hébert was successful in farming the rich land, and also evidently transplanted an apple tree that had been brought from Normandy. Sagard reported his observation of the plenty that was enjoyed at the Hébert home. He saw cattle, Indian corn and peas acquired by trading with Natives, and young vines, and declared that the Hébert homestead was "full of other little things that demonstrate the bounty of the earth" (Sagard 1866, 1:159). Likewise Champlain described the Hébert farm as productive, bearing not just peas and beans, but also squash, cucumbers, and melons (Champlain 1971, 3:205). However, no real profits from farming were successfully reaped in those first few years, as his contract with the company precluded participation in the wider marketplace. The injustice of this was also noted by Sagard (Sagard 1866, 1:53).

In 1620, when Champlain was given greater authority over the colony, he named Louis Hébert as king's attorney. Two years later, as such, Hébert petitioned for actual title to the land he had cleared and farmed. It was granted him in 1623, and three years later more lands were added to his holdings. Thus it was that the apothecary became somewhat of a gentleman farmer in New France. However, as a result of a fall on the ice, he died in 1627. Their servant Henri appears to have been killed in that year as well. Hébert's wife and children were left to go on alone.

The population of French Catholic women in New France was extremely low throughout the first quarter of the seventeenth century. Even by 1627, of approximately one hundred inhabitants, only eleven were women. Thus, from the time of her arrival, Marie Rollet Hébert was regularly expected to provide hospitality, supplying needed food and lodging to many. In 1618 she was the mother of the bride at the first Catholic marriage performed in New France, when her daughter Anne married Étienne Jonquet. Recollet Father Joseph LeCaron officiated at the ceremony. Three years later, her second daughter, Guillemette, married Guillaume Couillard, who took over the management of the Hébert lands (inheriting half of them upon the death of his father-in-law) as well as adding his own large land grant to the family's holdings.

The Hébert-Couillard household was an expansive one. It eventually comprised not only their son Guillaume (and after 1634 his wife, Hélène, and their three children); their daughter Guillemette and her husband and their ten children; two Innu young women, Charité and Espérance, who had been adopted by the navigator Samuel de Champlain and left to board with the family in 1629, but who left sometime during the next year or two; an African "servant" (likely from Madagascar, but perhaps from West Africa) named Olivier, who had arrived on an English ship and who had been given to Guillaume Couillard, also in 1629; and, as years passed, several other Native young women who had been placed in the care of the Jesuits; as well as a succession of several servants.[3] The Hébert-Couillard household was a gathering place for many of the early inhabitants of New France. Their farm was

---

3. The first chapter of Brett Rushforth's *Bonds of Alliance: Indigenous and Atlantic Slaveries in New France* (2012) is an invaluable and long-needed contextualization of both African and indigenous enslavement by French colonists in North America.

a resource upon which many colonists depended, particularly during the famine of the winter of 1628–29.

However, the notion of bountiful provision freely given was directly contradicted by Champlain, who, during that starvation winter, begrudged the Hébert-Couillard family's harvest and suspected they were not sharing everything they had. Champlain expressed dismay that every week he was given only nine and a half ounces of Indian corn, barley, and peas from the Hébert-Couillards. Champlain was convinced that Guillaume Couillard was keeping more for his own family.

The paucity of that winter was in great part owing to the actions of the Kirkes, four English brothers who, as privateers in the employ of the English, invaded Champlain's trading post at Tadoussac in 1628 and demanded the surrender of Quebec. Champlain demurred, but was forced to capitulate when the Kirkes cut off all supplies to the colony. Interestingly, the Kirkes were quite generous to the Hébert-Couillard family, and instead of despoiling them, allowed them the choice of being taken to London and eventually returned to France, or of staying in Quebec. Champlain recorded, perhaps with some slight ill will, the circumstances of the family's decision. He mentioned that they worried about being without a priest, and that he made quite clear to them that if the English remained in possession of their lands, they would be permanently without recourse to the sacraments. Therefore, Champlain advised the family to sell their possessions and abandon their land and return to France with the Kirkes (Champlain 1971, 6:72–74). Deciding against taking Champlain's advice, the Hébert-Couillard family remained in New France for the full three years it took for France to regain possession of its colony.

They were not alone in making this choice. Other French people remaining in Quebec were the families of Pierre Desportes (whose daughter would eventually marry Guillaume Hébert), Nicolas Pivert, Abraham Martin (after whom the famous "Plains of Abraham" were named), and Guillaume Houbou (who would eventually become Marie Rollet's second husband). During the English occupation, Guillemette Couillard gave birth to a daughter, Elizabeth, whose godfather was

Lewis Kirke. (It appears that in the absence of a priest, the family baptized the baby themselves.) Given this, it seems that the Hébert-Couillard family maintained a good relationship with the Kirkes. (The Kirkes' mother was a native of Dieppe—perhaps they had much in common with the Héberts.) It will be recalled that Étienne Brûlé and Nicolas de Marsolet had also elected to remain in order to continue their profitable careers.

Marsolet also had a somewhat accidental hand in expanding the Hébert-Couillard household. He had represented to the Kirkes that Champlain's desire to take Charité and Espérance with him to France was opposed by local Natives. Champlain claimed that this was untrue, and accused Marsolet of having indecent motives for wanting to keep the young women in Quebec. In Champlain's account, Espérance accused Marsolet of deceit and of betraying the French, and she threatened to kill him with a knife if he approached her again. Her sister Charité's words were just as strong; during dinner with the Kirkes, she told Marsolet that she would rather eat his heart than the meal on the table. Despite the girls' vehement protests, the Kirkes listened to Marsolet and refused to allow the girls to accompany Champlain; thus the two were installed with the Hébert-Couillards. Guillaume Couillard promised to care for them as if they were his own children (Champlain 1971, 6:114–22). However, despite his promises to reward the Hébert-Couillards, it seems that Champlain never saw the girls again.

When Champlain left, Marsolet, Brûlé, and fellow translator Jean Nicollet all remained in New France, living among the Natives and sharpening their linguistic, diplomatic, and trading skills. While Marsolet and Brûlé appear to have had no opposition to dealing with the English, Nicollet seems to have absented himself from European trade altogether during the period of English occupation. Other translators, notably Olivier LeTardif, left New France with Champlain.

When, in 1632, the French and the English signed the Treaty of St. Germain-en-Laye, Louis XIII granted Guillaume de Caën the trading monopoly for that year. Cardinal Richelieu also revoked the Recollets' permission to missionize in New France and transferred the spiritual monopoly to the Society of Jesus. Thus it was that three

Jesuits, Father Paul LeJeune, Father Anne de Nouë, and Brother Gilbert Buret, set sail for Quebec with de Caën. LeJeune reported the joy with which he was greeted by the Hébert-Couillard family upon their arrival in Quebec:

> But when they saw us in their home, celebrate the holy Mass, which they had not heard for three years, good God! what joy! Tears fell from the eyes of nearly all, so great was their happiness. Oh, with what fullness of heart we sang the *Te Deum laudamus* . . . After singing the *Te Deum*, I offered to God the first Sacrifice in Kebec. The Englishman, having seen the Patents signed by the hand of his King, promised that he would go away within a week, and in fact, he began preparations for going, although with regret; but his people were all very glad of the return of the French, for they had been given only six pounds of bread, French weight, for an entire week. They told us that the Savages had helped them to live during the greater part of the time. (Thwaites 1896–1901, 5:41)

It is possible that many of the French who had remained in Quebec gathered there for Mass that day. It is unlikely that Brûlé and Marsolet would have had any interest in doing so.

Rituals: The Hébert Women and Baptisms

In 1627 the first formal baptism of a Native young man in Quebec (as opposed to earlier and frequent baptisms of the sick and dying) was celebrated with a banquet at the Hébert-Couillard household. The young man, Naneogauchit, son of the Innu chief Chomina, was given the name "Louis" by his godparents, Marie Hébert and Samuel de Champlain. The banquet, said to have consisted of fifty-six wild geese, thirty ducks, twenty teal, two cranes, two barrels of biscuits, fifteen or more pounds of prunes, six baskets of corn, and even more, was prepared at the home of Marie Hébert.

This celebration is of particular significance because of its relevance to the role of Catholic women in New France. The conversion and baptism of Native people was, of course, the primary goal of the

Jesuit missionaries. Although the Jesuits were primarily interested in converting Native men, even male converts required both a godfather (*parrain*) and a godmother (*marraine*) for a proper baptism. Over a period of years, Marie Hébert and her daughter Guillemette (Hébert) Couillard served as the godmothers of dozens of people, including many of the Native young women who resided in their household while studying with the Jesuits (and later with the Ursuline sisters), as well as Guillaume Couillard's "servant," Olivier LeJeune.

In 1629 Marie Hébert remarried. Her new husband, Guillaume Houbou, seems to have been easily integrated into the family. As was mentioned, she and her new husband, along with her son Guillaume, her daughter Guillemette, and her son-in-law Guillaume Couillard, decided to remain at Quebec during the British occupation, which lasted until 1632. (Her daughter Anne had died in childbirth the year after her marriage.) Upon the return of the French, Marie continued to house Native girls studying with the Jesuits and to serve as godmother in their baptisms. Also in this year, the young man Olivier was given to Guillaume Couillard by a crewman of the Kirkes, who had purchased him from one of the Kirke brothers for fifty ecus.

It is tempting to speculate about Olivier's role in this extended family, but his description as "servant" rather than "slave" cannot be taken as the final word on this subject. As has been noted by Marcel Trudel, although slavery was not legalized in Canada until 1709, it was practiced long before then (*DCB* 1966, 1:452). It is evident that this young man was in a subordinate position in the Hébert-Couillard household. In his Relation of 1632, Father Paul LeJeune (the source of the patronym that the young man would eventually take as his own) described an incident in which this young man, not yet fluent in French, was asked if he wished "to be a Christian, if he wanted to be baptized and be like us." The young man agreed, but expressed some skepticism: "You say that by baptism I shall be like you. I am black and you are white. I must then have my skin taken off in order to be like you." The priest found this humorous, but the young man did not. Whether the young man feared the ritual would include flaying is unlikely; rather, it seems that he was simply well versed in the operations of racial hierarchies. When Father LeJeune laughed, he cried. When he was told that he could possibly be baptized after progressing further in his knowledge of French, he left his blanket with Father LeJeune, vowing not to reclaim it until he was baptized (Thwaites 1896–1901, 5:62).

Although it is impossible to exactly identify a specific cultural or symbolic meaning for leaving his blanket with the priest, Olivier's actions appear to reveal his strong desire to be fully integrated as kin. Upon his return to "his mistress" (presumably Guillemette Couillard), and being asked about the whereabouts of his blanket, he replied, "Me not baptized, no blanket. They said, 'Come, you be baptized,' and me not baptized. No return, no blanket." The priest LeJeune interpreted this to mean "that we had promised him the baptism, and that he did not wish to return" to reclaim his blanket "until he had received [baptism]" (Thwaites 1896–1901, 5:62). It is quite possible that Olivier's expectations of full kinship included liberation from enslavement. At the very least, he was willing to leave what was likely one of his few personal possessions with the priest, in token of the promise of baptism. He was baptized in 1633, and it is nearly certain that Guillemette Couillard served as his godmother. Given the young man's choice of baptismal names, the identity of his godfather is less certain; it may have been the head of the household in which he resided, Guillaume Couillard, or it may have been his namesake, the head clerk who had returned to Quebec, Olivier LéTardif. Father Paul LeJeune noted that he took great pleasure in catechizing and teaching Olivier, and related another story about his difficulties in learning French:

> Wishing to know whether the inhabitants of his country were Mahometans or Pagans, I asked him if there were no houses there in which they prayed to God, if there were no Mosques, if they did not talk there of Mahomet. "There are," said he, "Mosques in our country." "Are they large?" I asked him. "They are," he answered, "like those in this country." On telling him that there were none in France nor in Canada, "I have seen some," said he, "in the hands of the French and English who brought them into our country, and now they use them to shoot with." I perceived that he meant to say muskets and not Mosques; I smiled, and so did he. (Thwaites 1896–1901, 5:199)

The only other information about his life with the Hébert-Couillard family is a record of his punishment for slandering Nicholas Marsolet, Étienne Brûlé's fellow translator. For this transgression, he was "chained up for twenty-four hours." He signed his confession with the mark of X, which reveals that despite Father LeJeune's tutoring, he had not been taught to write his name. When he died in 1654, the word "servant" (*domestique*) rather than "slave" (*esclave*) was listed beside his name in the burial register (*DCB* 1966, 1:452). While it seems quite possible that Guillaume Couillard emancipated Olivier LeJeune, his death at such a young age may testify to the hardships he endured during his short life. In any event, the status of this young man, somewhere between slave and servant, is marked by "fluidity and ambiguity" (Rushforth 2003, 806).

Voyages: French Women Immigrants

Catholic women, both laywomen and women religious from European countries, were among the first colonists of North America. This is partially because the European colonization of North America was not only a mercantile venture, but was also a fundamentally religious enterprise. Conflicts between Catholics and Protestants, both in France and in England, were the backdrops against which French and English colonial policies were formulated. In the case of France, initial colonial efforts by Huguenot merchants were actively undermined by Cardinal Richelieu, who decreed in 1625 that only Roman Catholics might colonize New France. In addition, the deployment of religious missions to Native Americans eventually became a major factor in the French colonial enterprise.

While stated French colonial policy maintained that the establishment of permanent habitations was of primary importance, the mercantile agendas of the trading companies and their resulting disinterest in providing the economic support necessary for such an undertaking actually prevented a full effort toward colonization. Instead, owing in part to the post-Tridentine Catholic revival in France at the beginning of the seventeenth century, early financial support from French sources (particularly from pious laywomen) was directed toward the establishment of missions. In time some of these women were themselves moved to participate more directly in these missions.

In 1615 Recollet missionaries had been sent to New France. During the next ten years, operating primarily out of the settlement at Quebec, their efforts produced little in the way of converts (a mere fifteen Native converts over a twelve-year period have been documented), but they must be credited with establishing the groundwork for missions in New France. Like most early missionary efforts in North America, Recollet evangelization was directed toward Native men, given the European cultural assumption that males were heads of households and that their families would follow in conversion. Of course, this was not necessarily the case—some of the Native cultures the Recollets, the Jesuits, and later the Ursuline sisters would encounter (notably the Wendat and Haudenosaunee) were matrilocal and matrilineal, with uncles (mother's brothers) having more familial influence than fathers of children.

The Hébert-Couillard women were not the only godmothers in New France, although they were the earliest. As mentioned, the Catholic revival in mid-seventeenth-century France caused many French women to develop an interest in missions. Some funded Jesuit and other missions; others chose to become missionaries themselves. Most notable among these women were Marie-Madeleine de Chauvigny, Marie Guyart, Jeanne Mance, and Marguerite Bourgeoys.

Marie-Madeleine de Chauvigny (1603–71) became Madame de la Peltrie upon her marriage to the Chevalier de Gruel, Seigneur de la Peltrie. She was widowed at the age of twenty-two and was urged by her father to remarry. Having been caught up in the religious fervor of the time, she did not wish to marry again, but vowed to serve the mission to New France. In 1639, after inheriting her deceased father's fortune in addition to that of the Seigneur de la Peltrie, she chartered a ship and arranged for three Ursuline sisters and a postulant to accompany her to New France. She is recognized as the founding patroness of the Ursulines of Quebec. Madame de la Peltrie remained in Quebec for the remainder of her life, and was especially interested in the conversion and education of Native girls. Her devotion to the evangelization of Native girls was evident from the moment she arrived. Just days after disembarking, she visited Sillery, the Jesuit-administered Native Catholic settlement outside Quebec. She kissed every child she saw and before the day was over, Madame de la Peltrie served as godmother at the baptism of a Native girl.

Marie Guyart (1599–72), widowed at nineteen, entered the Ursuline convent at Tours at the age of twenty, taking the name Marie de l'Incarnation. She accompanied Madame de la Peltrie to New France; with Madame de Peltrie's financial support, and with her own business acumen and deep spiritual devotion, Marie de l'Incarnation founded the Ursuline convent and school in Quebec. A prolific writer, Marie de l'Incarnation produced two accounts of her spiritual life, another account of her vocation to mission work in New France, notes from retreats, notes from instructions on the catechism, notes from conferences, dictionaries in Iroquoian and Algonquin languages, a catechism in the Huron language, and an extensive correspondence that is estimated to have consisted of over thirteen thousand letters. She also wrote, with the Jesuit Father Jérôme Lalemant, the constitution of the Ursuline order in New France that established the autonomy of the sisters. The primary mission of the Ursulines in Quebec was made clear in this work: "to employ themselves to the best of their ability in working for the salvation of their neighbor ... especially in the instruction of girls and women, in particular, the Indians" (Lapointe 1974, 1). Although, in her correspondence, she does mention several "spiritual" sons and daughters (godchildren), it is clear that Marie de l'Incarnation's role, which she perceived as parental, centered on the academic and religious education of girls, both French and Native. Acculturation of the Native young women was her goal, and in this she was only partially successful. There is only one Native young woman (Marie-Madeleine Chrêtienne) who attended the Ursuline convent school who is known to have married a French man and remained in Quebec.

Jeanne Mance (1606–73), like Marie Guyart, was strongly compelled to mission work in New France. She deftly arranged for sufficient financial backing for a hospital, and upon her arrival in New

France in 1641, she established the Hôtel-Dieu de Montreal at Fort Ville-Marie, which fort would later become Montréal. Marguerite Bourgeoys (1620–1700), the foundress of the uncloistered Congrégation de Notre-Dame de Montréal, dedicated her life to the education of the girls of New France. In 1658 she began her school, located in a stone stable, for all the French children of Ville-Marie. Later, the boys were taught by priests, and Bourgeoys' congregation of nuns educated the girls. When the *filles du roi* (young women sent by the benevolent Catholic group called the Société de Notre-Dame, and later, by the French court, as prospective brides for the male colonists) arrived in Ville-Marie, Bourgeoys housed them and attempted to educate them on the finer points of managing a household in the environment of New France. In 1676 she established a boarding school for noble and bourgeois French girls, and later began domestic training schools for other girls at Lachine, Pointe-aux Trembles, Batiscan, and Champlain. Bourgeoys also began a mission school for Native girls at Montagne. Both Mance and Bourgeoys served as godmothers for many of the French infant girls of Ville-Marie.

French women also took part (and evidently took pleasure) in preparing the Native women at the Sillery réserve for the sacrament of matrimony. Many other French Catholic women shaped the colonial environment of New France by simply living their lives as devoted members of the Church. These women attended Mass, supported the Church materially and financially, sent their children to be educated by priests or sisters, joined religious confraternities, served as godmothers to each other's children, and sometimes took holy orders themselves. However, documentation of the lives of these women is sparse, particularly because contemporary records were most often kept by men, who were not interested in or privy to the details of women's lives.

Kinship: On Godmothering

The story of Catholic women in North America during the colonial period is not simply a tale of immigration and implantation of a French

Catholic culture. As has been illustrated, because of the Jesuit zeal for missions, which was foundational to the French colonial enterprise, many of the first Catholic women in New France were Native American converts.[4] Special attention has been given to Native Catholic women here, but not simply in a spirit of redress. Rather, an examination of the interactions between Catholic immigrant women and Catholic Native women is crucial to understanding the experiences of women in New France.

A greater understanding of these relationships can be achieved by recognizing that many of the women in New France were brought together sacramentally by means of the godmother/goddaughter relationship. Although the godparent/godchild paradigm is certainly reflective of colonialism's paternalistic understanding of Native and African people, godmother/goddaughter roles served as a means through which women of disparate cultures were brought into familial relation. As in France, the godparent/godchild relationship was taken seriously. Goddaughters were regularly named after their godmothers, and godparents had definite responsibilities. Godparents were charged with the moral and spiritual guidance of the godchild and were expected to raise the child should the child become orphaned. Godparents also provided a route of appeal and a source of refuge for the child should the parents prove unable to carry out their parental duties. In many cases during the early colonial period, the primary means of establishing intercultural relationships between women was religiously motivated and sacramentally mediated. With the passage of time, with the growth of the European-descended population, and with the introduction of slavery, the relation between godmother and goddaughter diminished in its potential to serve as an intercultural mediator. By the end of the colonial period, godmothers were most often family members or close friends of the same cultural background.

---

4. Unfortunately, many general histories of Catholics in North America in the colonial period tend to overlook or to minimize this important fact. One notable exception to this lack of attentiveness to Catholic Native people is Jay P. Dolan's *The American Catholic Experience: A History from Colonial Times to the Present* (1985).

In the case of immigrant Catholics, we do know that one of the primary relationships in New France was that of *premier voisin*, or "nearest neighbor." In the new environment, immigrants relied upon their neighbors in time of hardship and shared with them in time of abundance. When families grew, baptisms of children were, whenever possible, celebrated in the presence of neighbors and friends. While godparents of children were sometimes relatives of the parents, many new colonists did not have a pool of relatives from which to draw; in these cases, neighbors and friends (sometimes shipboard friends made during voyages of immigration) were selected. In choosing nonrelations as godparents, mothers forged sustained familial relationships between their daughters and their women friends and neighbors, ensuring a continuity between families into the next generation.

The Harvest: The Héberts as Ancestors

Marie Hébert died in 1649 and was buried near her home in Quebec (*DCB* 1966, 1:578). She was survived by her daughter Guillemette and by ten grandchildren. "[B]ecause of the numerous descendants of these children Couillard appears in the genealogy of almost all the old French-Canadian families" (*DCB* 1966, 1:236), including that of Abbé Couillard-Després, the primary organizer and recorder of the tercentenary celebration of Louis Hébert and Marie Rollet Hébert's arrival in New France.

Interestingly, the descendants of the Hébert-Couillard family also include in their ancestries the interpreters Olivier LeTardif and Jean Nicollet. In 1637 Nicollet married Guillemette Couillard's twelve-year-old daughter Marguerite, and a few weeks later LeTardif married her thirteen-year-old daughter Louise. LeTardif, in the employ of the trading companies since at least 1621, rose in prominence during his career. He had acted on behalf of Pontgravé in handing the keys to the habitation at Quebec to the Kirkes. Next he worked as an assistant clerk for de Caën, and later as head clerk for the Compagnie de Cent-Associés. The *Dictionary of Canadian Biography* reveals that he was a supporter of Jesuit missions, a godfather to baptized Natives many times over, and the adoptive father of at least one Native child. In 1644 this child, Marie Manitouabeouich, was the bride in the first Church-sanctioned Native/French marriage in New France. The marriage was performed by Jesuit Father Barthélemy Vimont, who had come to New France on the same ship as Marie Guyart and Madame de la Peltrie.

Originally a translator for the Compagnie des Marchands de Rouen et de St. Malo, Jean Nicollet was first sent by Champlain to various Algonquian-speaking groups along the Ottawa River. His service on Allumette Island drew him into kinship relationships with the Kichispirini nation led by Tessouat. He became a respected member of the nation, even participating in diplomatic councils and peace treaty negotiation. He also lived for nine years among the Nippising nation, during which time he fathered a child with a Native woman. He spent the English occupation years among the Wendat. When the French returned to power in New France, he became a clerk for the Compagnie de Cent-Associés in Trois-Rivières, married Marguerite Couillard, and with her raised two more children.

Much of the information in the *Dictionary of Canadian Biography* (DCB) has been gleaned from genealogists. The research done by French-Canadians interested in their ancestral ties to the first colonists of New France has made more accessible much of the information about relationships between French and Native peoples in the early decades of colonization. Every such genealogist is aware of the flawed but invaluable work of Abbé Cyprien Tanguay, the author of the seven-volume *Dictionnaire généalogique des familles canadiennes françaises depuis les origines de la colonie jusqu'à nos jours* (1871–1890). *Mémoires*, a quarterly publication of the SGCF (Société généalogique canadienne-française) is also liberally cited as a source in the *DCB*.

One descendant of the Hébert-Couillard family, Abbé Couillard Després, was the primary organizer and recorder of the tercentenary commemoration of the 1617 arrival of the Héberts in New France. This festival was a site wherein Francophone Canadians could celebrate—and romanticize—their heritage. In reading the documents produced in regard to this festival, it becomes quite clear that Louis

Hébert and his wife, Marie Rollet Hébert, were being held up as the mythic ancestors of the French-Canadian community in Canada. In the published records of this festival, the Hébert family was referred to as the first colonists and founding family of Quebec, and Francophone Canadians identified and described themselves as the descendants of these pioneer farmers.

In the preface to the official commemorative volume of this celebration, Abbé Azarie Couillard-Després, the noted author of *Louis Hebert: Premier colon canadien et sa famille* (1918), exhorted all descendants of "these pioneers" to remember that colonization and agriculture have been and continue to be the two main sources of the vitality of the (French-Canadian) race, and the primary basis of French-Canadian *survivance* (Couillard-Després 1920, 2). Collected in this volume are speeches, essays, poems, and letters from community, political, and religious leaders in praise of the Hébert family, most of which were contributed and/or recited on the occasion of the dedication of the bronze sculptures of Louis Hébert, Marie Rollet Hébert, and their son-in-law Guillaume Couillard, erected in Montmorency Park in Quebec City.

In the decades after the Riel rebellions in 1869 and 1885,[5] French-Canadian clergy, politicians, historians, writers, and poets were engaged, admittedly in various and sometimes polarized ways, in promoting a romanticized nationalistic mythology of the colonization of New France. From Benjamin Sulte to Louis Fréchette, from Jules-Paul Tardivel to Henri Bourassa, from Abbé J. G. A. D'Amours to Abbé Lionel Groulx, French Canadians were responding to a perceived crisis of culture, predicated in part upon the Canadian attacks on French and denominational schools in 1905 and 1912. Language, culture, and religion were, to Groulx and his compatriots, the keys to restoring (or constructing) a heroic sense of French-Canadian identity and to maintaining an impassioned opposition to an imposed British/English Canadian imperialism.

---

5. See Reid 2008.

In the past, historians of French-Canadian culture employed the term *survivance* to convey the sense of passionate mission that has characterized French-Canadian efforts toward cultural preservation in the face of British-Canadian cultural dominance. This term was used to signify "the three-fold concept of preservation of religion, language, and customs" that obtained over centuries of French-Canadian presence in the Americas (Wade 1981, 3:25). The term *survivance*, defined as the French-Canadian immigrant struggle toward preservation of religion, language, and customs, especially in the face of Anglophone, Protestant, and other post-Confederation Canadian forces, became an interpretive lens that simultaneously described, justified, and romanticized that struggle. While contemporary scholars of French-Canadian history have certainly acknowledged the ideological nature of survivance, the interplay between French Canadian religious history and the continuing desire to maintain a Francophone identity must also be recognized.

In the nineteenth century, French-Canadians often perceived the establishment and success of institutions of survivance as contingent upon clerical blessings, both religious and financial. At that time (as well as in the present), survivance also depended directly upon a mythologized understanding of the establishment and continuity of French-Canadian families and kinship networks. The erection of a monument to the Hébert family can serve, then, as a particularly salient locus in which to observe the interpretive frame of survivance and to witness the operations of the myths and symbols upon which this ideology is based.

Alfred Laliberté, the creator of the memorial to Louis Hébert, Marie Rollet Hébert, and Guillaume Couillard, known as "the Sculptor of the Rural Tradition," was a noted proponent of survivance. Born in Ste-Élisabeth-de-Warwick, Quebec, he studied in Montréal at La Société des Arts and at Le Conseil des Arts et Manufactures. In 1902 he traveled to Paris to study at L'École des Beaux-arts, and was profoundly influenced by the work of Rodin. Upon his return to Canada, he taught at his former school, Le Conseil des Arts, and during his career he enjoyed a number of commissions to create public statuary, including monuments to Sir Wilfrid Laurier, to Dollard des Ormeaux, and, of course, to the Hébert-Couillard family. His most famous works were smaller bronze sculptures in a series of more than two hundred pieces that he collectively named *Legends, Metiers et Coutumes*. These pieces represent men and women engaged in the various types of work carried out in the context of a rural Quebec community.

Literatures of all types were produced in service of survivance, and the tercentenary celebration of the immigration of the Hébert family was a perfect occasion for the florid expression of sentiments of this sort. The poems in praise of Marie Rollet Hébert epitomize these literatures and are provided in appendix 3.

Symbol: The Godmother of New France

At the center of Marc Lescarbot's last Relation from New France in 1612 is a list of prominent French persons, presumably potential donors to the missions of New France, who had been named as godparents to baptized Native boys and girls, men and women (Thwaites 1896–1901, 2:155–61). In this text Lescarbot reported that the secular priest Jessé Fléché had baptized 140 (mostly Mi'kmaq) Natives since his arrival in 1610. The list of absentee godparents includes seventy-three men, including the Prince de Condé, the Count de Soissons, the Duke de Nevers, and the Duke de Guise, as well as Fléché's three brothers, Jean, Mathieu, and Gregoire. In addition, one Monsieur Bertrand, described as "present and assisting in these baptisms," is named, and perhaps surprisingly, so is Father Fléché himself. Also included are the Bishop of Paris, the Bishop of Boulogne, the Bishop of Troyes, and the Abbé of Clervaux. (Thwaites 1896–1901, 2:155–59). The list of thirty-five women includes the Princess de Condé, the Countess de Soissons, the Duchess of Nevers, Madame de Guise, and Fléché's mother, sister, and three sisters-in-law (Thwaites 1896–1901, 2:159–61). The list gives the impression that Fléché provided godchildren to absolutely everyone of his acquaintance, but the fact that no women religious were included raises the possibility that Fléché was either unacquainted with many sisters or was unaware of their potential as financial (and spiritual) supporters of missions. However, the list also demonstrates Father Fléché's intention to tie all of these French people in some tangible way to the Native inhabitants of the land in which he labored. Despite the criticisms later levied against him by the Jesuits, Fléché's baptismal zeal, which does indeed seem to have been practiced without attention to proper proselytization, was a first step toward establishing fictive kinship relationships between French and Native persons. Admittedly, these initial godparenting relationships could not be realized in person. It would take a few more years for godparenting to be properly practiced by French persons actually present in the colony. However, Fléché did seem to understand that any mission would need to be grounded in and supported by a sense of relationship between potential sources of financial and religious support and those toward whom the mission was directed.

Through the religious role of godmother, the first and perhaps the most enduring familial relationships between Native people and French women were forged. The relationship between godparent and godchild seems to have functioned relatively well in New France, and appears to have been integrated easily by Native converts. This is likely because, as we have seen, many Eastern Woodlands Native cultures (including Innu and Wendat) themselves sealed alliances and created trading relationships through the exchange of gifts and the celebration of banquets, which then resulted in the establishment of kinship bonds. However, as the case of Olivier LeJeune so vividly illustrates, these familial ties did not necessarily ameliorate what would become the racial hierarchy underpinning and justifying slavery.

Nevertheless, the institution of godmothering was one critical means through which the inhabitants of New France negotiated the demands and crises of an early modern colonial context. Godmothering enabled French colonists to expand their fictive kinship networks across cultures. Godmothering enabled Natives to maintain one traditional modality of establishing alliance. Just as Marie Rollet Hébert passed her children through the hatchway to be bathed in the protection of Father LeCaron's blessing, the children of New France were placed in a site of sacred power during the sacrament of baptism.

Theologically, baptism did not merely make a person a Christian; it actually protected a person from being consigned to hell upon death—at least in the absence of the commission of a mortal sin after the performance of the sacrament of baptism and prior to the performance of the sacrament of penance. Socially, this ritual functioned to create relationships between unrelated persons, to expand the network of family to include the person being baptized. Important responsibilities were conferred upon the godparents as they were placed into relationship with the baptized person. In this ritual, the identities of the godparents and godchild were made public, and the duties of the godparents in regard to the spiritual well-being of their godchild were articulated.

Like the Native rituals of captive adoption, baptismal rituals conferred new identities and formally established new relationships. However, although baptism sacralized these relationships, these relationships were not egalitarian. Like parent/child relationships, godparent/godchild relationships are hierarchical. In fact, it is perhaps most accurate to interpret these godparenting relationships as continuous with all of the wrenching dislocations and coercive relocations of Native people that marked the early missionary and colonial period in New France: kin exchanges in which people are exchanged for empty gifts, baptismal rolls lengthened by the addition of the new names of the deceived and of the dying, artificial réserves populated by distressed, hungry, and bereaved people whose traditional ways of life had been irremediably disrupted. In fact, the displacements and dislocations of Native people from their traditional kinship structures and the repeated attempts to integrate Native people into French kinship structures were the primary religious strategies of the Jesuit missionaries in New France. These religious strategies of social dislocation set in motion the first geographic dislocations of Native people and laid the groundwork for even more dislocations of Native people from their traditional lands. In this way, the new religious structures imposed by the French missionaries were crucial forerunners to the settler colonialist structures that would be introduced in later decades.

6

Conclusion

When the context of your existence is imprisonment and murder, disease and death, you must determine what is of value. When you cross borders, you must hold this valuable material close to you as you would carry on your person the precious items without which you would be lost. When human beings are exchanged in a colonial context, when indigenous "total systems" and European missionary and mercantilist systems mix, there is danger: how can a human being retain his or her value?

Marcel Mauss's work on gift and exchange in indigenous cultures (1967) illustrates the conceptualization of value in these societies. In indigenous cultures, gifts were not held to have exchange-value (as Marx described commodities in industrial societies), but to have intrinsic value, which remained within the gift throughout its course of exchanges. Mauss noted that gifts were not held as possessions or built up as capital. Rather, they were continually exchanged. And as gifts were exchanged, their histories remained with them; they were inalienable from their sites of origin. Exchanging true gifts, then, was an essential part of the orientation of these indigenous cultures, as the exchange was the act that established relationship between persons and groups. The exchange of gifts also produced one important surplus: the obligation of reciprocity. Those bound in relationship through the exchange of gifts were bound to remain in equilibrium, in a constantly renewed reciprocal exchange with one another.

The persons exchanged between Champlain's group of Frenchmen and Tregouaroti's group of People of the Peninsula were operating, in a general sense, within differing frameworks of exchange. This is not to say that Savignon was a pure gift and Brûlé was a pure commodity; although there is no evidence that Wendat men were moving toward the accumulation of wealth through trade route ownership at the early date of 1610, there was assuredly an awareness on the part of the Wendat that any persons exchanged could serve as excellent hostages should alliances go awry. However, there was a deep chasm between the French and Wendat orientations toward this exchange. In the process of producing a truchement, the human value of Brûlé became compromised. He was loosed from his context of origin, and because of the pressing needs of the French mercantile economy at that time, his value was determined according to what he could produce in the system of trade rather than according to his human networks of obligation. He became a site of contestation for both the French and for the Wendat confederacy, and his value was in dispute. Even in killing Brûlé, it does not seem that the Wendat ever denied his primary relational value. He was murdered precisely for neglecting to incarnate the singular relationship between the French and the Wendat. He was killed because he attempted to skirt reciprocal obligation, the central value of the kinship system into which he had been incorporated.

While Joseph Chihoatenhwa was not formally exchanged in any such ritual of alliance, he actively sought participation in a system of exchange that operated in opposition to the kinship system of his people. In affiliating with the Jesuits, in seeking out a nontraditional route to power, he appeared to some of his countrymen to be denying the value of his site of originary meaning. He was likely killed for acting in a manner that was perceived by many as treasonous, and as endangering others. In his pursuit of survival during a period of great crisis, and in his creation of innovative relationships with sacred power, he did, however, remain faithful to what he held to be of central value: the protection of his loved ones and his generations.

In the case of Thérèse Oionhaton, as with numerous unnamed but palpably present Native women, we have seen a number of differing articulations of value as these women negotiated dangerous cultural boundaries. Some women voiced their traditionalist loyalties by curtly dismissing Jesuit interference, by resisting Catholic doctrinal threats by telling one another their dreams, and by attempting to escape the coercion they found in the Jesuit-ruled mission villages like Sillery. Others traveled the routes to relationship with sacred power recommended by the Jesuits, but remained able to articulate and act upon their central values by affiliating themselves with networks of other women modeled upon traditional kinship structures. They resisted reification, even as the Jesuits inscribed their names on the baptismal rolls and totaled up the harvest of souls for that year's report.

The other newly emergent orientation here is that of modern subjectivities, which reside not in the commodifications of French economic activity, but in the exercises of power and the internalizations of discipline demonstrated by these "converts." The historical moment under study here predates Michel Foucault's classical period, but the technologies of power deployed by the actors in this context do indeed prefigure Foucauldian modern subjectivities. In the Jesuit Relations, we witness the movement from the public enactment of rituals of mortification, humiliation, and punishment to the privatization of bodily disciplines, as the women "converts" pass on technologies of power to one another. While the Jesuits are clearly moving toward the reform of the soul through the use of the disciplines, the "converts" appear to be acting, for the most part, to position the body as a gift through which one establishes relationship with sacred power. The Jesuits were aware of this positioning; they condoned public punishments for Native sinners, but tended to discourage private mortifications of the body when Native people practice these disciplines. The missionaries at Sillery saw the production of docile bodies as their purview. One should not belabor the Foucauldian implications of this colonial moment, but movement toward this particularly European instantiation of the modern can indeed be perceived in this colonial encounter.

The most salient way in which modern sensibilities emerged in this colonial context is in the extension of notions of collective identity on the part of Native peoples. Philip Deloria has observed that while European and Euro-American instantiations of the modern seem to revolve around the creation of a sense of individual identity, Native modes of modernity focus on the establishment of collective identities. The expansion of Native notions of kinship to include persons of multiple nations (through adoption, alliance, and condolence) is an excellent example of the emergence of a specifically Native construction of modernity. Again, as Deloria rightfully insists, Native agency and participation in the construction of modernity is critical here (Deloria 2004).

In a certain way, the Wendat were correct in accusing the Jesuits of inscribing them to death. Each name on a baptismal roll represented a transformation. This is not to say that traditionalism died with so-called conversion, but that religious creativity was marshalled in order to survive the onslaught of colonialist practices. There were various materially visible modes of transformation enacted by the human beings participating in these colonial encounters, including dislocation from traditional geographies and the establishment of new alliances. Most significantly, new kinship structures were formulated in order to articulate these new orientations. The colonial reorientations that took place included the articulation of value, a value that was often denied by those who inscribed and commodified human beings. The emergent orientations of the human beings involved in this negotiation of disjunctive structures and overlapping discourses were material and symbolic orientations that could protect and nourish the people who created them. As the material and symbolic effects of colonialism conspired to construct these people as having value only in certain respects, these emergent creative orientations allowed them to negotiate the new landscapes in which they found themselves. Of necessity, these new orientations remain opaque. However, disclosures of these orientations can be found even in the colonialist inscriptions.

Marie Rollet Hébert's experience is instructive. Her efforts to maintain and establish kinship bonds through godmothering did indeed make an impact upon New France. The religious institution of godmothering ramified throughout her extended family (including her daughter's "servant" Olivier LeJeune), and throughout the network of young Native women who were taken into her home while being catechized by the Jesuits. The Ursuline sisters later took up this task, but prior to their arrival in New France, Marie Hébert and Guillemette

Couillard's doorway was the entrance to a new and expansive cross-cultural familial structure.

An analogy may also be worth exploring. Laurier Turgeon has written eloquently on the varied meanings and uses of the copper kettle in New France (and in contemporary museum exhibitions). Copper kettles were important trade articles in the colonial period. Copper had always been valued by Native groups in the Americas, particularly because of its reddish color, which represented

> fertility and vitality . . . red was likewise the color of power . . . Copper of European origin, however, acquired statutory and symbolic functions beyond those of native copper during the prehistoric period. Amerindian groups assigned greater value to European copper, no doubt because of its intrinsic properties and its singularity. It came in the form of something virtually unreproducible (kettles); it was also vastly more abundant and more rigid. Its provenance apparently increased its representational power. (Turgeon 1997, 9–10)

Because of the power that resided in European copper, it was highly sought after as a trade item. When acquired, the kettles were often transformed from their original shapes into "bracelets, rings, pendants, and earrings . . . These reworked kettle fragments were worn in battle or on diplomatic missions, for holidays or for funeral rites" (Turgeon 1997, 10). However, when the kettles remained in their original state, they were not used for everyday cooking, but in ritual. The Feast of the Dead was so named by the French; the Wendat referred to the ritual as "The Kettle," and an actual grouping of kettles was its focal point. In Brebeuf's famous description of the ritual, he reported that "[t]he Feast of the Dead is hardly mentioned, even in the most important councils, except under the name of 'the kettle.' They appropriate to it all the terms of cookery, so that, in speaking of hastening or of putting off the Feast of the Dead, they will speak of scattering or of stirring up the fire beneath the kettle; and employing this way of speaking, one who should say 'the kettle is overturned,' would mean that there would be no feast of the Dead" (Thwaites 1896–1901, 10:279).

The use of kettles also predominated in the ritual itself. Not only were kettles hung all about to ornament the scaffolding surrounding the central pit of the reburial, but in the center of the pit itself were three copper kettles, "which could only be of use for souls; one had a hole through it, another had no handle, and the third was of scarcely more value" (Thwaites 1896–1901, 10:297). In other words, the kettles were for use in the afterworld; therefore they were marked as such. "No longer operative . . . they could be of service only to the souls in the great beyond; they . . . became sacrificial offerings" (Turgeon 1997, 15).

Kettles functioned on several levels. First, the kettle in its everyday use was the object around which families and villages gathered for nourishment or for celebration and feasting. The hospitality of the kettle was the first and most inviolable mode of treatment of any person arriving peacefully in a strange village. Kettles transformed into body ornaments symbolized power. In the Feast of the Dead, the kettle symbolized the ingathering of kin, the unification of multiple clans, villages, nations, and allies. "The community was reconstituted in the reunited bones of its ancestors and even in those of outsiders in common ground, and its own identity reaffirmed" (Turgeon 1997, 16). While the last traditional Feast of the Dead was celebrated by Wendat and Ottawa people in 1695 (Trigger 1990, 131), a final Feast of the Dead was performed in 1999. On that solemn occasion, the remains of hundreds of Wendat people whose bones had been kept in the Royal Ontario Museum were returned to the site of the 1636 Feast of the Dead from which they had been excavated by archaeologists fifty years before. Three hundred boxes of Wendat bones were blessed by Madeleine Gros-Louis, the eldest Wendat woman present, as the remains of their ancestors were returned to the earth. Among the bones were also copper kettles (Seeman 2011, 142–44).

The kettle's multiple valences, as sign, as metaphor, as sacred object, and even as commodity, can provide some insight into the persons whose lives were transformed by the colonization and missionization of New France as well. It is not insignificant that Étienne Brûlé was excluded from "the kettle." His treason precluded his incorporation into the socio-religious body of the Wendat. It may aid in the understanding of Joseph Chihoatenhwa if, for a moment, one likens the source of the power he sought to a kettle. Instead of appropriating the powerful object and then turning it to his own ends, as did many Wendat who appropriated elements of baptism into recently dreamed curative rites or into the ritual torture of priests, Joseph brought himself into proximity with the sacred power of the Jesuits and was transformed thereby. Unfortunately, his inversion of appropriation was likely equated with treason by his own people. The women of the Wendat diaspora, like Thérèse Oionhaton, as well as women of other nations, created and recreated communities, as did the kettles in the Feast of the Dead. Marie Hébert provided hospitality and sustenance to men and women, to French and Native people, but because she and her husband received the gift of an enslaved human being, at least one young African man did not always have an equal seat at her table. And it is this legacy of inegalitarianism, of "not-quite-the-same-value," that she and her daughter Guillemette Couillard passed on to the generations. Soon enough, the structure of settler colonialism would amplify and codify the racial hierarchies and land dispossessions that began during this early missionary colonial period.

We surely cannot romanticize these men and women from our shared historical past, but one lesson abides. The successful negotiation of the modern world requires a willingness to create and maintain lasting relationships that extend across cultural borders. It also requires a demonstration of respect for the inherent value of others. The lives of Étienne Brûlé, Joseph Chihoatenhwa, Thérèse Oionhaton, and Marie Rollet Hébert can provide models for us to ponder as we attempt to develop our own strategies. The fate of Étienne Brûlé certainly demonstrates that it is at our own peril that we fail to do so.

Appendixes

References

Index

Appendix I

Kin Replacement in the Jesuit Relations

When a person was taken captive by members of the Wendat confederacy, that person was intended as a replacement for a particular absent (deceased or captured) member of a particular kin group, or as a trophy capture for a particular warrior. The *Jesuit Relations* provides ample documentation of the ritual nature of the adoption/torture of captives. Two especially illustrative excerpts from the *Jesuit Relations* are included here.

> 1. As soon as they have taken a prisoner, they cut off his fingers; they tear his shoulders and his back with a knife; they bind him with very tight bonds, and lead him,—singing, and mocking at him with all the contempt imaginable. Having arrived at their village, they have him adopted by some one of those who have lost their son in the war. This feigned parent is charged with caressing the prisoner. You will see him come with a necklace in the form of hot iron and say to him: "See here, my son; you love, I am sure, to be adorned, to appear beautiful." While thus deriding him, he begins to torment him from the sole of the feet even to the crown of the head with firebrands, with hot cinders,—piercing his feet and his hands with reeds or with sharp irons. (Thwaites 1896–1901, 18:31)

> 2. It is customary when some notable personage has lost one of his relatives in war, to give him a present of some captive taken from the enemy, to dry his tears and partly assuage his grief. Now the one who had been destined for this place was brought by the Captain Enditsacone to the village of Onnentisati, where the war chiefs held a Council and decided that this prisoner should be given to

Saouandaouascouay, who is one of the chief men of the country, in consideration of one of his nephews who had been captured by the Iroquois. This decision being made, he was taken to Arontaen . . . He was dressed in a beautiful beaver robe and wore a string of porcelain beads around his neck, and another in the form of a crown around his head . . . Meanwhile, they brought him food, from all sides,—some bringing sagamité, some squashes and fruits,—and treated him only as a brother and a friend . . . Meanwhile, a Captain, raising his voice to the same tone used by those who make some proclamation in the public places in France, addressed to him these words: "My nephew, thou hast good reason to sing, for no one is doing thee any harm; behold thyself now among thy kindred and friends." . . . [But the prisoner had sustained serious wounds during his capture which became infected, and instead of adoption, Saouandaouascouay decided to torture his adopted nephew to death.] This is a summary of the talk he had with him: "My nephew, thou must know that when I first received news that thou wert at my disposal, I was wonderfully pleased, fancying that he whom I had lost in war had been, as it were, brought back to life, and was returning to his country. At the same time I resolved to give thee thy life; I was already thinking of preparing a place for thee in my cabin, and thought that thou wouldst pass the rest of thy days pleasantly with me. But now that I see thee in this condition, thy fingers gone and thy hands half rotten, I change my mind, and I am sure that thou thyself wouldst now regret to live longer. I shall do thee a greater kindness to tell thee that thou must prepare to die, is it not so? Come then, my nephew, be of good courage, prepare thyself for this evening, and do not allow thyself to be cast down through fear of tortures." . . . While the Captain was conversing with him, a woman, the sister of the deceased, brought him some food, showing remarkable solicitude for him. You would almost have said that he was her own son, and I do not know that this creature did not represent to her him whom she had lost . . . Towards 8 o'clock in the evening . . . the people gathered immediately . . . Cries of joy resounded on all sides; each provided himself, one with a firebrand, another with a piece of bark, to burn the victim . . . [A]nger and rage did not appear on the faces of those who were tormenting him, but rather gentleness and humanity, their words expressing only raillery or tokens of friendship or good will . . . This one said to him, "Here, uncle, I must burn thee"; Another one asked him, "Come, uncle, where do you prefer that I should burn you?" . . ."Ah, it is not right," said one, "that my uncle should be cold; I must warm thee." Another one added, "Now as my uncle has kindly deigned to come and die among the Hurons, I must make him a present, I must give him a hatchet," and with that he jeeringly applied to his feet a red-hot hatchet. (Thwaites 1896–1901, 13:37–69)

Appendix 2

*John Steckley's Translation
of Joseph Chihoatenhwa's Prayer*

You who are master, God, behold now I know you. It is fortunate that now I know you. You are the one who skillfully made this earth and this sky. You are the one who made we who are called human beings.

Just as we are the masters of the canoes and the longhouses we have made, so you are our master because you made us. It is a matter of little importance that we are the masters of all that we possess as it is for a short time only that we are the masters of the canoes and the longhouses that we have made. It is for a short time that we are masters. As for you, you have become the permanent master of we who are called human beings. While it would not be a trifling matter that you are master when we are still living, it is principally at the moment that we die that you are master.

You alone are master; no one shares the position with you. You are the one we should greatly fear. You are the one we should greatly love. It is very true that human beings and spirits are not really powerful. Not only do spirits lack power, but they do not love us.

I now give special thanks that you willed that I should acquire knowledge of you; for you greatly love us.

Behold, I am now offering myself to you; I who am located here. Behold, I now choose you for my master. You are the principal master of I who am located here. Use your wisdom when you are thinking about I who am located here.

You have all of us in my family within your sphere of influence. If I am not present when something happens to my family, I will think that he who most assuredly has us within his sphere of influence is watching. As for me, I am not of such a stature. It will be of little import if I am present, as my family will die even if I am there.

Behold, I now express great thanks. Behold, I now know your plans. I should not think: 'what if something happens to my family?' I will think that God who loves us will reflect on the matter. And if he wills that my family should become poor, I will think: 'It is the will of God who loves us.'

And if my soul wishes to become rich, I will think that he does not think of God. I will greatly fear this and take care as to how I live. For it is easy for one who is rich to be one who offends, as, unknown to him, he is accompanied by a bad spirit.

Alas, those people who are rich brag in vain. For, either rich or poor, we do not surpass one another. You love us equally; both those who are rich and those who are poor.

Fortunately, I now know your intentions; you, God, who loves us. I express great thanks. I completely abandon myself to you, I who am located here. Behold, as we now cast away from us all kinds of things that we value while we are still living. Behold, they are no longer valued. Just you alone are valued. Apply your wisdom, great master, with respect to I who am located here.

It alone would have been providential if you had merely wished that human beings should come into being. Nevertheless, one should express thanks as there is good reason to rejoice here on earth in the many things that you have given us. You have greatly favored us by willing that people should go to the sky when they die, and that they should live forever.

I should not examine it for faults as things are quite perfect in the sky. I would have overestimated my ability if I thought that I could examine it, for I am not of such a stature. It is providential in itself that I am familiar with your word. Behold, I now believe that it is true. I do not doubt it as you do not lie. You speak only the truth, whatever you say.

You said that you will not refuse me anything in heaven as nothing is difficult for you. You love us. Your word is the subject of my prayer.

Truly, it is likely that we might suffer while we are living. There will be great cause for our rejoicing in the sky, and people will no longer cling tenaciously to life when they are sick. It is no longer a difficult thing to die. It is in vain that we fear to die while we are living. We are foolish. For at the moment of death, when one goes to heaven, one should be very happy.

It is like it is with those who go to trade. They suffer, those who go to trade. It is of little significance, however, that one expresses satisfaction when returning home and thinks: 'We are now returning home and are at the end of our suffering.' For it is only when one is at the point of dying that one should think: 'Now I will be at the end of my suffering.'

These are my thoughts, God, the master. I now no longer fear death. I will express satisfaction when I am at the point of death. I will not suffer or be sad when relatives of mine die. I will think that God deliberated on it and willed that he loves them very much, for he willed that people would depart for a place where they will be very happy. (Steckley 1981)

Appendix 3

Poems to Marie Rollet Hébert

Recited upon the tercentenary celebration in 1917.

A Marie Rollet

A l'épouse héroique et vaillant de Louis Hébert

Vaillance des coeurs maternels,
Vertus profondes et sublimes,
Toutes vos gloires anonymes
Remplissent ces jours solennels!

De la pénombre séculaire
Où dormait votre souvenir
Un jour vous deviez revenir
Et c'est ce jour qui nous éclaire.

Car c'est la fête des mamans,
De nos grand'mères bisaïeules
Et qui, dans nos memoires seules,
Avaient leurs dignes monuments.

Notre piéte filial
En cette fête a réuni
Tout un heritage béni
De gratitude cordiale.

Et, vers toi nous avons tendu
Nos mains franches et bénisseuses,
O mère des mamans heureuses
De qui nous sommes descendus.

Source féconde d'une race,
Epouse du "premier semeur"
Vois, comme une garde d'honneur
Ta grade famille qui passe . . .

Ce sont tes filles et tes fils
Qui sont groupés près de ce temple,
Tressaillant au sublime exemple
Des sacrifices que tu fis.

Ils ont grave dans leur memoire
Le cult ardent de piété
Que tu dictais avec bonté
Aux devanciers de notre histoire.

Ils savent les jours de douleur
Où tu laissas ta chère France
Pour te vouer à la sufferance
De l'exil ténébreux du coeur.

Compagne des jours solitaires,
Combien de fois sur le Rocher
Qu'il travaillait à défricher,
Tu suivis ce "faiseur de terre!"

Combien de fois, le long des nuits,
Où grondait l'inconnu sauvage,
Tu vins l'attendre sur la plage
En disant aux flots tes ennuis!

Ton âme généreuse et forte
S'etait donnée à ce héros

Et, pour adoucir ses travaux,
Tu sus les mots qui réconfortant.

Malgré l'hostilité des temps,
Malgré la distance et les genes,
Les pauvres enfants indigenes
Sous ta chaumière étaient contents.

Tu leur apprenais à connaître
La bonté puissante de Dieu,
Dans l'eau, dans la terre et le feu
Qui servent l'homme comme un maître.

Tu leur disais l'affection
Qui doit unir dans la concorde,
La chrétienne miséricorde
Et la sainte Rédemption.

Ils t'écoutaient. Leur âme fruste
Et ténébreuse, sous l'éclat
De ton suave apostolate,
Se redressait fière et robuste.

Ils étaient beaux dans leur fierté.
Et dans leur droiture touchante
Tu voyais l'aurore naissante
D'une utile fraternité.

Or, tes pieux enfants eux-mêmes,
Héritiers de ton dévouement
Ont conserve fidèlement
Tes leçons graves et suprêmes.

C'est pourquoi celles que tu vois,
Nos mères, nos soeurs, nos épouses
Restent les gardiennes jalousies
Des traditions d'autrefois.

Pour nous léguer, toujours fidèles,
L'heritage de tes vertus,
Dans les chemins par toi battus
Elles ont marché devant ells.

Elles on partagé le faix
Des nobles peines journalières,
Sachant bien qu'aux heures dernières
Leurs fils moissonneraient la paix.

Or, en évoquant la mémoire
Du Père des premiers colons,
C'est aussi toi que nous voulons
Couronner de la même gloire.

—Alphonse Desilets

Stances a Marie Rollet

Noble et vaillante était cette femme française
Digne épouse d'Hébert, défricheur et colon;
Pour elle, en sa maison, au bord de la falaise,
Loin de France, combine le triste hiver fut long!

La solitude planait sur cette colonie.
A la plainte des bois effrayant l'avenir,
Se mêlaient, on eût cru, les appels d'un genie
Qui disait: "Pleur un peu, je suis le souvenir."

Et Marie enseignait aux enfants la prière,
Devant l'âtre, le soir, pour couronner le jour.
Son âme s'éclairait à la douce lumière
D'un profound dévoument et de son grand amour:
Amour du Dieu regnant, dévoûment de la femme
Qui brave la tempête et traverse les mers,
Dans un nouveau pays où l'on sème son âme,
En dépit des frimas et des grands vents amers.

Loin du pays de France, au milieu des sauvages,
Elle bravait l'ennui qui sortait des grands bois,
Parfois elle tournait son regard vers la plage
D'où montait, sans répit, et des pleurs et des voix.

Des loups hurlaient là-bas, ces chasseurs d'esperance,
Quand elle bénissait le bon Dieu pour son pain;
Son âme s'attristait en rêvant de la France,
Et la brise chantait dans l'ombre des sapins.

On avait tout quitté sur la terre natale
Qu'elle ne verrait plus qu'en des songes, la nuit:
Pendant que le hibou passait dans les rafales,
Et pendant que Kébec s'enveloppait d'ennui.

Et le soir, près de l'âtre, on causait en famille.
On parlait de Dieppe et de tous les amis,
Et de toute la France, et la petite fille
Disait à sa maman: "C'est donc bien loin Paris?

S'en viendront-ils un jouir, en mon oncle et ma tante?
Et Claude de Latour, l'abbé Jessé Fleché?
Pourquoi nous laissent-ils si longtemps dans l'attente?
Ne nous aiment-ils plus? Nous ont-ils bien cherchés?"

Et la lune filtrait dans la rafale blanche.
La famille dormait, et tout semblait mourir;
Les hiboux hululaient tristement dans les branches,
Madame Hébert priait avant de s'endormir.

Le jour clair ramenait la gaieté dans son âme.
Elle enseignait à lire aux enfants des Hurons . . .
Comme elle, aimons le bien, et gardons notre flamme,
L'amour de notre sol par lequel nos vivrons!

La patrie est le fruit de nos âmes qui s'aiment:
L'amour est sacrifice, il compte en tous les temps,

Et l'épouse d'Hébert, par ses veilles suprêmes,
Rattache son hiver aux feux de nos printemps!

Marie Rollet aima Québec même aux jours sombres:
Elle lutta pour nous jusqu'au bord du tombeau;
L'avenir la grandit; elle sort de son ombre
Apportons-lui des fleurs; son souvenir est beau;

O femme qui luttez et souffrez dans la vie
Rappelez-vous souvent les mères d'autrefois.
Sachez qu'il faur des pleurs pour faire une patrie! . . .
Ecoutez dans le soir, vous entendrez des voix!

Voix des fils qui s'en vont loin du regard des mères,
Voix des soldats tombés aux rafales de mort.
La vie est un grand deuil, la vie est une guerre.
Le sacrifice est tout, et Dieu compte l'effort!

Mais votre coeur qui saigne entrera dans l'Histoire
S'il répand son amour pour la cause du bien.
L'effort ne sera pas plus grand que la victoire . . .
J'entends des cris monter de ce sol canadien!

O morts, vous qui dormez dans vos tombes de planches,
Est-ce vous qui rêvez de voir vos fils grandir?
Français, nous vous aidons à recueillir les branches,
Les rameaux éternels, qui pour tous vont reverdir!

—Louis-Joseph Doucet
(Couillard-Desprès 1920, 124–28)

References

Anderson, Emma. 2007. *The Betrayal of Faith: The Tragic Journey of a Colonial Native Convert*. Cambridge, MA: Harvard Univ. Press.

Aristotle. *Rhetoric*, Book 1, Part 2. Translated by W. Rhys Roberts. http://classics.mit.edu/Aristotle/rhetoric.1.i.html

Axtell, James. 1990. *After Columbus: Essays in the Ethnohistory of North America*. New York: Oxford Univ. Press.

Barker, Adam J. 2010. "From Adversaries to Allies: Forging Respectful Alliances between Indigenous and Settler Peoples." In *Alliances: Re/Envisioning Indigenous—non-Indigenous Relationships*, edited by Lynne Davis. Toronto: Univ. of Toronto Press.

Bishop, Morris. 1948. *Champlain: The Life of Fortitude*. New York: Alfred A. Knopf.

Blackburn, Carole. 2000. *Harvest of Souls: The Jesuit Missions and Colonialism in North America, 1632–1650*. Montreal: McGill-Queen's Univ. Press.

Byrd, Jodi A. 2011. *The Transit of Empire: Indigenous Critiques of Colonialism*. First Peoples: New Directions in Indigenous Studies. Minneapolis: Univ. of Minnesota Press.

Campeau, Lucien. 1987. *Fondation de la Mission Huronne (1635–1637)*. Monumenta Novae Franciae 3. Quebec: Les Presses de l'Université Laval.

———. 1989. *Les Grandes Épreuves (1638–1640)*. Monumenta Novae Franciae 4. Montreal: Les Éditions Bellarmin.

———. 1990. *La Bonne Nouvelle Reçue (1641–1643)*. Monumenta Novae Franciae 5. Montreal: Les Éditions Bellarmin.

———. 1992. *Recherche de la Paix (1644–1646)*. Monumenta Novae Franciae 6. Montreal: Les Éditions Bellarmin.

Cervantes, Fernando. 1994. *The Devil in the New World: The Impact of Diabolism in New Spain*. New Haven: Yale Univ. Press.

Cesareo, Francesco C. 1993. "Quest for Identity: The Ideals of Jesuit Education in the Sixteenth Century." In *The Jesuit Tradition in Education and Missions: A 450-Year Perspective*, edited by Christopher Chapple. London: Associated Univ. Presses.

Champlain, Samuel de. 1971. *The Works of Samuel de Champlain*. 6 vols. General editor H. P. Biggar. Publications of the Champlain Society, Extra Series (1922–36). Reprinted facsimile. Toronto: Univ. of Toronto Press.

[Cicero, Marcus Tullius.] 1954. *Ad C. Herennium de ratione dicendi (Rhetorica Ad Herennium)*. Translated by Harry Caplan. Cambridge, MA: Harvard Univ. Press. http://penelope.uchicago.edu/Thayer/E/Roman/Texts/Rhetorica_ad_Herennium/1*.html.

———. 1960. *De Inventione. Topica*. Translated by H. M. Hubbell. Cambridge, MA: Harvard Univ. Press. https://www.loebclassics.com/view/marcus_tullius_cicero-de_inventione/1949/pb_LCL386.15.xml.

Couillard-Després, Azarie. 1918. *Louis Hebert: Premier colon canadien et sa famille*. Montreal: L'Institution des Sourds-Muets.

———. 1920. *Rapport des fêtes du IIIe centenaire de l'arrivée de Louis Hébert au Canada, 1617, 1917*. Montreal: Imprimerie de la Salle.

Cranston, J. Herbert. 1949. *Étienne Brûlé: Immortal Scoundrel*. Toronto: Ryerson Press.

DCB (Dictionary of Canadian Biography). 1966. Vol. 1, *1000–1700*. Edited by George W. Brown, Marcel Trudel, and André Vachon. Toronto: Univ. of Toronto Press and Les Presses de l'Université Laval.

Delage, Denys. 1993. *Bitter Feast: Amerindians and Europeans in Northeastern North America, 1600–1664*. Vancouver: Univ. of British Columbia Press.

Deloria, Philip J. 2004. *Indians in Unexpected Places*. Lawrence: Univ. Press of Kansas.

Devens, Carol. 1992. *Countering Colonization: Native American Women and Great Lakes Missions, 1630–1900*. Berkeley: Univ. of California Press.

Dickason, Olive. 1984. *The Myth of the Savage and the Beginnings of French Colonialism in the Americas*. Edmonton: Univ. of Alberta Press.

Dolan, Jay P. 1985. *The American Catholic Experience: A History from Colonial Times to the Present*. Garden City, NY: Doubleday and Co.

Donnelly, Joseph P. 1967. *Thwaites' Jesuit Relations: Errata and Addenda*. Chicago: Loyola Univ. Press.

Eccles, William J. 1998. *The French in North America, 1500–1783*. Rev. ed. East Lansing: Michigan State Univ. Press.

Farrell, Allan P. 1938. *The Jesuit Code of Liberal Education: Development and Scope of the Ratio Studiorum*. Milwaukee, WI: Bruce Publishing Co.

Fischer, David Hackett. 2008. *Champlain's Dream*. New York: Simon and Schuster.

Fitzpatrick, Edward A., Mary Helen Mayer, and Asher Raymond Ball. 1933. *St. Ignatius and the Ratio Studiorum*. New York: McGraw-Hill.

Foucault, Michel. 1995. *Discipline and Punish: The Birth of the Prison*. Translated by Allen Sheridan. New York: Vintage Books.

Greenblatt, Stephen Jay. 1990. *Learning to Curse: Essays in Early Modern Culture*. New York: Routledge.

Greer, Allan. 2000. "Colonial Saints: Gender, Race and Hagiography in New France." *William and Mary Quarterly* 3 (57): 323–48.

———. 2003. "Conversion and Identity: Iroquois Christianity in Seventeenth-Century New France." In *Conversions: Old Worlds and New*, edited by A. Grafton and K. Mills. Rochester, NY: Univ. of Rochester Press.

———. 2005. *Mohawk Saint: Catherine Tekakwitha and the Jesuits*. New York: Oxford Univ. Press.

Hanzeli, Victor. 1969. *Missionary Linguistics in New France: A Study of Seventeenth- and Eighteenth-Century Descriptions of American Indian Languages*. The Hague: Mouton de Gruyter.

Harrod, Howard L. 1984. "Missionary Life-World and Native Response: Jesuits in New France." *Studies in Religion/Sciences Religieuses* 13 (2): 179–92.

Heidenreich, Conrad. 1971. *Huronia: A History and Geography of the Huron Indians, 1600–1650*. Toronto: McClelland and Stewart.

Hoxie, Frederick E. 2008. "Retrieving the Red Continent: Settler Colonialism and the History of American Indians in the US." *Ethnic and Racial Studies* 31 (6): 1153–67.

Jaenen, Cornelius. 1974. "Amerindian Views of French Culture in the Seventeenth Century." *Canadian Historical Review* 55 (3): 261–91.

———. 1976a. *Friend and Foe: Aspects of French-Amerindian Cultural Contact in the Sixteenth and Seventeenth Centuries*. New York: Columbia Univ. Press.

———. 1976b. *The Role of the Church in New France*. Toronto: McGraw-Hill Ryerson.

Jennings, Francis. 1976. *The Invasion of America: Indians, Colonialism, and the Cant of Conquest*. Chapel Hill: Univ. of North Carolina Press.

Jurgens, Olga. 1966. "Étienne Brûlé." In *Dictionary of Canadian Biography*. Vol. 1, *1000–1700*, edited by George W. Brown, Marcel Trudel, and André Vachon, 130–33. Toronto: Univ. of Toronto Press and Les Presses de l'Université Laval.

Keller, Mary. 2002. *The Hammer and the Flute: Women, Power, and Spirit Possession*. Baltimore: Johns Hopkins Univ. Press.

L'Incarnation, Marie de. 1989. *Marie of the Incarnation: Selected Writings*. Edited by Irene Mahoney, O. S. U. Mahwah, NJ: Paulist Press.

Lapointe, Gabrielle, ed. 1974. *Constitutions et règlements des premières Ursulines de Québec par le Père Jérôme Lalemant, 1647*. Quebec: Monastère des Ursulines de Québec.

Lawrence, Bonita. 2003. "Gender, Race, and the Regulation of Native Identity in Canada and the United States: An Overview." *Hypatia* 18 (2): 3–31.

Leavelle, Tracy. 2012. *The Catholic Calumet: Colonial Conversions in French and Indian North America*. Philadelphia: Univ. of Pennsylvania Press.

Lescarbot, Marc. 1907–14. *The History of New France*. Translated by W. L. Grant. 3 vols. Toronto: Champlain Society.

———. 1928. *Nova Francia*. Translated by H. P. Biggar. New York: Harper and Brothers.

Long, Charles H. 1995. *Significations: Signs, Symbols and Images in the Interpretation of Religion*. 2nd ed. Aurora, CO: Davies Group.

Martin, A. Lynn. 1988. *The Jesuit Mind: The Mentality of an Elite in Early Modern France*. Ithaca, NY: Cornell Univ. Press.

Mauss, Marcel. 1967. *The Gift: Forms and Functions of Exchange in Archaic Societies*. Translated by Ian Cunnison. New York: W. W. Norton.

Mémoires de la société généalogique canadienne-française. 1944–. Montreal: Société Généalogique Canadienne-Française.

Morrison, Kenneth M. 1990. "Baptism and Alliance: The Symbolic Mediations of Religious Syncretism." *Ethnohistory* 37 (4): 416–37.

———. 2002. *The Solidarity of Kin: Ethnohistory, Religious Studies, and the Algonkian-French Encounter*. Albany: State Univ. of New York Press.

Murphy, James J. 1974. *Rhetoric in the Middle Ages: A History of Rhetorical Theory from St. Augustine to the Renaissance*. Berkeley: Univ. of California Press.

Pagden, Anthony. 1993. *European Encounters with the New World: From Renaissance to Romanticism*. New Haven: Yale Univ. Press.

———. 1995. *Lords of All the World: Ideologies of Empire in Spain, Britain and France c. 1500–1800*. New Haven: Yale Univ. Press.

Parkman, Francis. 1983. *France and England in North America*. Vol. 1. New York: Literary Classics of the United States.

Poirier, Lisa J. M. 2004. "Godmothers and Goddaughters: Catholic Women in Colonial New France and New England." In *Encyclopedia of Women and Religion in North America*, edited by Rosemary Skinner Keller and Rosemary Radford Ruether. Indianapolis: Indiana Univ. Press.

Pomedli, Michael M. 1991. *Ethnophilosophic and Ethnolinguistic Perspectives on the Huron Indian Soul*. Lewiston, NY: Edwin Mellen Press.

Quintilianus, Marcus Fabius. 1933. *Institutio Oratia*. Translated by H. E. Butler. Cambridge, MA: Harvard Univ. Press. http://penelope.uchicago.edu/Thayer/E/Roman/Texts/Quintilian/Institutio_Oratoria/home.html.

Reid, Jennifer. 1995. *Myth, Symbol, and Colonial Encounter: British and Mikmaq in Acadia, 1700–1867*. Ottawa: Univ. of Ottawa Press.

———. 2008. *The Creation of Modern Canada: Mythic Discourse and the Postcolonial State*. Albuquerque: Univ. of New Mexico Press.

Ronda, James P. 1972. "The European Indian: Jesuit Civilization Planning in New France." *Church History* 41 (3): 385–95.

———. 1979. "The Sillery Experiment: A Jesuit-Indian Village in New France, 1637–1663," *American Indian Culture and Research Journal* 3 (1): 1–18.

Rushforth, Brett. 2003. "'A Little Flesh We Offer You': The Origins of Indian Slavery in New France." *William and Mary Quarterly* 60 (4): 777–808.

———. 2012. *Bonds of Alliance: Indigenous and Atlantic Slaveries in New France*. Chapel Hill: Univ. of North Carolina Press.

Sagard, Gabriel. 1866. *Histoire du Canada et Voyages que les Frères mineurs recollects y ont faicts pour la conversion des infidèles depuis l'an 1615 . . . avec un dictionnaire de la langue huronne*. 4 vols. with consecutive pagination. Paris: Edwin Tross.

———. 1939. Sagard's *Long Journey to the Country of the Hurons*. Edited with introduction and notes by George McKinnon Wrong. Translated by H. H. Langton. Toronto: Champlain Society.

Seeman, Erik. 2011. *The Huron-Wendat Feast of the Dead*. Baltimore: Johns Hopkins Univ. Press.

Smith, Jonathan Z. 1993. *Map Is Not Territory: Studies in the History of Religions.* Chicago: Univ. of Chicago Press.

Smith, Wallis S. 1970. "A Reappraisal of the Huron Kinship System." *Anthropologica* 12 (2): 191–206.

Steckley, John. 1981. *Untold Tales: Joseph Chihoatenhwa, Eustace Ahatsistari, Estienne Annaotaha.* Ajax, ON: John Steckley (R. Kerton Printing).

———. 1987. "An Ethnolinguistic Look at the Huron Longhouse." *Ontario Archaeology* 47:19–32.

———. 1993. "Huron Kinship Terminology." *Ontario Archaeology* 55:35–59.

———. 2004. *De Religione: Telling the Seventeenth-Century Jesuit Story in Huron to the Iroquois.* Norman: Univ. of Oklahoma Press.

———. 2007. *Words of the Huron.* Waterloo, Ontario: Wilfrid Laurier Univ. Press.

Tanguay, Cyprien. 1871–90. *Dictionnaire généalogique des familles canadiennes depuis la fondation de la colonie jusqu'à nos jours.* Quebec, Canada: Eusèbe Senécal; Ottawa, Canada: Library and Archives Canada.

Thomas, Nicholas. 1991. *Entangled Objects: Exchange, Material Culture, and Colonialism in the Pacific.* Cambridge, MA: Harvard Univ. Press.

Thwaites, Reuben Gold, ed. 1896–1901. *The Jesuit Relations and Allied Documents: Travels and Explorations of the Jesuit Missionaries in New France, 1610–1791.* 73 vols. Cleveland, OH: Burrows Brothers.

Todorov, Tzvetan. 1984. *The Conquest of America: The Question of the Other.* Translated by Richard Howard. New York: Harper and Row.

Tooker, Elisabeth. 1991. *An Ethnography of the Huron Indians, 1615–1649.* Syracuse, NY: Syracuse Univ. Press.

Trigger, Bruce. 1988. *The Children of Aataentsic: A History of the Huron People to 1660.* Reprinted with new preface. Kingston, ON: McGill-Queen's Univ. Press.

———. 1990. *The Huron: Farmers of the North.* 2nd ed. New York: Holt, Rinehart, and Winston.

Trudel, Marcel. 1966. *Histoire de la Nouvelle-France, Le Comptoir, 1604–1627.* Montreal: Fides.

———. 1973. *The Beginnings of New France, 1524–1663.* Toronto: McClelland and Stewart.

Turgeon, Laurier. 1997. "The Tale of the Kettle: Odyssey of an Intercultural Object." *Ethnohistory* 44 (1): 1–29.

Turner, Dale. 2006. *This Is Not a Peace Pipe: Towards a Critical Indigenous Philosophy.* Toronto: Univ. of Toronto Press.

Veracini, Lorenzo. 2010. "The Settler-Colonial Situation." *Native Studies Review* 19 (1): 101–18.

———. 2013. "'Settler Colonialism': Career of a Concept." *Journal of Imperial and Commonwealth History* 41 (2): 313–33.

Wade, Mason. 1981. "The French Parish and '*Survivance*' in Nineteenth-Century New England." *A Franco-American Overview.* 3 vols. Cambridge, MA: National Assessment and Dissemination Center for Bilingual Education.

Weiner, Annette. 1992. *Inalienable Possessions: The Paradox of Keeping-While-Giving.* Berkeley: Univ. of California Press.

White, Richard. 1991. *The Middle Ground: Indians, Empires, and Republics in the Great Lakes Region, 1650–1815.* Cambridge, UK: Cambridge Univ. Press.

Wolfe, Patrick. 2006. "Settler Colonialism and the Elimination of the Native." *Journal of Genocide Research* 8 (4): 387–409.

———. 2013. "The Settler Complex: An Introduction." *American Indian Culture and Research Journal* 37 (2): 1–22.

Zoltvany, Yves. 1969. *The French Tradition in America.* Columbia: Univ. of South Carolina Press.

Index

Aataentsic: and myth of illness, 172–74; and origin of Three Sisters, 147
adoption: and mutuality of relationship, 151; of Thérèse Oionhaton, 129; paralleled with baptism, 195; as strategy of alliance, 3, 37, 68, 151; and torture, 27
Aenons, 66–67, 96
agnatic inheritance, 63, 137, 140
Agnus Dei, 45–47
agriculture, 154, 191
alcohol, 92
alliance: baptism as, 98, 106; Brûlé as symbol of, 52, 57; with Champlain, 19n3, 24–30, 33–42, 70; Chihoatenhwa and trade, 116; and Feast of the Dead, 141; and godparenting, 196; -*hwatsir*-, 88; and kinship, 64, 68, 124, 139, 199; and trade, 50, 116, 194; Wendat, 124, 129–31, 136
Amantacha, 56, 58, 60, 61, 71
Ancienne Lorette, 129, 133
Anderson, Emma, 13–14, 84
Annieouton, Joachim, 104
Aonetta, Marie, 106, 113, 127, 169
Arendarhonon (Rock People), 24, 28, 29, 30, 32–36, 39, 136, 137
Arenhatsi, Cecile, 166
Aristotle, 79, 85

Ataronchronon (Bog People, subgroup of Attignawantan), 111, 137
Attignawantan (Bear People), 24, 39, 40, 46, 52, 66–67, 99, 100, 105, 137, 138, 146
Attigneenongnahac (Cord People), 24, 56, 137
awendio, 123

baptism: and alliance, 97, 98; Annieouton's resistance to, 104; of Joseph Chihoatenhwa, 73, 93, 105–10, 112, 117; and godparenting, 181–83, 186, 189, 193–95; and healing, 98–99; Hébert women and, 183–85; Innu understandings of, 97, 98, 103, 155, 156, 161; and kinship, 14, 100, 166, 196–97; missionary perspectives on, 96, 97, 98, 130, 153; Ragueneau's expansion of, 130; Wendat ritual appropriation of, 102–4, 132, 202; Wendat association with murder, 7, 93, 100–101, 199; Wendat man refusing, 149; Wendat women resisting, 6, 154, 164–65
beaver: depopulation of, 49, 154–55; and Feast of the Dead and, 141, 143; given to Champlain, 34, 36; revaluation of, 8–9; Wendat trade in, 48

Benedicite, 54
bereavement, 16, 26, 149, 168–69
Blackburn, Carole, 11, 75, 93
Bourgeoys, Marguerite, 185, 187
Brébeuf, Father Jean de: and baptism, 99, 100; and Joseph Chihoatenhwa, 105, 107; death, 132; and dreams, 118; and "esken," 146; and *khiondhecwi*, 147; on language, 83, 85–86, 89, 92; and myth of lost sister, 172–74; and 1636 Feast of the Dead, 62–67, 142, 143, 200; and 1636 Relation, 77, 97, 139–42, 173; and relativism, 96; on writing, 93
Brûlé, Étienne: background, 21; as embodiment of alliance, 37–38; escorting LeCaron, 40; exchanged for Savignon, 29–32; and Feast of the Dead, 66–67; journey to secure Susquehannock allies, 40, 43, 44–45; journey to Wendake, 32; murder of, 62, 67–68; participation in ritual of exchange, 35–37; remonstrated by Champlain, 59–61; and Sagard, 53–55; Seneca captivity, 45–48; as symbol, 69–72; wages, 50; and women, 51–52
Burridge, Kenelm, 151

Caën, Emery de, 55, 56, 58
Caën, Guillaume de, 180, 181, 189
Cahiagué, 40, 42
captives, traditional Iroquoian rituals regarding, 25–28, 144, 149–51, 205–7. *See also* torture
Caragouha, 40, 52
Carantouan, 43–45
Carigonan (Innu medicine man), 91

Champlain, Samuel de: adopted Innu nieces, 178, 180; alliance with Wendat, 33–34, 36–38; background, 19–20; Brûlé's emerging independence from, 48, 57; denunciation of *truchements*, 59–61; habitation and first winter at Stadacona, 22–24; and Louis Hébert, 175–79; joins Wendat in raids on Haudenosaunee, 40–43; and kin exchange, 29–32; and Kirkes, 58; meets Wendat, 24–28; observations of Wendat culture, 134–37; and religion, 39, 43
Chaudron, Guillaume, 66–67
Chauvigny, Marie-Madeleine de, 185
Chihoatenhwa, Joseph: baptism, 105–8; concern for relatives, 109–10; defense of Jesuits, 102, 110; as evidence of missionary success, 73; Ignatian retreat, 111–12; illness, 105; murder of, 114–16; nieces of, 106, 109, 114–15; prayer of, 122–26, 209–11; recovery from illness, 108–9; redefinition of kinship, 112–13; as symbol, 120–23; taunted by Wendat, 74; translation of theological concepts, 90, 111; and writing, 90–93
Cicero, 79–82
commodification: Brûlé's, 16, 71, 197; of Joseph Chihoatenhwa, 120, 122; of corn, 163; and exchange value, 196; of human beings, 3, 4, 199; of kettle, 201; of languages, 94; and market economy, 4; secularization of, 4, 38, 57, 68; of translators, 83
condolence: hybridized, 166; and kinship, 199; traditional, 86, 131, 145, 168

conversion, 53; Champlain and, 38; of Joseph Chihoatenhwa, 104–14; Innu women's resistance to, 161–64; LeJeune on reason and, 80–81, 95; missionary assumptions about, 2, 53, 185; of Thérèse Oionhaton, 127; Wendat woman's opposition to, 144–47, 151; Wendat women and, 164–71
copper kettle, 200–201
corn, 49, 114, 133, 135, 147, 163, 174, 177, 179, 181
Couillard, Guillaume, 178, 179, 180, 182, 183, 184, 191, 192
Couillard, Marguerite, 190
Couillard Després, Abbé Azarie, 191
coureurs de bois, 50, 51, 72
courtship, Wendat, 135
Cramoisy, 77, 105

Daniel, Father Antoine, 83, 99, 138
Davost, Father Ambroise, 99, 138
Deloria, Philip, 15, 198, 199
De Noüe, Father Anne, 82–83, 138, 181
DePaul, St. Vincent, 155
Devens, Carol, 14, 162–64
disease. *See* epidemics
donné, 130
double-consciousness, 151
dreams: Chihoatenhwa's, 117–19, 124, 125; Wendat, 17, 62, 92, 93, 102, 104, 118–19, 139, 198, 202; Wendat women's, 143–45. *See also* myth-dreams
DuBois, W. E. B., 13, 151
Duval, Jean, 22–23

Ekouandaé, Michel, 128
epidemics, 92, 98–105, 107, 133, 161, 171, 196; Joseph Chihoatenhwa and, 105–8, 116, 120
Etionnontateronnon (Tobacco Nation), 114, 116

Feast of the Dead (*yandatsa*, "the kettle,") 63–64; Joseph Chihoatenhwa and, 107; converts unwelcome in, 145–46; and *hatisken*, 146; and kettles, 200–201; in 1636, 65–72, 139–41; reclamation of pelts from, 142–43
fides ex auditu, 95
filles du roi, 187
fishing: Basque, 20; Wendat, 41, 45, 58, 84, 117, 118, 135, 136, 137
Fléché, Jessé, 176n2, 193–94
Fort Ville-Marie (Montreal), 19n3, 33, 128, 187, 192
Foucault, Michel, 15, 198
French River, 32, 40
fur trade, 3, 20, 49, 55, 57, 58, 63, 140

Gahoendoe (Christian Island), 132
Garnier, Charles, 114
gender: Champlain and, 133–37; at Sillery, 153–60
gendered division of labor, 136
Georgian Bay, 1, 32, 40
gift: and alliance, 116, 129, 130, 194; and courtship, 135; empty, 70–72; and Feast of the Dead, 64, 66, 141–43, 145; and reciprocity, 28, 150–51; and reparations, 131; and trade, 49. *See also* Mauss, Marcel

godparenting: as alliance, 98; begins in New France, 181–82; as establishment of kinship, 188–89; Jessé Fléché and, 193–94; as institution, 194–95; Marie Rollet Hébert and, 182, 199
Gravé, François, Sieur du Pont (Pont-gravé), 20, 21, 23–25, 31, 34, 36, 189
Greer, Allan, 13
Gros-Louis, Madeleine, 201
Gua, Pierre de, Sieur de Monts, 2, 19–23, 57
Guyart, Marie (Marie de l'Incarnation), 185–86, 190

Haudenosaunee (Iroquois Confederation): and Brûlé, 44–48, 68; and captives, 27; and Joseph Chihoatenhwa, 115, 117; and Champlain, 29, 34, 35, 38, 40–45, 48; and dispersion of Wendat, 129–33; and language, 26n8; and Thérèse Oionhaton, 6, 128–29
Hébert, Anne, 176, 178, 182
Hébert, Guillaume, 176, 178, 179
Hébert, Louis, 175–77, 189, 190, 191, 192
Hébert, Marie Rollet: as ancestor, 189–91, 194; as godmother, 181, 182; and hospitality, 178, 181; poems to, 213–18; remarriage, 179; shipboard blessing of children, 175n1, 177
Hébert Couillard, Guillemette, 176, 178, 179, 182, 183, 189, 199–200, 202
Hébert-Couillard family: as ancestors, 189–93; household, 177–82, 184

hell: baptism as protection from, 195; Innu incorporation of, 162, 166; Jesuit illustrations of, 147–49; Wendat critique of, 148–49, 151, 164; Wendat fearlessness of, 148–49; Wendat reappropriation of, 145; Wendat relativization of, 96
Houbou, Guillaume, 179, 182
Huguenot, 19, 20, 57, 184
hunting, 35, 49, 84, 118, 128, 129, 135, 136, 138, 154–55
-hwatsir-, 88
hybridity, 16, 17, 102, 113, 121, 122, 132, 166

Ihonatiria, 66, 99, 105, 138
illness. See epidemics
individualism, 4, 10, 14, 15, 63, 66, 116, 140, 142, 161, 198
Innu (Montagnais): and baptism, 97, 98, 103; and Brûlé, 31; and Champlain, 23, 24, 26, 29, 178, 181; and LeCaron, 82; and LeJeune, 83–84, 91, 93; and Marsolet, 55, 59; at Sillery, 128, 154–64; and Wendat, 22n5, 36, 49
Iouskeha, 101, 104, 174
Iroquet, 24, 25, 29, 30, 33, 35, 37
Iroquoian language, 26, 186
Iroquoian warfare, 26, 27, 149

Jesuit Relations: composition, 76–77; interpretation, 77–78; publication, 77; rhetoric in, 80–82; use in financing mission, 77
Jeune Lorette, 133
Jogues, Father Isaac, 114, 127

khiondhecwi, 147, 174
Kichesipirini, 25, 36
kin exchange, 29–32, 37, 134, 195
Kirke brothers, 58, 60, 179–80, 182, 189

Lachine Rapids, 30, 32, 33, 35, 40, 43, 48
La Conception. *See* Ossossané
Lake Huron, 1, 32, 46, 49, 54, 76
Lake Nipissing, 32, 40
Lalemant, Father Charles, 50n13, 55, 73, 132
Lalemant, Father Gabriel, killed by Haudenosaunee with Brébeuf, 132
Lalemant, Father Jérôme, 77, 94, 102, 103, 113, 115, 117, 119, 122, 132, 148, 149, 186; Jesuits blamed for disease, 92
Laliberté, 192
Lawrence, Bonita, 14–15
LeCaron, Father Joseph (Recollet) 39, 40, 52, 53, 138; shipboard blessings, 177, 194; wedding officiant, 178; Wendat dictionary, 82, 85
LeJeune, Father Paul: and Carigonan, 91; and death of Brûlé, 67, 68; education, 78; establishment of Sillery, 111, 154–58; and Hébert-Couillard family, 181–84; and images of hell, 147–48; and *Jesuit Relations*, 62, 75–77; and native languages, 82–84, 90–94, 94n3; and reason, 95; and rhetoric, 78–82; and women, 163
LeJeune, Olivier (Guillaume Couillard's slave), 180, 182–84, 194, 199
LeMercier, Father François Joseph, 77; and baptisms, 100, 164; and Joseph Chihoatenhwa, 90, 104–12, 125, 169; and language, 86; and relativism, 96
LeMoyne, Simon, 127
Lescarbot, Marc, 32, 175n1, 193
LeTardif, Olivier, 180, 183, 189
locative re-situation, 149
Long, Charles H., 3–6, 13, 94, 151–52
Loyola, Saint Ignatius, 112

Makheabichtichiou, 155
Mance, Jean, 185–87
Manitouabeouich, Marie, 190
Marsolet, Nicolas de: 24, 55, 59–61, 83; and Kirkes, 180, 181; and Olivier LeJeune, 184
matriliny: Wendat, 52, 62, 63, 88, 139, 140, 168, 185; Champlain's evidence of, 136, 137
Mauss, Marcel, 4, 15, 27, 196
Membertou, 20, 176
mercantilism: and Brûlé, 48, 71, 197; and Champlain, 57, 58, 60, 61; conflict with missionization, 184, 196; and Jesuits, 95; and the secular, 4, 9, 38; and Wendat, 142, 171
Mi'kmaq, 20, 176, 193
Mohawk: adoption of Thérèse Oionhaton, 127, 129; Champlain's raids upon, 25, 26, 28, 30; raids upon Wendat, 47, 127–28, 130
Montmagny, Governor, 131, 155, 158
Morrison, Kenneth, 11, 97, 98, 103, 161, 163, 165, 172
myth-dreams, 153, 154, 175

Naneogauchit, Louis, 181
Negabamat, Nöel, 155

232 • Index

Nenaskoumat, François Xavier, 155
Neutral Nation (Wenrohronon), 28, 67, 92n2, 127, 128, 132
Nicollet, Jean, 182, 191, 192
Nipissing, 28, 49

Ochasteguin, 24, 25, 28, 29, 33, 137
Oëntara, 92
Oionhaton, Thérèse, 5, 6, 16, 127, 128, 197, 202
oki (plural *ondaki*; sacred powers), 88, 89, 90, 99, 119, 124
Oneida, 136
Onondaga, 41, 129, 130, 133, 136
Ononharoia, 139
Onontchataronon, 24, 25, 28, 29, 30, 33, 36, 136
opacity: and Long's hermeneutic, 13, 17, 94; of myth-dreams, 151–52, 173
Oquiaendis, 99
Ossossané (La Conception), 66, 74, 101, 104, 105, 106, 111, 113, 116, 127
Ottawa, 49, 138, 163, 201
Ottawa River, 32, 40, 48, 49, 137, 138, 190
Ottawa Valley, 18, 26, 38, 47, 49, 138

Pastedechouan, Pierre, 13, 83–84
path of souls, 147
Peltrie, Madame de la, 185–86, 190
Petite Nation (Weskarini), 28
Pigarouich, Étienne, 156
Pomedli, Michael, 12, 88–90, 119, 146
Port-Royal, Nova Scotia, 2, 20, 175, 176
Poutrincourt, Jean Biencourt de, 175
premier voisin, 189

Quintilian, 78, 79

Ragueneau, Father Paul, 104, 113, 130, 131, 143, 144, 145, 147, 150, 151, 165, 167
reciprocity, 3, 4, 15, 17, 27, 28, 95, 131, 142, 149, 150, 151, 162, 196, 197
Recollet, 3, 4, 12, 13, 32, 39, 40, 53, 55, 57, 69, 70, 82, 83, 87, 138, 176, 178, 180, 185
redistribution, 49, 63–66, 137, 140–42
ren (sacred power), 89
reorientation, 6, 112, 169, 199
rhetoric, 16, 74, 75, 77–82, 96, 111, 114, 122, 144, 166, 169
Richelieu, Cardinal, 58, 180, 184
Richelieu River, 25, 26, 29, 32, 48
Riel rebellions, 191
Ronda, James, 160–63
rumor, 143–54

Sagard, Brother Gabriel (Recollet): and Brûlé, 52–55, 57, 67, 70; dictionary, 53–54, 82, 87; and *oki*, 88, 89, 138; and story of Héberts, 176, 177
Savignon, 29–37, 69, 70, 137, 197
Seeman, Erik, 13
Seneca: and Brûlé, 45, 47, 48, 68; and Chihoatenhwa, 115, 122; new Wendat policy, 129, 130
Sillery, 17, 111, 128, 133, 153–63, 186, 187, 198
slavery, 178n3, 188, 194, 202; vs. "servant," 182–84
Smith, Jonathan Z., 5
Smith, Wallis, 52, 63, 140, 143
Soranhes, 60, 71

soul, Wendat conceptions of, 62, 139, 144–47, 173, 201
Steckley, John, 12, 89, 90, 116, 117, 122, 124, 146
Ste. Marie, 111, 128, 130, 132
Ste. Marie II, 132
St. Jean Baptiste (Contarea), 113, 145
St. Lawrence River, 2, 21, 49, 128, 168
survivance, 191–93
Susquehannock, 28, 40, 42, 43, 44, 45

Tadoussac, 22, 23, 24, 26, 29, 33, 59, 179
Taenhatentaron, 131, 132
Tahontaenrat (Deer People), 24n7
Taiaeronk, Louis, 166–69
Tawiscaron, 101, 174
Teanaostaiaé (St. Joseph), 111, 131
Tehorenhaegnon, 101–2
Teondichoren, Joseph, 127
Tessouat, 36, 190
Three Rivers, Trois-Rivières, 48, 128, 131, 155, 190
Tionnontaté, Etionnontateronnon (Tobacco Nation), 28, 74, 114, 116, 132
Toanché, 39, 40, 134
Tobacco Nation. *See* Tionnontaté, Etionnontateronnon
torture: Brûlé escapes, 45–47; hybridized with baptism, 132; kin replacement in *Jesuit Relations*, 205–7; and kinship, 68; traditional Iroquoian rituals regarding, 25–28, 144, 149–51; Wendat critique of heaven and hell as, 147–50
trade routes, 47, 51–52, 65, 123n4, 125, 143, 153, 197

transparency, 9, 93, 94, 151–52
Tregouaroti, 28, 29, 30, 32, 33, 35, 137, 196
Tsondihwane, Rene, 117, 119

Ursulines, 6, 13, 14, 127, 128, 165–68, 170n2, 182, 185, 186, 199

Viel, Father Nicolas, 53, 138
Village of the Dead, 147, 164, 172–74
Vimont, Father Barthélemy, 76, 115, 190

wampum, porcelain collars, 34, 36, 39, 67, 131, 135, 137, 167
warrior complex, Wendat, 27–28, 136–37, 149
Wendake, 1n1
Wendat confederacy: and baptism, 99, 114, 116, 124; and Brûlé, 57, 71, 72, 197; Champlain and, 2, 3, 4, 5, 9, 24, 26, 28, 30, 36, 37, 38, 42; dispersion of, 128, 129, 130, 132; and Feast of the Dead, 141; and trade, 47–52
Wendat language: and Brébeuf, 83, 85; and Brûlé, 47, 49, 57; and Joseph Chihoatenhwa, 91, 109, 113, 122, 124; concept of self, 146; opacity of, 95; and Sagard, 6, 53, 82; and translating the sacred, 87–90
-*wendio*-, 123

yandatsa, "the kettle." *See* Feast of the Dead

Lisa J. M. Poirier is an assistant professor in the department of Religious Studies at DePaul University in Chicago. Her scholarly interests center upon Native American new religious movements, and she is particularly interested in constructions and operations of gender.